This book may be kept

FOURTEEN DAYS

A fine of TWO CENTS will be charged for each day
the book is kept over time.

Dec 9 '54			
Jan 4 '55			

DUKE UNIVERSITY PUBLICATIONS

HIGH TIME
TO TELL IT

WILLIAM J. LONG, Lawyer
Noscitur a sociis

HIGH TIME
TO TELL IT

"Ah, distinctly I remember"

Mary Alves Long

DURHAM, NORTH CAROLINA

DUKE UNIVERSITY PRESS

1950

920.7
L85h

COPYRIGHT, 1950, BY THE DUKE UNIVERSITY PRESS

27096
mai '51

In memory
of my whole family,
especially my sister
Jane Taylor Long
and
Cadwallader Jones V
"A verray parfit gentil knight"

With Grateful Acknowledgments

to

DR. WALLACE ROLLINS, without whose inspiration
this book would never have been begun;

DR. GEORGE COFFIN TAYLOR, a most valued friend,
without whose faith and encouragement it would
never have been published;

and

PHILLIPS RUSSELL

CONTENTS

ILLUSTRATIONS

HIGH TIME
TO TELL IT

BOOK ONE

Childhood

1

OFF TO A START

IT WAS INTO a crowded Dixie-Land household already running over with children that I was born in Randolph County, North Carolina, "early on one frosty mornin' " in December, 1864, exactly two weeks to the day before Christmas, a bad time for a birthday, and certainly in those dreadful last days of the War between the States the worst possible time anybody could have picked, just before the surrender.

Surrender! That word was one of my childhood's puzzles. People were always saying "before the surrender," or "after the surrender." I thought it was a month as it sounded like the months ending in "ember"; but I noticed it never came. "When will surrender come?" I would ask, and everybody would laugh and say it had already come, leaving me as bewildered and mystified as ever.

By all the laws of proportion I should have been a boy; for our family, beginning with four girls and then surprisingly adding three boys all in a row, certainly should have wound up with a fourth boy. But nature knew best, for lacking all the manly attributes, I should have been a crooked stick of a man; and it was far better to have been a girl, of whom little was expected, than a boy, merely for the sake of symmetry.

Then, besides not being a boy, I broke another rule of three; for hitherto my mother's children had come every two years, but after the last boy was born, I had waited seven.

Anyhow when I became the eighteenth member of the family circle, I had made it even instead of odd.

Things had happened fast in our family just before I was born, for Uncle James and Aunt Agnes Long, who lived in Greensboro, had both died of what in those days was termed "consumption." Uncle James was nearest my father's age, and if Father loved and admired one brother more than another, it was Uncle James. Like Father he was a lawyer and also the editor of the Greensboro *Patriot*. Uncle James, who wasn't afraid of anything or anybody, wrote as he pleased, let the chips fall where they may, and according to Father, when he wanted to be particularly sarcastic, went to Shakespeare for the invective which made him bitter enemies. One man threatened to kill him on sight with a sword cane he carried for that purpose; but Uncle James paid no attention and took his walks abroad unarmed as usual.

Mother said Aunt Agnes was the most beautiful woman she had ever known; all her children with one exception inherited her beauty, and all of them her curly hair and her talent for singing and drawing. Mother had curly hair, too, and a really fine voice; but every one of us had Father's straight hair; and most of us his inability to carry a tune. "Why," we used to ask her, "didn't you, like Aunt Agnes, pass those gifts along?" When Father died at the age of sixty-eight he did not have a white hair in his head; and I made up my mind that as long as I had his straight hair, I wouldn't have any white hairs either. And I almost haven't!

People said Uncle James had left his children to the Lord, but Father said "No," he had left them to him. And so after the funeral he took the three eldest—Lizzie, Eleanor, and Agnes—to Grandma Long's and brought Edwin, Loraine, Alex, Mary Shepherd, and their aunt Miss Lizzie Caldcleugh—no kin of ours—to a household most people would have said was "full up"; there being, besides these newcomers, four others—three of these, children of mother's sister Anne, who had married Dr. Michael Holt, were also wards of father. Last but not least was Miss Margaret Jane Taylor, "Aunty" to us, an idolized though very distant cousin on Mother's side of the house, so distant that nobody but a Southerner would have counted her as kin. These two households were a big responsibility to Father, who now had to feed in those last days of the war sixty people, black and white. But Confederate money being practically worthless, it was either this arrangement or the poorhouse. Luckily Uncle James had left three hundred dollars in gold, without which Father, being unable to pay the taxes, might have lost both the plantations. Prices had gone sky high, Sister Annie's new calico dress costing ninety paper dollars.

People on plantations went without what they didn't raise, or else used substitutes. Whenever the word "Confederate" appeared in a recipe, it meant some sort of substitute, as lard for butter or sorghum molasses for sugar. The dreadful stuff called coffee was made from parched sweet-potato skins. Only Grandma Long continued to use real coffee, to get which Father had performed a near miracle.

More dreadful in those last days was the havoc wrought by "deserters" from our armies hiding by day and roaming the country by night. Many a time our trembling family, roused by a sky lit with flames from some house which had been robbed and burned, watched in terror, afraid to go back to bed again.

In my very own family, besides Father, who always signed himself William J. Long, and my mother, formerly Mary Webb of Hillsborough, there were my six brothers and sisters. After my arrival they could now say, "We are seven"; though in the Wordsworthian sense we were eight, as one of us in the churchyard lay—the "first little Johnny." My mother, like my Grandmother Long, named two of her children John. When my grandmother was asked why, she said she liked the name. So I suppose my mother did too.

People in those days took the business of christening their children very seriously, usually calling them after some member of their family, either to honor him or to carry on a famous name. Cousin Sallie Webb of Alabama, for instance, wishing to preserve her father's phenomenal name given to him because he was born on a phenomenal day, the like of which was never before seen, named her son "Memorable Frost." One of our neighbors, Roddy Kimry, saying he had nothing to give his children but names, gave them each three apiece: William Henry Harrison, Mary Margaret Alice, Virginia Ann Glenn, Sylvina Helen Josephine, and John A. Gilmer, though not knowing what the A stood for.

Our parents, more frugal, gave us only two—all family names. The first two daughters, Sabra Ramsay and Annie Webb, were named for their grandmothers; and the next two, Jane Taylor and Elizabeth Strudwick, for Mother's cousin and for her sister living in far off Alabama, whom we called Aunt Betsy. Her family, Mother told us, was like Job's, seven sons and three daughters. Her first boy, John Webb, Mother named for her favorite brother and our favorite uncle, always joking and laughing, besides bringing us French candy or Roman candles to shoot off at Christmas. Then, varying the pattern slightly, she called her next boy William Osmond after Father and his oldest brother. Grandmother Long had found Uncle Osmond's name in a novel, an amazing circumstance, as the Grandma I knew did not believe in novels and would even burn them up. This particular one had disappeared, nobody ever having seen it or heard its name. And then came the second Johnny, named John Henry for Father and one of my Mother's brothers, though there were lots of other Johns whose

MARY WEBB LONG

Beloved by all who knew her

WILLIAM OSMOND LONG
at the Age of Four

namesake he might have been: my mother's grandfather, John Huske; Grandfather and Great-grandfather Long; and Father's brother John Wesley. Strangely enough, the two sons Grandmother had named John were never called that, but William and Wesley. When my turn came, I also was named for two people, Mary for Mother and Alves for Grandma Webb, and was called Mary Alves.

In those times and in such a household how could there possibly have been any welcome for this little Mary Alves? But, though Mother was always saying "a baby is a wellspring of pleasure *redolent with care,*" I do not remember ever having any doubts of her affection or anyone else's in those early days of family life. I think no child was ever more loved by a whole family than I was then and afterwards, perhaps because I was the youngest, for certainly I possessed no qualities or endowments to justify my untimely coming. I was not only loved but was conscious of being loved. Even when my father, despairing because his broken health did not permit him to practice law, would look at me sadly, clasping and unclasping his hands in a way he had, and say, "She ought never to have been born," my feelings were not hurt; for I felt dimly what I knew later, that this was not a denial but a proof of affection inspired by the desperate feeling that here was a world in ruins and there was nothing he could do for it or for me.

II

Father could never bear to see any of us punished, no matter how much the whipping was deserved. How Mother ever maintained discipline was a mystery, for when she was giving Will and John some sorely needed whipping, Father would stand by begging her to stop. I was made of sterner stuff, for, though adoring Will and John, I was all for having them obey the rules.

Once, finding the door of the locked closet open, I

looked inside and saw John eating out of the sugar bar-rel—a thing strictly forbidden. Horrified, I ran to tell Mother. "I never could stand a tattletale," she told me. And I had felt so virtuous, trying to help make the sugar barrel last the year out till time to buy the next one; something by the way that never happened, no matter how much sorghum molasses we ate on our bread, or how often we made Confederate cake instead of sponge or pound. And anyway sorghum wouldn't do for every-thing. You just had to have sugar to put on clabber or to make hard sauce for blackberry and peach dumplings. Hurt and bewildered, I crept upstairs, and climbing on the big bed in the middle room turned my face to the wall and cried myself to sleep. But I was cured of tale-bearing, henceforth to be a "shalt-not" like that of false witness in the Ninth Commandment.

Generally I minded very well, but occasionally there was a temptation too strong to resist, especially if it meant going anywhere. Every once in a while some child in a big hurry for a drink would, instead of unwinding the rope slowly and carefully, let the windlass go as fast as it could; and the bucket, banging from side to side, would drop off into the bottom of the well. And there it stayed, often for days, until we could find Bud, the only Negro able to do the ticklish job of climbing down and up the sixty slippery feet of rock wall.

In the meantime every drop of water had to be brought from the spring, a quarter of a mile away at the bottom of a hill. Some job! For there must be water for Auntie's hothouse flowers, as well as for all other pur-poses. So twice a day every child able to carry a pot or pail would join the bucket brigade. Since it was easier to take the clothes to the water than the water to the clothes, the family wash that day was being done at the spring; so when Lou Elvie Savannah, a nice little darkey, came in search of her mother, our washerwoman, she was told to go to the spring. Of course, I begged to go with her, but Mother flatly said no, I couldn't. I loved to go to the spring, too far for me to go alone, watch the water bubble up through the rising and falling sands, and take at last a cool drink from the big gourd lying on the stone wall. There was much ceremony to be gone through first. I'd look fearfully to see if there was a snake in the stones, then rinse the gourd off very carefully, and search for the most unlikely place anybody else would think of using, before I finally took a drink. Mother was like that, too, never drinking from the same glass any of her children had used, but having a fresh one brought.

I thought of all those joys, and now I had this little darkey for company; how could I resist such a heaven-sent opportunity? I couldn't, and I didn't.

Mother was waiting for me when I returned, and indignantly switched my legs. Father looked on with deep concern. "Did it hurt very much?" he wanted to know. It hadn't, and anyway, I think I felt as did my cousin John Webb of Alabama who was overheard saying to his younger brother, "Aw, come on, Mem, let's go; the fun's goin' to last a long time, and the switching'll only take a minute."

III

I never remember either of my parents giving us any formal instruction on morals, seeming to rely, instead, upon the commandments, catechism, and Bible reading to guide us in the straight and narrow path. This thing called my conscience was a sadly undeveloped affair hardly worthy of the name. Personally I felt far guiltier over breaking a lamp chimney, for which I was always punished, than over telling a lie.

We got, no doubt, much profit from the Bible, but also thrills, and even fun. John had nicknamed Will "Bildad," a name he had found in the Book of Job—not exactly a pet name but one mightily pleasing to our fancy. Job was not a book any of us would have chosen for our private devotions, but as it was my mother's custom to have us read the Bible aloud from "kiver to kiver" and then start all over again, Job took its turn along with Deuteronomy, the Psalms, Romans, Hebrews, Lamentations, Proverbs, and the Song of Solomon, Ecclesiastes, and Ruth.

Sunday was a day for getting ahead on Bible reading, and Mother several times a day would assemble us in a semicircle, calling on each to read in turn. We were supposed to read only five verses at a time, but John, who abhorred being "fenced in," often read ten; I, though wanting terribly to do the same, would think indignantly, "Why doesn't Mother stop him?" and because she never did, envied and admired this darling irrepressible.

It was also a day for singing hymns; Mother gathered us round the piano, letting each choose his favorite. Mine was the one beginning:

> Where, oh where, is the Prophet Elijah?
> Where, oh where, is the Prophet Elijah?
> Safe now in the Promised Land. . . .

and continuing verse after verse with a different name. Most of us, being tone deaf like Father, were sadly off key—a hopeless lot, but Mother never gave us up.

Father told us about his going to singing school when he was a boy. He said he learned the names of the notes: do, re, mi, fa, sol, la, ti, do; how to beat time; pass the books around; build the fire and sweep out the room; but he never learned to sing.

Sunday in our house was kept as a Day of Rest in the manner prescribed by those old Hillsborough Presbyterians, in accordance with the Fourth Commandment and the Shorter Catechism, which allowed only "works of necessity and mercy"—a phrase permitting more latitude than its makers ever dreamed of. For your Sabbath-keeper, no matter how strict, is rarely consistent. Why, I wondered when we began preparing on Saturday the dinner to be eaten cold on Sunday, did we have hot

coffee and biscuits for breakfast? And though I thought
grown-ups could do no wrong, still it looked queer to
see Father reading the weekly newspaper. No stories
for us children except those found in Sunday school
books, usually most unpleasant tales about sickly children
on deathbeds or disobedient ones breaking the Sabbath
by going on the water and invariably getting drowned.
I would no more have put to sea in a boat on Sunday
than I would have jumped overboard, both meaning
to me certain death.

Our toys were all put away, no games of any kind
being allowed. You might sit in the swing, but only if
you kept perfectly still. No studying lessons, thank goodness! That was as sinful as picking cotton or planting
corn, the way Joel Pike did, who was the scandal of the
neighborhood. When somebody stole his horse, it was
regarded as righteous retribution.

After breakfast we were sent off to learn a hymn and
the Shorter Catechism. I had a morbid taste in hymns,
always choosing ones about hellfire and chains or the
Judgment Day:

> Day of Doom, that dreadful day
> When Heaven and Earth shall pass away.
> What power shall be the sinner's stay,
> How shall he meet that dreadful day?

How indeed! It still gives me the shudders. Another favorite of mine was:

> Lo, on a narrow neck of land
> Twixt two eternal seas I stand,
>   Yet how insensible!
> A point of time, a moment's space
> Removes me to yon heavenly place,
>   Or shuts me up in hell.

Years passed before I ceased to wake up in the night
trembling from some horrid dream of the Judgment Day.

The Shorter Catechism gave me no trouble till I
reached the question, "What is Original Sin?" I couldn't

learn the answer, and I told Mother I wouldn't try any longer: "If you don't learn it, then you can't go to church," she said; and seeing by my face that that was no punishment, she added, "nor have any dessert." That went home, for unless there was company we had dessert only on Sunday, and I knew that we were going to have greengage plums out of one of Mother's glass jars.

But Sister Lizzie, whose understanding heart recognized that I really couldn't learn that "ole" answer, took me off to the parlor and, sitting beside me on the haircloth sofa, soon had me letter perfect.

IV

Sunday was a day of rest for the horses, too, all being turned out to pasture, not to be driven anywhere except to church. There being no Presbyterian Church in the neighborhood, Mother took us by turns to the once-a-month services of the Methodists, Baptists, and Lutherans at their churches: Liberty Grove, Mount Pleasant, Mount Zion, and Richland.

The custom then was for the men to sit on the right side facing the pulpit, and the women on the left. I loved to sit by a window where I could watch the young men escorting their sweethearts to the door, taking off their hats, and bowing as a parting gesture. Miss Emily Patterson in a white dress, leaning on Mr. Louis Henry Smith's arm, was a treat for anybody's eyes.

Like other little girls in the neighborhood I was allowed to carry in "season" sweet shrubs tied in my handkerchief, a red June apple, or a colored Easter egg. And there were many envious eyes when we displayed our treasures after church. I seldom had the biggest June apple, but my Easter egg, dyed by Marthy Ann Black, the miller's daughter, couldn't be beat. She put designs in wax on the ends and sides of the eggs before boiling them in the dye, and when the wax was removed, there were the patterns against a colored background.

At Richland, the church of the Lutherans, after hearing the scolding delivered to the members present for the sins of those absent, I told myself fairy stories, never paying any attention to the minister, until one Sunday afternoon I suddenly began listening to Dr. Jacob Henry Smith, a Presbyterian who had come all the way from Greensboro to preach to us. He was comparing God to a great eagle teaching its young to fly by spreading its wings underneath to catch them if they fell. It was the first time I had ever thought of God's all-seeing eye watching over me with love and care, instead of trying to catch me doing wrong.

Dr. Smith was not only a great preacher but a wonderful father, daring to defy public opinion and bring up his children according to his own ideas. He was much criticized for taking them to the circus every time it came to town, but kept right on doing it. The circus people were very proud of this, and at the opening performance the clown would always come out and, turning a somersault, ask, "Is Dr. Jacob Henry Smith present?" Whether he was or not the crowd would yell "Yes," and the clown would say, "Then the circus can begin." The Smith boys would rather go fishing and tramping with their father than anybody else, and home was such a pleasant place that none of them ever went uptown at night. His five boys all became men after his own heart, three being eminent divines, and two, college professors, one of them becoming the president of Davidson College.

v

On the Sundays when we went to Richland, Mother always took us to little Johnny's grave under a cedar tree next to that of my great-grandmother, Mary Dudley Ramsey. The marble slab topped a brick foundation so high I had to be lifted up to look at the inscription fast becoming obliterated. I loved Johnny's little upright marble tombstone which under the inscription bore a broken chain—four links with one all by itself at the end, and below that a rosebud. The four links joined together were of course my four sisters, and the one little link was Johnny. From there we went to look at the graves of Uncle Wesley and Grandpa Long, on whose tombstone we read that "An honest man is the noblest work of God."

Time to go then, and we wandered to the gate looking curiously at the strange names such as Reitzel and Fogleman—for ours was a Dutch settlement. The name Luttlerloh in letters so large you could read them from the road interested me most. I pronounced it to myself in three syllables as spelled and was astonished when I learned that the name was the same as that of the man my father called Louis "Letlow."

During World War I, I said to a friend, Eggert by name, that I was surprised to see so many names on the lists of killed and wounded that were not American.

"Miss Long," he asked, "What is an American name?"

"Sitting Bull, I guess, or Pocahontas," I told him with a red face.

I remembered that conversation when I visited the cemetery at Belleau Wood a few years later. The day was cold, and the straining flagpole creaked and groaned dismally in the fierce bleak wind that swept over "the crosses row on row." The name on the first cross I looked at was "Cohen." And today thousands of American boys lying in graves under alien skies all round the world bear names belonging to all races, creeds, and colors, even American Indians and Negroes, "in one red burial blent." May they sleep well!

"Who was the first man?" asked the teacher.

"Washington," said Jimmie.

"Why, Jimmie, how do you make that out?"

"Well, he was first in war, first in peace, and first in

the hearts of his countrymen; so Washington was the first man," Jimmie stubbornly insisted.

But that teacher would not agree. "Adam was the first man," she told him.

"Oh, well," said Jimmie, "if you want to drag in foreigners."

VI

My four sisters, all being bright girls, were not content to sit at home without money, and though having only a limited education they succeeded in becoming teachers with salaries even more limited than their education.

Annie and Lizzie and also Cousin Lizzie Long, Valley of Humiliation Girls as they were, actually became governesses in that Mountain of Conceit—Virginia. Sister Lizzie, being the youngest, had had very little education, though she had attended Edgeworth in Greensboro a short time; but her natural ability, sweet disposition, and pretty face made up for other deficiencies.

Sister Annie, the only one who had inherited Mother's talent for music, had the gift of laughter. Witty and gay, wherever she went there was fun and frolic. When she left home, it was just as if somebody had snuffed out the candle. She was pretty too, with quantities of long hair piled up in a chignon. And she was perfect in the Grecian bend. She loved to wear pretty clothes herself, and was always making some pretty dress as a surprise for somebody.

Sabra taught school in the Foulkes family, living in Greensboro, all of whom she loved and admired, prefacing her remarks on returning home with "Mrs. Foulkes says—"

Jane was the best educated of all my sisters, having studied under Mr. Sterling at Edgeworth, and in Charlotte under Mrs. Robert Burwell, Mother's former teacher, who was considered the finest woman teacher in

North Carolina. Jane was "particular." Things had to be just right. She would work for hours getting her guimpes to fit perfectly, and when she was dressed, if not "the glass of fashion and the mould of form," she had every detail practically perfect. And she looked like Mother with her arched eyebrows, large brown eyes, and lovely though determined mouth. She had practically a permanent position in the Masonic Orphan Asylum in Oxford, at twenty-five dollars a month and board. Chicken-feed now, the salary seemed princely then. There were naturally no vacations at the Asylum, and you could teach as long as you liked; and Jane, anxious to make all she could, had no mercy on herself, being determined to educate John and me. She was in our family the torch-bearer of learning.

The destinies of this institution were in the hands of Mr. Mills, who not only had to help raise the money but whose task was also to make the machinery run smoothly. As there was no fixed income and contributions were uncertain, there were many ups and downs in the larder. Too much salt pork, bread, and molasses, not a happy combination for a meal. Jane's health suffered under the diet in spite of the many invitations to dine with friends and relatives like Cousin Lucy Cooper or Colonel Edwards, whose every meal was an epicurean repast, even cornfield peas tasting like some rare delicacy when served on his table. And as for the fried apples, all perfectly cored, fried a luscious brown, and arranged in neat little stacks as symmetrical as if they had been silver dollars, they would have graced a Lucullus's feast.

There were many problems besides food at the Asylum, for instance, finding homes for the children. One little girl was indignantly returned because she had lost *the* needle.

Even if my sisters had been at home, they were of course much too old to be my playmates; but what was even better, they were always ready and delighted to make clothes for me and for my china doll, sole survivor of their childhood manhandling. Anna Belle had survived, it is true, but not without injuries. There were silver strands among the jet where the paint had rubbed off, cheeks pale and wan, and eyes a faded blue. The worst though was a broken shoulder! That was really something, as it prevented her wearing tarleton and muslin dresses in summer, no matter how hot the weather. But with all her faults I loved her dearly, and no little girl was ever prouder or happier than I when I spied her under the Christmas tree, dressed up in a brand new outfit beautiful beyond dreams. That dress! What pen could do justice to that dress? Sister Annie, my most stylish sister, had made it—a black silk that shone and rustled. Oh, the liquefaction of that dress when my Anna Belle took her walks abroad! The term "two-piece" was then unknown; but a two-piece dress it was, with a long, voluminous skirt ballooning out, its many flounces piped with green silk, and a basque all buttoned up in front with green silk buttons. The open sleeves were edged with a knife plaiting of green silk over a lace frill; and round the neck was a little white lace fichu; on her feet were black silk slippers with green silk bows —the only thing that didn't come on or off. When I looked underneath, there was a whole set of new underclothes, chemise, petticoat, and pantalettes, feather-stitched, herringboned, and edged with tatting. Tatting was Sis Jane's specialty; so I ran to hug her as hard as I could.

When I showed all this finery to Sister Lizzie, she took me on her lap and told me I must be very proud of this dress for it was a piece of the silk dress Judge Gilmer, a great friend of Father's, had given Mother because Father had done him a favor.

This was the way it happened. After court was over in Graham, a crowd of lawyers all got on the train going to Greensboro. Much conviviality! And when it was time to get off, Judge Gilmer couldn't find his hat. If Judge Gilmer arrived without a hat, it would be the talk of the town, whereas, if Father appeared hatless, no one would say a word, as everybody knew Father was never in a "condition," he being one of those people who always knew where to stop. So Father lent Judge Gilmer his hat; and Judge Gilmer sent Mother the black silk dress with a beautiful letter about Father's being such a wonderful friend. Now the dress was all worn out, just enough left to make my doll a dress.

Father was always doing favors for people. It was a habit he had. There was the one he had done for Mr. Matt Ransom, who was running for the legislature. He sent Father word he needed every possible vote, and there was a man of considerable influence whose support Ransom knew he could get if Father would only speak to him. There was no time to be lost, as the election might come off any day; so Father immediately left on horseback for the long ride to Raleigh, finally arriving there at two o'clock in the morning. Instead of waiting, Father rode to the man's house and waked him up.

Putting his head out of the window the man asked, "Who are you, and what do you want?"

"I'm William J. Long," Father answered. "And when I heard yesterday that the election is going to be pretty close, I got right on this horse and have been riding ever since, to ask your support for Matt Ransom."

"Well, Mr. Long," the man said, "if you want my vote that bad, you can have it."

There is a New England saying something like this: "Wear it out; make it do." I had done my share of wearing out, hand-me-downs being the order of the day. Cousin Mag in Charlotte sent us Anna's clothes, and Aunt Rob Webb in Hillsborough, Belle's. My youngest Long cousin, Mary Shepherd, being three years older than I, got them first, and when she outgrew them, handed them on to me. A new dress bought or specially made for me was something I never dreamed of. And then Sister Annie, after searching trunks and closet shelves, pretty bare after four years of war, produced a masterpiece from the scraps she had unearthed.

The pleated skirt was of striped black and gray silk, the stripes being very narrow indeed, which had once belonged to a great-grandmother; and the waist was a little jacket of black cloth trimmed with a white fur called "ermine," though I'm sure it never came off the back of any stoat. There was a hat to go with it: an old black felt found in the yellow press had been twisted into shape for my head, with a little piece of the ermine put rakishly on one side. Sunday morning before church, Sister Annie dressed me up in this creation, stood me up in front of the fire downstairs, and turned me round and round before an admiring family, even Will and John being impressed. As for me I was completely bursting, and feeling that it was up to me to say something, I made one of those remarks greeted by ribald laughter that become a family classic: "I may *look* proud, but I don't *feel* proud."

VII

By the time I began to take notice, Uncle James's children had become an integral part of the family, no difference being made by my parents between us and them that I ever observed. Father and Mother were those cheerful givers beloved by the Lord. Having taken these children into their home, they had taken them into their hearts with no regrets or repinings. As for me, they were heaven-sent, especially Mary Shepherd. Like Will and John, we seemed to be an entity, never spoken of separately but always linked together—Mary Shepherd and Mary Alves. But our names being more of a mouthful than theirs became contracted to "Mayshepherd" and "Myralves," which, as we grew older, we didn't like and complained of bitterly with no results. Professor Maria

Sanford out in Minnesota used to say that Southerners have lazy lips. Ours were not the only names contracted, my sisters Annie and Lizzie becoming "Stannie" and "Slizzie," and it was years before I knew that the real name of "Bobbrellen" Keck, our tenant's daughter, was Barbara Ellen.

Tasks performed with my darling Mary Shepherd never seemed very difficult, perhaps because she did most of the work. Together on Saturdays we clayed the hearth; together we made lamplighters out of old letters, rolling the strips at the bottom firmly together for a handle and curling with the scissors the slashed parts at the top; together we set the table, and every Monday, that being washday, did the dinner dishes; and together cleaned, with brick dust and an Irish potato cut in half, the steel blades of our ivory-handled table knives. It was fun I thought to see the stains disappear like magic, and one day, thinking Mary Shepherd was not letting me do my fair share, I took perfect aim and heaved the brickbat at her head—being caught in the act by Aunty, who happened to be standing near. I was her pet and darling, but, this she could not overlook; taking me into the garden, she cut a tiny switch and telling me what a wicked girl I was, whipped me tenderly on the legs. I felt no repentance—only thankfulness that it was Aunty instead of Mother doing the whipping.

Luckily, the brick had done little harm, and Mary Shepherd held no grudge.

And most important of all we went together on errands. Naturally a timid child, I had been made more so by the darkies' tales of devils dwelling in our gateposts, or ghosts seen in graveyards. Nat reported having seen and heard a devil rattling chains in a darksome spot near the millpond, henceforth given a wide berth. If a covered wagon came down the road, the darkies, yelling, "Speckerlaters!" ran into the back yard out of sight.

"What is a 'speckerlater'?" I wanted to know.

MARY SHEPHERD LONG
Daughter of Agnes Caldcleugh and James Long, editor of the
Greensboro Patriot

Aunt Agnes Caldcleugh Long

Uncle James Allen Long

"Men who buy darkies, and sell 'em down south where overseers beat and work 'em to death," they told me.

Of course the war being over, speculators too had gone; but not understanding this, I trembled at the sight of a covered wagon.

Besides these imaginary fears, there were the very real ones of "biting dogs" and stray cows, especially bulls bellowing and pawing the ground, which sometimes came down the road in front of our house.

Mary Shepherd, though taking due precautions, like everybody else in our family was afraid of nothing; and when together we went to the Brown Place after apples or in search of the blackberries, dewberries, and strawberries growing in the fence corners and fields far and near, I felt no fear.

Nothing in the world is sweeter than a wild strawberry. Mary Shepherd and I knew all the best patches, and with our tin pails would set out early in the morning to pick them before the sun got too hot. We had long conversations on those tramps. One was about slavery. I had just read *Uncle Tom's Cabin,* a forbidden book, and how we ever came to have it I never knew. Some leaves were missing, and it stopped when Cassie was playing ghost in the attic. I never knew how it ended until after we moved West many years later. The book made me hate slavery, and I told Mary Shepherd that I thought slavery was wrong.

"It can't be wrong," she said, "because if it was wrong, Uncle William wouldn't have owned slaves."

Her logic was unanswerable, for I too thought my father could do no wrong, but, while in some inscrutable way I didn't condemn him, my mind was henceforth a closed shop on the question of slavery. Open minds are fine things, but it is a mistake to keep them open too long, or they become an open pit into which you fall, than which no fall is worse.

Later I found that I was right on both counts, for I learned that Father himself thought slavery wrong and would have freed his slaves except, as he said, there was no place in the South for a free Negro. Aunt Delphina Mendenhall had freed hers on the death of her husband, Mr. George Mendenhall, and sent them to Ohio, where they dragged out a miserable existence. Then, as now, freedom to starve is a sentence of death.

Sometimes we quarreled. Once, and only once, Mary Shepherd began to cry, saying that she was an orphan, whereupon I also burst into tears, crying so bitterly that it all ended in her comforting me, the cause of our quarrel being completely forgotten.

Generally, though, when I would say mean things she would just look at me and curl her lip—a strange device reducing me to the status of a worm, completely speechless and feeling myself absolutely in the wrong. This curious power went with her through life and proved exceedingly useful when she was dealing with those hateful principals infesting the public schools of Minneapolis in the gay nineties. The ability of devastating with a look while preserving a complete silence is a powerful weapon, perhaps because it leaves your enemy feeling baffled and defeated yet with no room for complaint.

Without Mary Shepherd there would have been nobody for me to play dolls with, a thing I loved to do more than anything else. Our tastes were not exactly the same, for she loved to sew for them, whereas I loathed all needlework, wanting only to dress and undress them and have tea parties.

Her wax doll far outshone my Anna Belle, being much larger, able to open and shut its blue eyes, and, when squeezed, to say "Papa" and "Mama." Its curls were real hair, though unfortunately there was a bald spot requiring a cap or other headdress to conceal it.

We could have not only tea parties but even a

wedding when Mother, returning from Hillsborough, brought me a man doll. He was neither a "store doll" nor rag doll, but a truly marvelous creation, the very latest thing in knitting, which Mother had just learned how to do. As he was clearly a soldier, belted and buttoned with stripes on his sleeves and pantaloons and a cap on his head, I promptly named him Stonewall Jackson. A museum piece, if I only had him now; but those fine clothes being made of pure wool, he fell an easy prey to moths, enough of him being left for a nice funeral under the smoke tree.

But his was a gay life while it lasted, for weddings had become the order of the day. Mary Shepherd had turned out a bridal dress and veil that would be decorated with real orange blossoms if Aunty's tree was in flower. Nor was my Anna Belle the only bride. Little girls bringing their dolls for an afternoon visit clamored to wed them to Stonewall Jackson, borrowing for the occasion Anna Belle's veil and letting her be a bridesmaid. The best doll tea set belonging to Uncle James's children carefully kept in a basket in the yellow press would be brought out, and Aunty, being appealed to, always found something in her cupboard fit for the wedding feast. Yes, Stonewall Jackson, like other men, made a wonderful difference in our lives.

It was about this time that Mary Shepherd and I decided to collaborate in writing a novel, each contributing a hero and heroine. I named my heroine Topaz Pearl, my taste at that time running to jewel names such as Opal, Ruby, Garnet, and Chrysoprase. As we thought we had to account for every minute of time in our novel, the first day was a very long one filled with games and much feasting, for which we chose all our favorite dishes for breakfast, dinner, and supper. There was no description and nothing that could be called dialogue. There were going to be proposals of course, but not yet. And, of course, no caresses. In our creed kisses came only after engagement, and maybe not until after marriage, as in the case of Cousin Lily and Cousin John Webb, of Bell Buckle, Tennessee. Finally after a supper of cold ham, Sally Lunn, spoon bread, damson preserves, brandy peaches, and deep-dish apple pie, followed by a game of "I Spy," it was time to put our characters to bed. How to accomplish this caused a grave dissension, Mary Shepherd wishing to chronicle "they retired," and I holding out for "went to bed." Neither of us yielding, this literary partnership came to a timely end.

Together we sought to achieve a beautiful complexion, a *sine qua non* in those days and not to be bought in a box. No, it must be perfectly natural, like that of a celebrated beauty in New Orleans who, hearing a Yankee soldier say as she passed him, "By God, she's painted!," turned on him with the retort, "Yes, and by God only."

Instead of tying our split sunbonnets round our waists to keep cool, thereby getting tan and freckles, we resolved to bury our heads in them hereafter, no matter how hot the day. We tried to remove those defects already there by nightly applications of a cucumber and milk lotion compounded from a popular recipe. A treatment wholly barren of results. So when our black Maria told us that if on the first day of May we washed our faces in dew and wiped them on some part of our body, preferably feet and legs, the freckles would be transferred to those parts, we determined to give this treatment a trial. When the looked-for day arrived, there was no dew. A whole year to wait! It seemed too much. When this second May Day appeared, there was no lack of dew but, just as everybody told us, a complete lack of results. Not a freckle was transferred.

In Mary Shepherd's case it made no difference, her complexion already being practically perfect. Unlike me she had the wonderful gift of beauty with none of its attributes missing. She had them all: lovely features, smooth, fair, rosy complexion, curly hair, large brown eyes with long lashes, slender ankles, small feet with an instep so high water flowed under it, and a taper waist. It was what I envied most as we grew older—that taper waist. Never any gaps between her skirts and belts! When she fastened her belt, things always stayed put, while mine, no matter how much pinned or how tightly belted, always wriggled loose.

What a difference beauty makes in one's life! Loraine had all sorts of good qualities, but no beauty or glamour. Always wanting to grab off for herself every mean job, she was self-sacrificing almost to the point of mortal sin. "If self-sacrifice is such a fine thing, why not let the other fellow have a fair share?" I'd tell her, trying vainly to hold her back, partly because I hated to see her doing such horrid things, and partly because of the guilty feeling I had when I wouldn't help.

When Loraine returned home from her first experience as governess, she spent most of her salary in gifts. Mine was the first hat ever bought for me and never to be forgotten. It was a white chip with a plaited band of pink velours running over the crown centered with a wreath of pink roses. I thought it the most beautiful hat in the world, wearing it with gratitude, pride, and joy.

In her own quaint fashion, Loraine was an artist— never, it is true, painting a picture, but doing better than anybody else with the preposterous fads that swept the country in the seventies. Spatterwork, for instance, which took the country by storm. This was the truly difficult art of arranging leaves on a white cloth in such a way that, when the leaves were removed after the cloth had been spattered by a brush dipped in ink, you had a picture in black and white with which to decorate a screen for the fireplace in summer. Loraine's screens acquired much local fame, and neighbors came from miles around asking to see Miss Loraine's "spattered" work.

Her hanging baskets were also the wonder of the neighborhood, not only the one formed by lichens and sycamore burrs, but the white one made from Canton flannel torn into strips, raveled out on both sides, and then miraculously twisted in the shape of a basket, finished off at the bottom with a huge tassel. This fleecy white marvel becoming, when depended from the center of the ceiling, a wonderful dust-catcher very attractive to flies, it soon found its way to the ash can.

> Like the snowflake on the river
> A moment here, then gone forever.

Mother had taught Loraine to sing and play the piano both by ear and by note. I adored her repertory of popular songs, especially the rash of "darling" melodies then afflicting the country, "Molly Darling," "Katie Darling," and other plaintive bits:

> I'm nobody's darling
> Nobody cares for me.

> Into a ward of the whitewashed walls
> Somebody's darling was borne one day.

On Sundays she sang only hymns, and I can see her now as she sat at the piano one morning under Uncle Edwin's portrait singing:

> The Lord has come!
> Let heaven and nature sing!

Such lives as Loraine's meet with few earthly rewards, and hers was no exception; but I'm sure that now, "a harp within her hand" and many stars in her crown, she is singing in Zion the song of the redeemed. Else what's a heaven for?

Loraine, Mary Shepherd, and Alex—a wonderful trio, never giving trouble to anyone, always doing their part, they brightened all the lives in our household.

VIII

I loved my sisters, but the feeling I had for my brothers was something very like worship. Never did brothers have a more devoted slave, my main idea being to stick around, ready and proud to do their bidding, no matter what, or how varied their orders:

"Sis, go get me a drink of fresh water; and look out how you let down the bucket—don't let go of the handle to the windlass."

"Sis, go to the woodpile and bring me the axe."

"Sis, go to the loft and bring me the hammer; be careful now and don't fall off the ladder."

"Sis, my knife's so dull it won't cut a thing; turn the grindstone while I sharpen it."

"Here, take this bucket of slop and throw it into the pig trough, and don't spill it."

"Run down to the May apple tree and pick up a basket of apples."

Sis was the name they used most, though they often called me "Sisser my She" or "Woman Old," pet names of their own invention, of which I was very proud, certain that nobody had ever had brothers like mine. I was their special pet, always tagging along at their heels like a little puppy, almost everywhere they went except swimming.

"Hurry up and eat your breakfast," they would call, preparing to make the rounds of their rabbit and partridge traps. I would grab a biscuit, run outside, and off we'd go, with the dogs, Mum and Rollo, scampering on before. The boys were not expert trappers, and I can't remember our ever finding any partridges though we never failed the night before to press our noses to the pane and recite the magic charm:

> Star light, star bright
> First star I've seen tonight
> Wish I may, wish I might
> Catch a whole heap of partridges tonight.

But hope sprang eternal, and disappointment never dampened their spirits long. John, returning from a fruitless hunt, said cheerfully, "No, I haven't caught anything, but I like to have scared up a rabbit."

Great fun too to ride on their ox cart drawn by their pet oxen Dick and Buck. "We're going to the woods, Sis; want to come along?" "Going down to the meadow after walnuts, Sis; hurry up if you want to go." And I would always come running.

Once when John took me to the woods to get sticks for our woodpile, he smelled smoke and, leaving me in charge of the ox cart, went off to investigate. Coming back he was all excited, and after making me promise "cross my heart" never to tell anybody, for if I did, I would be an "informer" and might get shot, he told me that there was a still down there run by one of our neighbors, Clay Coble. I promised, shivering, for I knew about stills and "Revenuers," those bluecoated men everybody hated who went around smashing stills and hauling men off to prison in Greensboro, where they were kept in dirty jails and caught fevers, as had Bing Smith, whose tongue all dried up just like a piece of fried bacon.

Going home John told me a funny story about a Negro who was being tried for making illicit whiskey.

"What is your name?" asked the Judge.

"It's Joshua, Jedge," he replied.

"Joshua," repeated the judge, and, trying to be funny, asked, "Are you the Joshua that made the sun to stand still?"

"No sah, Jedge, I ain't. I's de man what made de moonshine."

IX

Will and John didn't exactly swear, God's name being omitted from their assortment of expletives: "dog-gone," "I'll be dog if," and, strongest of all, "Dad dim it," a curious, faintly reminiscent expression probably of their own coinage, used only in times of stress and great moment. I was never tempted to employ any of these, and if I had done so, they would have promptly slapped me down, for the code of that day limited the use of strong language to men only; and even they had bounds beyond which they must not go. No gentleman then would swear in the presence of ladies. Even the Negroes, if you came where they were ploughing knew better than that, and would revert to Gee, Haw, Gid up, and Whoa.

Father himself never used any strong language no matter what the provocation. Once I saw him at white heat over a package to be sent by freight to my sister in Georgia, the tying up of which had taken days, but which was finally accomplished to his complete satisfaction. The foundation of this package was my crib, standing up high and foursquare like a regular bed except that it had rockers and slats to prevent the baby from falling overboard. The legs and rockers were carefully wrapped, and all sorts of things such as bags of dried fruit, black walnuts, and big hominy were crammed into the space between the slats with pillows and blankets to make everything snug; a log cabin quilt placed firmly around that, and the whole covered over with newspaper and firmly bound up with odds and ends of string, clothes-line, leather harness, and even an iron chain or two. There was never anything like it. It had exhausted the energies of the whole family, and everybody was glad to see it hoisted into the wagon and hauled to Greensboro twenty miles away, Will and John going along to hold it down and prevent too much jolting. When they came back and told my father the freight office had refused to accept it until repacked and crated, it seemed like the end of a beautiful dream. You knew by the way Father kept twisting his hands and crossing and uncrossing his legs that he was perfectly furious, but all he said was, "It's enough to make a body swear."

x

Most brothers like to "plague" you, and perhaps the unmerciful teasing mine administered was just what I

needed to give my sense of humor the third dimension
without which life becomes a sorry thing. The first two
dimensions: see a joke, make a joke, you cannot acquire
—you have to be born that way. But luckily the third,
"take a joke," greatest and rarest, can be ding-donged
into you; and that's what my brothers did for me by
everlastingly keeping at it. No letup! There was nothing physical or "practical" in their tripping. They didn't
pull my hair, stick out a foot, pull out a chair, or threat-
en me with dead snakes; but they tried to catch me
napping by asking trick questions such as: "Who is the
father of Zebedee's children?" "What is the color of
Job's blue turkey hen?" "If a herring and a half cost a
penny and a half, what would three herrings cost?" And
I would always bite and come back for more.

And if I begged for a story, there was much riga-
marole to be gone through first; beginning with the
never-ending tale of Pharaoh's Crib with a million
bushels of corn, and a locust came in and carried off a
grain of corn, another locust came in and carried off
another grain of corn, and so on ad infinitum. Or the
tale of the old yellow cat which went no farther; or

The Three Little Girls

Once there were three little girls. One was named Sugar;
one was named Salt; and the other, Hush Your Mouth. Sugar
stood too close to the fire and melted. Salt fell in the spring
and got drowned.

Now what was the name of the other little girl? I can't remember. You tell me what her name was.

And when I would answer, "Hush Your Mouth," he
would say, "Oh, you told me to hush my mouth and I
will. I won't say another word."

Then, suddenly relenting, he would begin "Once
upon a time . . ." and we were off into a world of enchantment with Sinbad and his roc, Ali Baba, and the
magic "open sesame," or Cinderella and her glass slipper
—a world where lovers lived happily ever after, where

wicked sisters and stepmothers got their come-uppance; or a world of genii, ghouls, and giants whose curdling rhyme:

Fee-Fi-Fo-Fum, Peach and a Plum,
I smell the blood of an Englishmun

made you afraid to go to bed upstairs alone, and somebody had to come along and keep you company.

XI

Will, who had a mechanical turn of mind, tried his hand on toys for the Christmas tree, astonishing me with a doll house and a wonderful bedstead with cords instead of slats for the mattress. Mother had just learned how to weave willow baskets, and one of these which he mounted on runners like a sled was the first and only doll carriage I ever had. The fact that I had to drag it along by a string bothered me not at all. One good thing about living on a big plantation away off is that there is nobody around to poke fun at your belongings. But Will could do bigger things than toys. With his limited assortment of parts such as a round hollow thing he called a cylinder, some chains, iron rods, and a few wheels, he succeeded in turning out a strange contraption which could actually thrash out dock seed. Years afterward he invented a nickel-in-the-slot machine for cigars, but it never made his fortune, for when he tried to patent it, he was too late—somebody else had beat him to it.

Dear, dear brothers! Lovely and pleasant in their lives, in their death they are not divided. The grasses have long been growing on their graves side by side under Minnesota skies where I, the last living member of our household, will someday once more make our family circle even. In life their love for me never faltered or failed. I was always their little sister to be specially loved and cherished—the one to whom their hearts turned for comfort in sorrow or distress. They always wanted me along.

2

GRANDMA LONG

GRANDMA LONG was the only grandparent I ever knew, the others all having died before I was born. Her house was in sight of ours though a mile away. Both houses were on a hill; and there, across the open fields that lay between, you could see the roof, red chimney, and even people, very tiny, almost like ants, walking down the path to the spring. The two-story house was so rambling that I sometimes lost my way in it, not knowing how to get back to the starting point. Across the front of the house was a long piazza at one end of which grew a large multiflora rosebush, and on top of the railing there were pots of "hen and chickens." How we longed to sit and climb on those porch railings! But never did, not even asking.

Opening on this porch were Grandmother's room at one end, the parlor in the middle, and the dining room at the other end; and, off the parlor with a window on the porch side, was the middle room where guests were put. At the back of the parlor was a door into the hall where the stairs were, and at the end of the hall was another door opening into the back yard. I remember going up those stairs once, but have completely forgotten what I saw up there.

Grandma's bedroom—also her sitting room—had a four-poster bed in each of the two outside corners,

Grandmother's being next to the porch between two windows.

Once my sister Jane, sleeping in the other bed, waked up to find bending over her a strange Negro man who promptly ran out when she screamed. This, I think, is the only occurrence of the kind ever heard of in our neighborhood.

There was a big chair at the head of Grandma's bed next to a table under the window, where she kept her Bible. In the chimney corner next to the porch was a candlestand on which was a brass candlestick rising out of a kind of saucer on which was a pair of brass candle snuffers. In the other chimney corner, instead of a closet, was an enormous black press. One red-letter day when I happened to be there, the top of this press got a vigorous going over, yielding up a copy of the *Fairy Ring* which Grandma herself had once tossed there out of harm's way, but which, now in her old age, she put into my eager hands. Hours of delight were in store, for it contained practically every fairy tale in the whole world. When I took my treasure home and told my story, the family could hardly believe their ears.

Behind Grandma's room was another large bedroom where I sometimes, when spending the night, slept with my cousin Eleanor for a bedfellow. The mattress on this bed was stuffed with shucks, from one of which the maker had neglected to remove the cob. No matter how carefully I disposed myself upon retiring, this corncob always disturbed my slumbers by burrowing into the small of my back. As I lay there trying to get back to sleep, the stillness would be shattered by loud reports, amounting almost to a fusillade; and though I had been told that these were noises all old houses made, they scared me just the same as I snuggled closer to my beloved Eleanor.

Beyond the bedroom opening into the hall, was another, smaller one containing Uncle James's handsome mahogany secretary where his Masonic emblems were kept. These Eleanor would sometimes show me with great pride—the apron, the red plume, and gold triangular pin.

II

Grandma, christened Sabra Shepherd, the Shepherd after her mother's stepfather, belonged to a large family, all girls but one. Hanging on her parlor wall was one of those pictures done in embroidery (still preserved) showing the family grouped round a table. She had outlived them all, and most of her own family as well, being now all alone in the world except for my father and her grandchildren.

Great-grandfather Ramsay, a shipwright, whose invention of a boat had won him the honor of a letter from George Washington, had died early in life, leaving to his wife, Mary Dudley, the struggle of bringing up the family. There was a legend to the effect that her Uncle Joseph Dudley, who lived in London, had left his large fortune to his only brother's heirs, of whom she was the sole survivor. Unable to produce the vital statistics necessary to establish her claim, she never received a penny of this vast sum, which remained tied up in chancery.

Though unaided, Mary Dudley Ramsay seems to have done very well by her family. Great-aunt Eleanor had become a teacher in Wilmington at the fabulous salary of a thousand dollars a year, and had married a gentleman named Stanley. I thought Eleanor Stanley the most beautiful name in the world, especially as it belonged to my idolized cousin Eleanor Stanley Long, the beauty of the Long family, who told me such wonderful fairy tales and who let me comb her hair—long, thick, and wavy. Aunt Eleanor Ramsay and all the other sisters had married well; but with one exception nobody ever heard a word from their families, nor knew where they were—living in Georgia maybe.

GRANDMA SABRA SHEPHERD RAMSAY LONG

*A woman who did what was right in her own sight, deeply loved by
her husband and children, and highly respected by all who knew her*

GREAT-GRANDMOTHER MARY DUDLEY RAMSAY SURROUNDED BY HER CHILDREN
An Embroidered Picture

That exception was Washington Hilliard, Father's first cousin, who lived in Atlanta. He had been Ambassador to Brazil and had also written a novel called *Godolphin,* a copy of which he had sent to Father and which I read again and again, remembering only the statement that once fled, the joy of the morning hour could never be recaptured.

What had become of the only son, Jack Ramsay, was a mystery. He had gone to live in South Carolina, where he became rich. All that was known about his fate was that he had gone on a trip to New York and had never been heard of afterwards.

That made two mysteries in our family. Exciting like fairy tales. Grandpa Long's half-brother Alphonso had also gone to New York and had never been heard from again. Rummaging around I had discovered a dagger in a leather case, which I was told belonged to Uncle Alphonso. Nobody would ever tell me why he had left home; so I liked to imagine that the stain on the blade was blood from somebody he had killed, perhaps in a duel; and that that was why he never came back. I early acquired the habit of telling stories to myself, which stood me in good stead at church and was also a very good way to put myself to sleep. The family called it "daydreaming."

III

Grandpa and Grandma had met by chance, the usual way, as Charles Dudley Warner says about the bear he encountered in a blueberry patch. And the place—that very Richland Church in the graveyard of which they both lie side by side. It was the custom after church for people, especially young people, to go down to the spring, and there Grandpa had handed Grandma a drink and lost his heart. Now Grandpa was a Quaker, and Quakers were forbidden to marry anybody not a Quaker; so he got turned out of the church for marrying Grandma. But Grandpa didn't care; he thought Grandma was worth it. They offered to take him back if he would say he was sorry; but he said, "I'm not sorry, and I won't say so." And I truly believe he never was sorry. Theirs was a fairy-tale ending—"and they lived happily ever after."

My grandfather John Long also belonged to a big family, all girls but one until Uncle Alphonso's arrival. His father, another John Long, had come to North Carolina from Loudoun County, Virginia, one of that state's richest and most prosperous counties, and settled in Chatham County, where his large family grew up and married. Grandfather's sisters, all Quakers of course, had married Quakers; so though Grandfather himself was not a Quaker, he was surrounded with Quaker relatives living near him. There was my great-aunt Becky Long, who had married Jonathan Newlin, a man of substance and strong will, who was remembered for having thirteen law suits about one mill, finally, I believe, winning the case. Great-aunt Polly had married a Lindley whose son, Dr. Alfred Lindley, moved to Minnesota. Another sister had married a Hadley; and there may have been others. Father's first cousins could literally have been reckoned by the dozens, and luckily I cannot straighten them all out. The list would be too long. Descendants of the Hadleys and the Newlins also moved west, where they all prospered, as Quakers generally have a habit of doing.

Great-grandfather Long's second wife, much younger than himself, was a Mrs. Wilson with two daughters, Oriana and Delphina, who, being about the age of my father and his brothers, proved wonderful companions to these sisterless boys. Oriana married a Nixon and moved west; while Delphina, whom we always called "Aunt," married Mr. George Mendenhall and lived in a house overlooking Deep River.

Grandfather finally became a Congressman, representing for many years Rowan, Chatham, and Randolph counties.

IV

Grandma had a strong will, and her word was law to her five sons, maybe sometimes to Grandpa, and even to neighbors, as you could see in the matter of nicknames. Her own was "Sibby," which she detested. She didn't like nicknames for anybody and then called four of her sons Edwin, James, William, and Wesley; and people called them just that—never Ed, Jim, Bill, or Wes. She said they should all have a college education, and they did—Uncle Edwin graduating from West Point, and the other four from the University of North Carolina.

Grandma needed that strong will for all she had to do in life. It was a lonesome place to which Grandpa brought this Fayetteville girl, only a quarter of a mile from Richland Church, and the nearest neighbor miles off. Grandpa had to go away on business, leaving a white girl named Matilda to keep her company. One dark night Matilda slipped out to meet her lover and didn't come back. So at midnight Grandma took the lantern and went to find her, going down the road almost to Richland Creek, a scary place if ever there was one, under all those dark overhanging boughs, calling, "Matilda, oh, Matilda," over and over; but no answer ever came; so Grandma had to go back and finish the night alone, Matilda never coming back then or ever.

Grandma had to get used to doing without Grandpa during all those years when he was a Congressman, for it was a long journey to Washington, and there was no running back and forth during the session. You had to stay put. Grandma had to use her own judgment and did. When she started to build a barn, the neighbors came to remonstrate. "Doesn't thee think thee should wait till John comes back and ask him what to do?" they said. The barn was built.

Grandpa made his apples into brandy, and, like all other candidates, just before election would take along to the meetings a barrel or two which he was accustomed to dispense freely, a good many people taking much too much. Grandma went with him to one of these meetings and didn't like what she saw. When she got home, without saying a word to anybody, she went down into the cellar and opened the spigot in every barrel, letting all the brandy run out on the floor. After this the apples might rot on the ground, but there was no more brandy. Maybe that had something to do with her sons' habits of self-control.

Grandma used her judgment even about the law, doing what was right in the sight of her own eyes. It was forbidden to teach Negroes to read, but Grandma taught hers, on the ground that everyone should read the Bible, and how could they read if they were not taught? So when her boys started to school riding horseback, she put a little Negro behind each one and sent him along too. Probably she could never have got away with this if there had not been a great many Quakers in the neighborhood and if the school to which they went had not been run by Quakers.

Grandma seemed to know how to handle Negroes, for her slaves were exceptional for ability and conduct. Grandpa owned a flour mill and was accustomed to send a load of flour as far away as Petersburg, Virginia. Uncle Jack was always the driver in charge; Uncle Osmond, being the eldest son, generally went along. When they arrived too late to sell the load, they would drive into a wagonyard and wait till morning. Once Uncle Jack was wakened by hearing someone trying to rob the wagon. He captured the robber and fastened him to the wagon wheel in some peculiar way so that the Negro wouldn't even try to get loose—like a bull who has a ring in his nose—and calmly went back to sleep! Next morning everybody was crowding around to see the Negro, and one man was so impressed that he offered Uncle Osmond five thousand dollars for Uncle Jack. Uncle Osmond turned the offer down cold. "There isn't enough money in the world to buy Uncle Jack," he told the man proudly.

Mother had spent the first six years of her married life in my grandparents' home and told me this story about Grandma.

There were no hotels in those days except in towns, and when people were traveling through the country they would always stop at mealtime at whatever place they happened to be and ask if they might have dinner or stay all night. Two men came to Grandma's one day, and she invited them into the dining room. There was a roast chicken for dinner, and Grandma asked one of the men if he would carve, but he declined. Then she asked the other man to carve, but he also refused. "Well," said Grandma, "let it set." After a while, one man pulled the chicken over to him and helped himself; and then the other man pulled it over and carved himself a portion.

There was also a story about Grandpa.

Whenever he went off on business, Grandma would put a silk handkerchief in the pocket of his overcoat, and Grandpa had lost so many that Grandma scolded him a little. As he was starting off one day, Grandma gave him a brand new one and told him to be very careful not to lose it. Grandpa rode along in the buggy for some time before he used it and, as he thought, put it back into his pocket. In a few minutes he had occasion to use it again, but, to his amazement, it was not there. He decided that he must have dropped it on the road at the place where he had last used it, and, as it wasn't very far, drove back to look for it. Just before he got there, he saw a woman climbing back on her horse and, not seeing the handkerchief anywhere, asked her if she had found it; but she said no, she hadn't. Grandpa didn't believe her, but as there was nothing he could do about it, he had to go and tell this story to Grandma.

Some time afterward Grandma, before putting the

overcoat away for the summer, searched the pockets, and, discovering a hole in the right hand one, looked further and found that all the missing handkerchiefs, including the one he was sure the woman had found, had slipped down between the coat and the lining.

Grandfather after this incident said that he never would convict anyone on circumstantial evidence. Father, however, did not agree; he insisted that facts didn't lie, while people did. "The trouble is," he said, "that people don't get all the facts, as in the case of the handkerchief."

Mother was very fond of Grandfather and said he was the most sympathetic person to people's shortcomings she had ever known.

"Mary," he would say, "we ought not to be hard on people who we think did wrong, for we don't know how strong their temptation was. Just because some sin doesn't appeal to us, why should we condemn them, when, like everybody else, we yield to our own peculiar temptations, perhaps not nearly so powerful as the one these sinners you think so wicked were unable to resist?"

Grandfather's salary as Congressman had been a big help to the family finances. Grandfather had brought home from Washington many handsome gifts—a Chippendale sideboard, blue and white china on the washstand and in the cupboard, and silver marked with a shell. And I still have the ladle! They maintained a home where there was freehanded hospitality for all who came, and charity for the poor. How many people they fed, only the recording angel knows. It was so easy to write an order to the miller calling for a bushel of cornmeal or even flour. And sometimes Grandpa would hand out bacon from the smokehouse. No wonder they were respected and even loved by the whole community.

Grandma went on taking charge of everything—plantation, mill, and tan-yard; and with the help of Grandpa's salary they educated their boys, all of whom became men of character and ability respected in their community and in their state.

v

By the time I came on the scene Grandma was well in the eighties and gave no sign of being the strong-minded person described in these pages. In winter she sat by the fire picking the seed out of the cotton in the basket on her lap. She could not see to read, sew, or knit, and did this, she said, to keep from having the "hippo." She could not bear to be shut up and always kept the door of her room open even in winter.

Going to visit her was a frequent and always looked-forward-to event; only once did I rebel when, after a week of rain, Mary Shepherd and I were sent to ask how Grandma was. We had on heavy leather shoes, and the mud was thick and sticky. Our feet picked up mud as a snowball gathers snow, until we could hardly lift them up. I became indignant and told Mary Shepherd when we got back home that I was going to pronounce abusive e-pith-ets on the family for sending us through all that mud. After that, Will and John were always asking me when I got angry if I was going to pronounce any e-pith-ets.

Visiting Grandma made a nice break in the long Sunday afternoon. For though visiting our neighbors was a deadly sin, strictly forbidden, it was not, as Mother explained, any sin to visit Grandma, but, as she was old and feeble, one of the Christian virtues.

It was a long mile to Grandma's for a little girl all alone, but a pretty safe one as far as stray cows and bulls were concerned; these, turned out to graze by their owners, roamed the country at will, being one of my childhood's greatest terrors by day and also by night, for they were the cause of many a nightmare. But the way to Grandma's led across fenced fields, or between high fences one could climb if a stray cow appeared. The greatest hazard was Tige, the big black and yellow dog at the Blacks. If Tige saw you, he would jump right over the fence, barking and growling, and scaring you almost to death. He had seen me many times, but always acted as if I were a total stranger. He was supposed to wear a block but hardly ever did.

After passing Tige, I kept close to the fence, skirting the mill yard and safely crossing the bridge over the mill creek. Here, if I saw nothing to be afraid of, I often went to look at the big water wheel turning round with its dripping buckets. Then, hugging the fence till I reached the big poplar said to be the largest tree in North Carolina, I crossed the road and climbed the fence into the Big Field, comprising eighty acres. Plain sailing now except for snakes, which you had to watch for in the fields.

Once as I was walking along the narrow path through old field sedge up to my waist I got so close to a snake crawling across just ahead of me I had to jump over it.

There were the dreaded copperhead, the pilot, spreading adder, and water moccasin which I knew were poisonous, but I was afraid of any snake, large or small. The darkies had seen to that with tales of racers that would stand up on their tails, survey the landscape, and then take off after anything, even a man on a galloping horse, and whip both to death. There was also the terrible hoop snake which, taking the form of a hoop, would roll rapidly along until it reached its prey and then, after resuming its natural form, it would strike.

The part of the road I liked best was crossing the log over the meadow branch and the road past the meadow. Grandma's meadow was full of sweet grass which we used to gather and put in the bureau drawers. In the spring it was white with meadow lilies. Between fences all the way now past the tan-yard, where I shivered a little, remembering how the deserters had robbed it, killing the watch dog. It was now an empty shed, with

wide, yawning doors, and a huge pile of tanbark in front.
Not for worlds would I have gone through the yard, being in deadly terror of falling in the narrow water-filled
vats, which I had seen only once when piloted by John.

When you went to Grandma's house, if you were
walking, you climbed the fence into the apple orchard,
always stopping at the spring for a drink, clear, cool, and
tasteless. The sort of water you would dream of if lost
on a desert. Over the branch from the spring was a
spring house where the milk and butter were kept cool
in a long box down in the water. Then up the path at
least one city block to the gate at the privet hedge, and
there you were.

If you were riding, you went on past the house, turning at the big gate into a road bordered on one side by a
row of cedar trees and on the other by sprawling rose
bushes climbing over the rock wall of the garden. Beyond the cedars were tall sycamore trees shading the
"office," and a shed for the carriage and wagons.

Grandma's garden was in front of the house, separated from the yard by a paling and enclosed on the other
three sides by ivy-covered rock walls just made, but never
used, for pilgrimages by children's feet.

In the yard, between the house and garden, were
three huge oak trees with roots so high that all you had
to do was lay some sticks across, thatch, and carpet with
oak leaves—and there was the prettiest little doll house
you ever saw. A June apple tree leaned so slantingly
across the garden paling that you could and did—first
asking Grandma—walk right up into the branches and
pick apples. It was understood that when you went to
Grandma's you must always "ask first," even if it was
only to pick up an apple from the apple-strewn ground
under the May apple tree.

When you went in, you always asked her how she
was, and she always said, "I'm tolerable." Once when
somebody at home asked me how I was and I said, "I'm

tolerable," everybody laughed. Before I left she would ask me to read the Bible, which I was very proud to do, finding the chapter she wanted.

Her few oft-repeated maxims still linger in my memory: "To your aunt's house, but not every day," and "It'll never show on a trotting horse"—my favorite, which I've often said to myself when I felt all was not right with my apparel.

She never went anywhere and hardly ever left the porch. Once she took me into the yard and down into the field back of the house and told me this was where Grandpa was when he was stricken. He came into the house saying, "Oh, Sibby, my head, my head." She had put him to bed and sent for Uncle Wesley, who was a doctor. But he could do nothing, and before morning Grandpa was dead. That was the only time I ever saw Grandma sad.

She liked taking me to the dining room and giving me one of the wafers we always looked forward to getting when we went to Grandma's. These were round, about the size of a saucer, very thin, and had blisters all over them. No sugar was in them, and I think we liked them because they were different. Grandma's bread was different too, the kind called salt rising. I liked it better than ours. Grandma's kitchen was a large room behind the house with a huge fireplace and a wide hearth paved with large flat stones. Grandma had no kitchen stove; all the cooking was done on the hearth. There were cranes in the fireplace which you could pull out, hang pots and kettles on, and push back over the fire. The salt rising bread was baked in a big oven with legs, coals being put underneath and also on the top of the lid. The skillet was just like the oven only shallower, just right for biscuits and corn bread. The frying pan had a very long handle which kept the person holding it over the fire from getting her face burned. For the iron and the coffee pot, there was a little trivet. Potatoes were often roasted in the ashes and tasted better to me than ours cooked in the stove. I liked those burnt charcoal skins.

Grandma's only servant was a white woman because she had to sleep in the house and look after Grandma at night. The first one I remember was Mandy Moore— a tall silent woman who had a little girl who was not white or black either, but yellow, all very puzzling to us children. When one of my cousins asked why Patty was yellow, she was told that she was sunburned. "Feet sunburned, too?" she wanted to know.

Mulattoes were rare in that part of the South, and I do not remember being curious about Patty's color; I thought her a nice little girl and liked playing with her. I also liked the slices of bread with honey her mother used to give us. The beehives in the backyard belonged to Mandy, and I loved to watch the bees buzzing around in front of them. It was a long time before I knew that Patty's father was Wilson, one of father's most trusted slaves, the one to whom father gave his saddlebags every night during the war, as he thought no one would think of looking in Wilson's cabin. Mandy belonged to respectable people who had cast her off, and she hadn't a friend in the world except Grandma. What made the matter worse was that Wilson had gone off with Mandy's niece, whom he had actually married. Both women paid dearly, for they were outcast by both blacks and whites. What became of Patty and Mandy I never knew. They went to Greensboro, and I never heard of them again.

Grandma's last illness was a short one. Aunty went over and nursed her till the end. She never suffered, and just quietly fell asleep at the good old age of eighty-eight.

A man was put on a fast horse and sent to Greensboro carrying telegrams summoning Alex and Uncle Osmond's daughter, Cousin Lily. Cousin Lizzie Long was already there, and when Cousin Lily came, neither said a word

—just threw their arms about each other and kissed. Grandma was buried on one of the hottest of July days. When I went over, the yard was full of people, and horses and wagons were everywhere there was a place to put them. The whole neighborhood, black and white, had come to honor the woman who had befriended everyone who needed a friend. A neighbor had sat up all night to make Grandma's coffin out of black walnut, the finest wood for coffins. It was covered with black cloth—a good background for the handles that shone like silver—and was already on a bier out in the yard. Father was standing at the foot, his face working. I went up and threw my arms around his neck and kissed him, something I had never before done. Ours was not a demonstrative family, and we kissed only when we said goodbye or on returning from a long absence.

The pallbearers were Grandma's former slaves who had come to carry Ole Miss to her last resting place. They took up the bier, and the procession started down the hot, dusty road to Richland graveyard, everyone walking the short distance, not a wheel turning.

> Under the sod and the dew
> Waiting the Judgment Day.

3

AUNTY

WHEN YOU ASK people in the South, "Do you know her?" if it is anyone they like, they will lift their hands ecstatically and exclaim "Do I know her! Why I raised her." A visiting girl's version of this one summer in the late eighties: "Do I *know* him? I've reposed on his bosom," turned the town of Hillsborough into a debating society endlessly arguing whether she had, or had not, the most charitable claiming it was merely her "line."

Well, Miss Margaret Jane Taylor, whom we called "Aunty," had really raised my mother. She had become a member of Grandfather Webb's family the day he had found this little orphan of seven struggling through a snowdrift on her way to school, practically freezing to death, as little girls of that day wore no pantalettes!

With characteristic decision and indignation, he promptly picked her up and took her home to his wife, whose cousin she was, both being descended from the Hoggs. And there she remained till the day of his death, being as much a part of his family as his own children, most of whom named a child for her—all Margarets except my sister Jane. She, by the way, hated her name, and when my sister Lizzie wanted to name a daughter after her, she objected vigorously, finally compromising on Joan.

Aunty had a gift for nursing and was always the first to be sent for when there was sickness, or a baby coming.

She loved babies, and there was nobody like her to still their cries or make them laugh. If Aunty so much as pointed her finger towards baby's middle and made those indescribable gurgling noises, peals of delighted laughter would instantly burst forth. Babies bathed and powdered by Aunty never chafed; and those square pants she pinned on never cramped nor slipped. Even colic was obedient to her coaxing fingers; for screaming babies laid in her lap flat on their tummies, after a little patting, soon ceased to cry and went peacefully to sleep. Splinters, thorns, and fishbones all responded to her magic touch, and being quickly removed from fingers and throats, were laid on your palm for inspection. She was also a master hand with bread-and-milk poultices or plantain leaves, and any finger she tied up began right away to get well. To have Aunty on call was as good as having a doctor in the house.

II

Mother loved Aunty dearly, and after Grandfather's death, there being no other place for her in Hillsborough, she brought her home from the funeral to live in the country with us, thirty-two long miles away.

Aunty of course paid no board, for, aside from the fact that her income after the war was only thirty dollars a year, such an idea would never have entered Mother's head.

Being much older than my parents, Aunty was always helped first at the table, given the best seat by the fire, which incidentally she never took without being urged, and, as every child knew, must be the first to have her wood box filled, night and morning.

Mother gave her the best bedroom upstairs, soon to be mine too, for needing to be free for the many cares of so large a family, Mother turned me completely over to Aunty. This room at the north end of the house had a window on each side of the fireplace and a third open-

ing on the roof of the piazza towards the east. The north-
west window, overlooking the well, Father's old law
office, and a sort of barn, was a favorite perch of mine,
for here I could watch all the doings near the well: maybe black Maria washing clothes; and maybe chickens,
geese, and other poultry at feeding time, trampling on
the weak ones and pecking viciously as they crowded forward to snatch more than their fair share of the morning
meal. Here too I could see the never-ending show put on
by the pigeons nesting under the eaves of the barn, as
they strutted back and forth, billing and cooing, or
preening their feathers, my mouth watering as I thought
of pigeon pie on my plate at dinner; or, better still, a
squab all wrapped round with slices of bacon, stuffed to
bursting with sage or peanut dressing, and roasted, crisp
and crackling, to a rich brown.

After all, there wasn't much difference between me
and those feathered bipeds down below scrambling and
fighting for their daily ration.

Except perhaps, that I sniffed eagerly the scent of the
white microphylla rose under the parlor window just below; admired the ivy growing so luxuriantly on the
chimney of father's office, or the multiflora rose climbing
over the window; and one summer, leaned every night
from this same window, to look awesomely at the tail of
Halley's Comet, which some people said meant the
world was coming to an end.

III

Aunty had brought from Hillsborough her very own
furniture accumulated through the years, every piece
a gift with its special story. First and foremost, a present
from Grandfather Webb, was the four-poster bed he had
had made from a cherry tree growing in his garden. It
had a big feather bed and mattress that were changed
with the roll of the seasons, from top to bottom, or from
bottom to top. In the winter you snuggled down luxuri-
ously into the depths of the feather bed; and in summer

you lay stretched out comfortably cool on the flat level surface of the mattress. A split-bottomed chair stood conveniently near, to help us climb into this mountain of a bed.

The fine old mahogany bureau, with its small mirror on top of a little drawer where Aunty kept our combs and brushes, was a gift from Grandmother Webb. There were many keepsakes in this bureau, among them one little box of mine which Aunty would show me as a special treat. Looking back, it seems so little; but in those difficult Reconstruction days the tiny fan made of a jay bird's tail feathers tied with blue ribbon, the silver three-cent piece, and the little lace-edged handkerchief seemed to me priceless as rubies. The sad thing about that silver piece is that I have no recollection whatever of ever having had the fun of spending it.

The other three large pieces of furniture, not so grand but indispensable: press, washstand, and cupboard, made by a local carpenter and painted gray, were all given by grateful mothers who had named their babies Margaret Taylor.

Aunt Helen, Mother's oldest sister, who had married Father's oldest brother, Uncle Osmond, when Mother was only ten years old, was the first to do this, having presented Aunty with the press when Cousin Mag was born. Aunt Sarah, Uncle James Webb's wife, had given the bulky old washstand with a top drawer for towels, underneath which, on the two shelves behind double doors, was kept a vast assortment, including our tin foot tub. The blue and white china pitcher and basin were a gift from Uncle John, and beside them, adored by me, was a water pitcher of glazed brown stoneware around the sides of which circled huntsmen, horses, and dogs, in the never-ending chase of a madly running deer. My clumsy hands were strictly forbidden to touch this cherished piece, it having belonged to Aunty's mother.

Over the washstand, hanging in a Hogarth frame,

was a very beautiful sampler which, now moth-eaten but not faded, still lends distinction to my wall. The letters of the hymn on each side, labeled respectively "Morning" and "Evening" were done in stitches so fine you would think they were written in red ink. In these hymns I became well acquainted with the old-fashioned letter *S*, useful knowledge, as it appeared in many other books we possessed. As Aunty washed the night's sleep out of my eyes, we repeated together faithfully each day the Morning hymn until I knew it by heart; though I now remember only the first stanza:

> Awake, my soul, and with the sun
> Thy daily stage of duty run;
> Shake off dull sloth, and joyful rise
> To pay thy morning sacrifice.

There were many embellishments along the sides and top of this sampler and at the bottom it said: "Worked by Lydia Hogg in the 11th year of her age. 1772."

Little Lydia lived then in London, and in the course of time married a sea captain and came to live in Wilmington, North Carolina, where Aunty, her only child, was born. How and why, after the death of both her parents, Aunty came to live in Hillsborough, she never told me, perhaps because she herself didn't know. Hillsborough was her home until she came to live with us, and dearly did she love both the town and its people, making them live again for me in the tales she told.

One romantic story concerned her uncle. His ship had been destroyed by the French, who were supposed to make restoration. People kept on hoping to collect, and in Aunty's will I was left her gold thimble and one fifth of her French Spoliation Claim!

But dearest to me of the three pieces of furniture was the big cupboard which Uncle Tom's wife, Aunt Rob (short for Robina), gave when her first girl was born, Margaret Taylor the second. Never, I thought, was a treasure house equal to this. No matter what the emergency, Aunty could always find something here which just filled the bill.

The gem of the collection nearest Aunty's heart was the glass goblet-shaped sugar bowl, deep red in color, and ornamented with white bunches of grapes and their leaves. The top, curving upward, ended in a cunning little finial which served as a handle. Aunt Rob's mother, Cousin Annabel Norwood, whom Aunty dearly loved, had sent this over for a birthday gift by Alves, then a little boy—destined to die in the war.

IV

Most amazing and delightful was it one day to find tucked away in Aunty's cupboard, of all places, a copy of Byron's complete poems. Having already learned to love Byron by reading in *Hours of Idleness* "The Assyrian came down like the wolf on the fold," and "She walks in beauty like the night," I felt very like the astronomer when "a new planet swims into his ken"; Aunty, however, though she had never read a word of this book given her by her Uncle John, hesitated to let me take it, but, unable to deny me anything my heart was really set on, soon gave in. And so, completely ignorant of Byron's reputation, I went happily off with the book to my little black rocking chair on the piazza, no one ever noticing that here I was at the age of eleven reading *Don Juan*.

It was just as well, for I never found anything in those pages to corrupt my mind. Strange that the most profligate man of his time wrote of love without those sexy, physiological details so common in modern literature. I feel certain that if Byron were now to read many of the modern novels, he would turn away shocked and disgusted. At any rate, reading of Haidee's beauty and Don Juan's admiration, but nothing of passion, when suddenly "a fair and sinless child" appeared, I thought it merely sweet and lovely.

It was the same in George Eliot's *Adam Bede:* a stolen kiss in the buttery, a tryst on a mossy bank; and the next thing you know, Hetty is abandoning Arthur's child by the roadside!

Overwhelming grief and tragedy, but without any salacious details to defile one's mind.

Perhaps the age of innocence is the best time to read some of the world's masterpieces, missing all the implications and understanding only what is beautiful and noble. That is how I read *Gulliver's Travels* and *The Vicar of Wakefield,* which left me completely puzzled by everybody's joy on finding Olivia really married to the detestable Thornhill. How, I wondered, could anybody be glad for my darling Olivia to have a husband like that!

Always the greatest skipper that ever sailed the seas, I tried all of Byron's poems, reading only what I liked, and getting, I think, the cream as I reveled in that night of joy before the battle of Waterloo; the thunderstorm where Jura answers through her misty shroud; the wild farewell that rose from sea to sky, the watchdog's honest bark, and the dying glory over Venice throned on a hundred isles.

When we read that passage at Peace Institute, Lila Anderson raised her hand; "Miss Jane," she said, "there are only seventy-two of those islands."

But, better than all, are those immortal lines that kept my faith alive during two World Wars:

> For freedom's battle once begun
> Bequeathed by bleeding sire to son,
> Though baffled oft, is ever won!

They ought to be engraved on the Arch of Triumph, underneath that inspired sculpture of Rude, when the dying father hands his sword to his son, while above, a woman strides magnificently forward, pointing the way to victory, and shrieking what could only be the Marseillaise: "Marchons, marchons!"

V

Aunty was an early riser, and after we were both dressed, taking me in her lap, she would sit leisurely down by her candlestand near the window and read to me from her large illustrated Bible the greatest stories in the world, fascinating even to the modern child. A little boy, asked recently what book he wanted read to him, exclaimed, "Oh, the Bible; for you never can tell what God will do next." Also on the candlestand was a beautiful copy of the Psalms in very large print from which she read the Twenty-third Psalm so often that I soon knew it by heart. This little book had been given her by Cousin Mag, her first namesake, who had married General Rufus Barringer, the only rich man in the whole connection, and as generous as he was rich.

Aunty found time for catechism and even a little theology, teaching me the awful truth, "Thou God seest me," always and everywhere, no matter how dark the place. Worse still to learn that I had an immortal spirit that would go on living forever and ever. I didn't want this "never dying soul," a completely terrifying and insupportable idea which made me weep so bitterly that Aunty had to give up in despair.

It was the same way when she told me that I must love Mother better than I did her. With floods of tears, I protested that I didn't, and I couldn't, until Aunty, knowing that some day I would, naturally and of my own accord, ceased to argue.

It was the Hillsborough custom for the lady of the house herself to wash the breakfast dishes and count the silver. Aunty had relieved mother of this task, and, as soon as I was big enough, made me her helper. When the weather permitted, we performed this painstaking and solemn ritual on the back platform, first meticulously scraping the plates and dishes before carrying them outside. This being accomplished, the cook brought from the kitchen the large kettle full of boiling water, carefully setting it on a trivet. This was all the water we would have, and not a drop must be wasted. Using a mop, Aunty daintily washing while I wiped, we first did the glasses, teaspoons, saucers, and cups, in the order mentioned. This same water we used to rinse all the remaining dishes, after which Aunty carefully washed out the mop and dish pan in clean, hot soapsuds, removing all traces of grease. All the dishes were then put back in the pan and given a second lavish and final hot rinse. And then with the last of the hot water, carefully saved for this purpose, we again washed out the mop and dish pan, hanging them and the towels up to dry, all as clean as when we started. It was the Hillsborough tradition that mop, dish pan, and dish towels should never be used for any other purpose; and ours never were. Everything connected with food and body belonged in two hemispheres and "never the twain must meet."

I couldn't help thinking of Aunty and myself when at the University of Chicago I saw the girls in Foster Hall use the same washbowl for their faces, hair, lingerie, and dishes. I too washed my dishes at, but not in, that same bowl, holding them carefully under the faucet, but never putting them down in the basin. And I thought of us again when one of the girls studying for a Ph.D. in chemistry, on returning from a visit home invited us to her room for a salad and calmly, before our eyes, washed the lettuce in her basin.

But the high point of our ceremonial dish washing was doing the glasses, Aunty insisting they must shine and show no trace of lint. She impressed this idea upon me by the oft repeated, sad story of a young lady who invited her lover to dinner. The tumblers, alas! were very linty, and he never came back.

VI

Aunty had brought with her not only her furniture, but her flowers. These were the apple of her eye—all hothouse plants, of course, which during the winter were kept in a square pit, with windows on the east and south sides, but a little room overhead, instead of a glass roof, such as the pits in Hillsborough had. Moving these plants backwards and forwards, every spring and fall, was a real job requiring strong men to slide them up or down the planks placed for the occasion over the steps into the pit.

On a sunny shelf under the windows, growing in various pots and boxes, were the many smaller flowers: geraniums, oxalis, fuchsia, cowslips, primroses, tennella, heliotrope, and a marvelous amaryllis.

Kipling tells us: "A garden is not made By singing, 'Oh, how beautiful,' And sitting in the shade." And that eternal truth holds good concerning the watering of hothouse flowers, especially in dog days; and especially from a well sixty feet deep, distant from the flowers a full city block. We children murmured but never shirked; Mother saw to that. The thirsty tubs took a bucket apiece. And it required a lot of strain and will power, even with a watering pot, to pour the water into these boxes kept on high shelves where the dogs couldn't bother them.

Little Alex, the least vociferous and most faithful, when he grew up never could be prevailed upon to water his wife's flowers, telling her he had done enough of that, back in old Randolph, to last a lifetime.

But now, looking back, I know those citrus trees alone made it worth all the effort and strain. They were the only orange and lemon trees the people in our neighborhood had ever seen; and whenever there was somebody burning up with fever, they would come and ask Aunty for a lemon to cool a parched tongue, which she never refused, if there was one on the tree. Aunty kept these lemons as a sort of sacred trust, never taking one for her own pleasure, but always ready, whenever any of us needed it, with hot or cold lemonade.

ANNIE ALVES HUSKE WEBB
Wife of Dr. James Webb of Hillsborough

DR. JAMES WEBB OF HILLSBOROUGH
Physician, Merchant, and Banker

And she always saved an orange for mother to put
in the toe of our Christmas stockings.

VII

The Hillsborough Aunty talked of so much was an
insignificant village of about five hundred people, possessing, however, an importance completely incompatible
with its size and appearance. There was considerable
wealth there, yet no fine houses like those you see in
Virginia; even Mr. Paul Cameron living in one no better
than his neighbors, though reputed to be the richest
man in North Carolina, once owning a thousand slaves
down on his cotton plantation in Mississippi. The court-
house with its fine tower and clock given by George III,
still going strong, was the only show place in town. None
of the churches was at all imposing, nor either of the
principal schools, though the barracks of the Military
Institute had a decided edge on the Misses Nash and
Kollock's fashionable boarding school for young ladies.

Many fine young men, coming to read law or medicine in the offices of the various celebrated lawyers and
doctors, made a welcome addition to society, often marrying Hillsborough girls. One of these lesser lights, the
same, I believe, who afterwards said he was speaking
for Buncombe, blundered into immortality. Having
noticed that many young ladies using the fashionable
new spelling "ie" were signing themselves Sallie, Fannie,
or Marie, he asked one of the Norwood girls in all seri-
ousness, "Miss Belle, why don't you spell your name
with the French termination?"

The streets were mean and often impassable. There
were large flagstones on the sidewalks of Main Street,
but none elsewhere; and when it rained the unpaved
streets became quagmires of deep red mud through
which pedestrians picked a painful and uncertain way,
no lady, it is said, ever being able to lift her flounced and
embroidered petticoats high enough to prevent their becoming scarlet as sin.

The station was over a mile from town, having been placed there for the convenience of Mr. Jones, one of "the people," and, while not so intended, for the enrichment of the hack drivers.

The river Eno divided the town very unequally, only a few families—the Norwoods, James Webbs, Manlys, and Collinses—living "over the river." Between the low river bank and the high bluff where their houses were situated was the Dark Walk, gloomy and dismal even on sunny days, black as Erebus by night, requiring lanterns, yet still the most romantic spot in town, the very mention of which sent thrills and chills running up and down your spine. No one knew how many proposals had resulted there from the sudden involuntary shrinking of timid maidens against their escorts.

Here in this small village lived "the people" and "the other people," attending the same churches, doing business together, exchanging friendly greetings when they met abroad, but in their homes living an entirely separate existence, never exchanging visits or intermarrying. Once when I stopped for a short visit, my cousin Belle said to me, "Mary Alves, you won't have a good time, for there are only two men in town, Jim Kirkland and Winder Webb."

Presently espying a handsome young man approaching, I whispered, "Look, Belle, there's a man."

"He," she told me after saying good morning very pleasantly, "is a Green."

The same unbending attitude prevailed when an important industrialist bought the old Norwood Place and began agriculture on a large scale, building huge barns for his blooded stock. They were not impressed. "He," they said, "had married a Morris."

Beautifully mannered, conscious of their long descent, they went their way serenely, often in shabby clothes, but always looking like the real ladies they were. Even when working their fingers to the bone for a pit-

tance, earned by "Baltimore work," they were not to
be abashed by wealth of "Ormus or of Ind" or by royalty
itself.

"Baltimore work," so-called because carried on from
Baltimore, was the manufacture by hand of exquisite
white garments for infants, children, and even brides.
Notwithstanding the infinitesimal wages paid for the
finest handiwork Southern women were capable of, this
needlework was, nevertheless, a lifesaver for Southern
women, since it was the only way they had of earning
cash money. When in the summer of 1889 I visited my
Hillsborough cousins over the river, they would go
out on the piazza after breakfast, and, stopping only for
meals, stitch away, herringboning and featherstitching,
until it was too dark to see—and yet earn only about ten
dollars a month. Ten dollars—but independence!

Living in this small village were some of the most influential persons of North Carolina: Governor Graham,
who was also Secretary of the Navy during the adminis-
tration of President Fillmore; Judge Nash; the Ruffins,
father and son, both Chief Justices; the Manlys; and
many others, all people of high ideals, with a noble tradition of true hospitality, gracious living, and sincere
friendship, forming, I truly believe, as civilized and delightful a society as ever existed. Except for the institution of slavery! And even this they carried on with
humanity and friendliness.

Among "the people," there was naturally much intermarrying until finally they were all kinfolks. This had
its drawbacks, especially for the young girls, as whenever there was a death, they, like their elders, had to go
into the deep mourning of that time and give up going
to parties. Mary Ruffin, one of the most popular girls,
became a married woman without ever being able to attend a single one of the commencement balls at Chapel
Hill. Anna Huske, more independent, was the talk of
the town upon her announcing when in mourning for

her grandmother Norwood that she was going to the balls, wearing jet ornaments and a white dress with flounces piped in black. Her Aunt Rob was very sarcastic, saying: "Well, Anna, if you have no mourning in your heart, why bother with any mourning in your dress?"

VIII

Somebody had given father a complete set of Walter Scott's works, all destined to be read by me, with the exception of *The Life of Napoleon*. They were tall, heavy volumes bound in faded green and printed in letters small enough to ruin the finest pair of eyes in the world. Having discovered *Tales of a Grandfather*, I was telling everybody who would listen about the derring-do of the Black Douglas, William Wallace, and Robert Bruce; and, since I was of both English and Scotch descent, demanded to know what side I should take at the battle of Bannockburn. With never a neutral bone in my body, long accustomed to glorying in the invincibility of the English at Crecy and Agincourt, I found this was a very real and painful problem; I decided of course in favor of my beloved Robert Bruce.

One well-remembered day Aunty, interrupting my reading, took out of her bureau drawer a little box and showed me, yellow with age, a newspaper clipping announcing that "the amiable and accomplished Miss Elizabeth Hogg" had married Mr. John Huske of Wilmington.

Hogg and Huske! It made me think of the prodigal son, but Aunty said such an idea was sacrilegious, and went on to tell me that John Huske, a splendid young Englishman, becoming shortly after his arrival secretary to Governor Burke, had distinguished himself besides in many ways during the Revolution. These two young people had both died young, leaving two children: Annie Alves, my Grandmother Webb; and a son, John Huske, progenitor of the Wilmington and Fayetteville Huskes.

And finally, she told me that through my great-grandmother Elizabeth Hogg I was a cousin of Walter Scott.
This big news set me all agog, and I was for running
right away to broadcast it to the Sellers children; but
Aunty said that on no account was I to go around saying,
"Cousin Walter Scott," as that was bragging and would
make people laugh at me. This seemed hard lines at
the time, but now when I hear people speaking of Cousin Alfred the Great or Cousin Charlemagne, I see that
as usual Aunty was right.

Continuing to run up the family tree, she told me
that when Elizabeth Hogg's parents, James Hogg and his
wife McDouell Alves, had come to this country, they had
left behind them their youngest daughter Robina, in the
care of McDouell Alves's cousin, in whose home Walter
Scott, another cousin, was a frequent visitor. The friendship begun by these two young people lasted through
life, and when Robina married Judge William Wall
Norwood, Walter Scott presented her with a copy of
his portrait painted by Raeburn. And this portrait
being tragically burned together with her home in Gran-
ville County, he sent her a second copy, now in possession of Barry Bingham of Louisville, Kentucky.

In "Marmion" the Introduction to Canto VI, line
95, Scott describes their common ancestor Walter Scott,
known as "Beardie," because he refused to cut his beard
until the Stuarts were restored:

> With amber beard and flaxen hair
> And reverend apostolic air.

In my eyes the name of Alves now shone with a luster
bright as the morning star.

Robina Hogg Norwood, after her husband died, lived
until her death with her daughter, who had married Mr.
Andrew Mickle of Chapel Hill. Another daughter,
Eliza Norwood, married Mr. William Bingham, head
of the famous Bingham School at Oaks, whose original

methods used by himself so successfully no one could ever copy.

Aunty loved to tell the story of Uncle John's passage at arms with the great man. Mr. Bingham, who did not spare the rod on occasions, often punished the boys by sending them to meditate on their sins in an old shack called "Mahogany," thinking, perhaps, that boredom might be more of a deterrent than pain. Uncle John and his pal Cincy Ashe were on the carpet, and Mr. Bingham, after talking the matter over with the boys, pronounced sentence, saying to Cincy Ashe, "Go to Mahogany for the rest of the day," and then, turning to Uncle John, said, "and you follow him."

Cincy Ashe, however, had other plans. "Let's go fishing," he said, and Uncle John promptly agreed. The next day, Mr. Bingham, having heard of this, called them before him again.

"Cincinnatus Ashe," he said, "didn't I tell you yesterday to go to Mahogany for the rest of the day?"

"Yes, sir."

"And didn't you go fishing instead?"

"Yes, sir."

"This will hurt you more than it does me," said Mr. Bingham, picking up a whip and laying it on with a heavy hand.

Then, whip in hand, he said sternly to Uncle John, "Didn't I tell you to go to Mahogany?"

"No, sir, you didn't," gabbled Uncle John, "you told me to follow Cincy Ashe, and I did, sir. I followed him all day long."

And Mr. Bingham, with that fine sense of justice which made him admired and respected, didn't whip Uncle John.

One of Mr. Bingham's slaves was an ancient Negro woman over ninety, but still active and vigorous. When Mr. Bingham found her planting peach stones, he said, "Why Aunt Nancy, what are you doing that for? Don't you know it takes five years before a peach tree can bear fruit?"

"Laws a massy, Marse William, what if it do? Who can't live five years?"

After his death his sons Colonel Robert Bingham and William Bingham, a distinguished Latin scholar, moved the school to Mebanesville, where it became known as the Bingham Military Institute.

James Hogg and his children held an honored place in the community of Hillsborough, where their father finally pitched his tent. During the Revolution, being completely loyal to the American cause, he raised and financed a regiment to fight against the British.

None of his numerous descendants now living in North Carolina bear his name. And, since Hogg is not a pretty one, probably all of them prefer their own— Webb, Norwood, Long, Mickle, Bingham, Cheshire, Huske, Barringer, and so on ad infinitum.

His eldest daughter, Helen Hogg, was twice married, first to William Hooper, only son of the signer of the Declaration of Independence to reach maturity. He was a professor at Chapel Hill, and his interesting monument is one of the famous landmarks of the campus. Her second husband, Joseph Caldwell, the first president of the University, proved an excellent stepfather to her only child, whose descendant, Louis Graves, is now fittingly enough editor of the Chapel Hill *Weekly*.

Helen Hogg's brother Gavin, who took his mother's name of Alves, had a good deal to do with founding the University of North Carolina; and a letter of his, falling to pieces, but with its fine old handwriting still clear and beautiful, is preserved in the archives of the University. He died unmarried and is buried near his niece, Annie Alves Huske Webb, in the Presbyterian church-yard in Hillsborough.

James Hogg's wife's maiden name of Alves was destined to follow the course of empire westward. Walter

Hogg, eldest son of his parents, did not like the name of Hogg. The story goes that the hated commander Tarleton riding up one day, and seeing Walter standing near, threw his bridle to him, saying insultingly, "Here, you damned Hogg, you, hold my horse." Soon afterward, Walter took his mother's maiden name of Alves, and, going to Kentucky, settled in the town of Henderson, where his numerous descendants and those of other pioneer families still live and have formed an order called "The Transylvanians," honoring their ancestors—among them, James Hogg.

It was natural and beautiful that Aunty should end her long and useful life in the Hillsborough she loved so well, surrounded in her own room by her own cherished possessions, at the home of her beloved cousin, my Aunt Rob. Natural and beautiful too, that she lies buried in the Presbyterian churchyard beside those nearest and dearest to her heart—my Grandfather and Grandmother Webb.

4

WE GO A-VISITING

My oldest sister, Sabra Ramsay, who had Grandma Long's name and also some of her great qualities of strong will and determination, was fated by her ability and initiative to exercise a great influence on all our destinies.

My earliest recollection of her was that here is one who must be obeyed; and when she said, "Stop rocking" or "Quit playing with your fork," you did. And even if she found you were doing something you had no idea was wrong, like climbing on the big bed in the middle room upstairs and jumping off hard when there was company down below, and she suddenly came and slapped you, you quit cold without a single word of complaint, just trying very hard not to cry, though all stirred up inside with wonderment and anger. Thoughtlessness was no excuse with Sabra. There was the summer she came home with a beautiful new white percale dress with blue polka dots. I, wanting to help, persuaded the washerwoman to let me iron it, and of course scorched it a little and thereby earned a dreadful scolding. "You ought to have known better," Sabra told me.

Like all people of great ability she had the faults of her virtues, and I, who profited so much by those abilities, looking back across the years, feel only love, pride, and deep gratitude.

In our family it was Sabra who took the lead when

there was anything disagreeable to be done like telling
Miss Lizzie Caldcleugh after she had stayed with us a
year that she must go to live with her brothers out in
Arkansas. There didn't seem anything Sabra couldn't
do and do better than anybody else. She knew everything Aunty and Mother had to teach about sewing and
knitting, and there wasn't anything they didn't know.
Chemise yokes she embroidered were marvels of eyelet
work, and the sort of stitch required to make tiny roses
and ears of wheat. She was quicker and better than
anyone else in picking berries, cutting stones out of
cling peaches, or fashioning watermelon rind for preserves and pickles into leaves and other designs. And she
would not hesitate to tackle the impossible such as re-
lining the leather curtains of the carriage and making
a good job of it. Nothing daunted my sister Sabra.

Sabra had gone to the Misses Nash and Kollock's
School in Hillsborough and had taken lessons in drawing. She brought home two pictures done in colored
crayons which hung on our parlor walls along with
"Shakespeare and His Friends," and an oil portrait of
Uncle Edwin in his lieutenant's uniform with epaulets,
all of which I greatly admired, hardly knowing which I
liked most. Of the two crayons, I liked best the one
called "The Wedding Ring," which portrayed a beautiful girl in a pale pink dress, dark hair bound with a blue
ribbon, gazing at a gold circlet she was putting on her
finger.

We had one bond in common: we both loved poetry.
Our front piazza was over fifty feet long, and if you
walked it one hundred times you had walked a mile.
We loved doing that especially on rainy days, reciting
poetry as we walked. In that way Sabra taught me her
favorites: "The Bridge of Sighs," "The Raven," and
"The Song of the Shirt." I thrilled to the lines as I did
to the creepy tales of giants and ogres.

Stitch, stitch, stitch, in poverty, hunger, and dirt!

I learned a little of Poe's "Bells," too. Big words were
greatly to my taste. Polysyllabic marvels like "tintinnabulation" were everlastingly fixed in my memory.
And thinking to astonish people, I would try to use them,
getting laughter instead of applause when I spoke of the
"tintinnabulation" of our cowbell.

Such words would come to me when playing games
at church socials in Minneapolis long after I was grown
up. In one game you were asked to write on a slip of
paper a word and a question. After drawing from a hat
full of the folded slips, the players had to write a verse
answering the question and using the word correctly.
On my slip I wrote, "Where do you want to go?" and
"concatenation." The clever author who drew mine
turned in the following: " I long to roam to some lonely
station and find out the meaning of concatenation."

II

The spring I was seven years old Sabra decided to
take me with her on a round of visits, the greatest event
of my short life.

The first visit was to one of her Hillsborough schoolmates, Mrs. Banks Holt, who everyone, in the parlance
of the South, still called "Miss Cattie." The Holts owned
many cotton factories and were among the richest people
in North Carolina. The Banks Holts lived in a big
white house, a quarter of a mile from his father, Mr.
Edwin Holt, who had many sons, all great friends of my
father's. Long years afterwards Sabra met one of them,
Mr. Tom Holt, then governor of North Carolina, in
Chicago, where she had gone for the Columbus Day Celebration in 1892.

"Miss Sabra," he said, "there was never anybody like
your father. When I would come home from the factory,
and the old darkey who came to take my horse would say,
'Mr. William Long's here and is going to stay all night,'
I couldn't get into the house fast enough; for I knew

I was going to hear all the latest talk, and news of the world discussed as only William J. Long could do it."

And then she would go on to tell what great excitement there was whenever Governor Holt's carriage passed in the streets, the crowds always shouting, "It's a long time between drinks."

It was a very happy time for me at the Holts', where there was plenty of everything, and nobody wondering as we did when there was company, "What in the world are we going to give them to eat?" Here there was fried chicken almost every day, peach preserves, and Miss Cattie's specialty, mammoth jelly cakes—with four layers.

Then there were the two little girls, Mamie and Bettie, to play with, and lots of toys such as I had never seen. I loved to follow Miss Cattie with her big string of keys as she made the rounds of her storehouses and see the great cans of lard, big home-cured hams, boxes of raisins, and the other goodies in which those shelves abounded.

Among other things the Holts had which we didn't was a private burying ground that I could see from our bedroom window. I would rise up in bed at night, look fearfully at the shining white tombstones, dreading, but half hoping I might see a ghost, which the darkies had told me often haunted graveyards at night.

III

There was a great day coming, and it finally arrived. There had been an invitation to spend the day, children and all, at Mr. Edwin Holt's, the occasion being the bringing home of the bride by his youngest son, Mr. Lawrence Holt. The entertainment given for the bride by the bridegroom's parents was called an "infare," one of those old Chaucerian words that last as long as the custom survives.

The Holt family came from far and near to attend this celebration. Besides the Banks Holts and the Will

Holts, who lived in the neighborhood, there were the
Tom Holts from Haw River with their daughters,
Cora and Daisy; the James Holts from Graham; and also
from Graham Mr. Holt's married daughters and their
families, the Williamsons and the Whites. It was a great
concourse, but I had my share of attention, Cora and
Daisy taking me up to their mother's room and putting
some cologne on my handkerchief out of a cut-glass bottle
on the bureau which had a mirror so big you could see
yourself clear down to your toes.

And then we all went downstairs to see the bride,
Miss Maggie Erwin, from Morganton, said to be a great
beauty. And certainly when she burst upon my sight
she was the vision of loveliness that every bride would
wish to be. The vision has never faded, for I can still see
her as she looked that day in her beautiful lavender silk
dress, sitting in the center of the room, smiling at all
those who crowded around to greet her. I gazed till
somebody dragged me off to the yard for games with the
other children.

There were so many grown-ups that we children ate
at the second table, feasting on turkey and a dish I had
never seen before called macaroni but which I immediately liked on account of the cheese. I thought of
Yankee Doodle and wondered why he had ever called
the feather in his cap macaroni.

IV

After dinner we children went into the garden to look
at the flowers where a Negro woman we called Aunt
Hannah busily raked and weeded. She was very friendly,
and when we admired the hyacinths in full bloom she
told us we could pick as many as we liked. That sounded
very strange to me, for at home any child caught picking
hyacinths would be whipped. So I hung back at first,
but as everybody else was plucking great handfuls, I
gathered a big armful too. Then, as children do, the

others started off to show their flowers to their mothers. I
was distinctly reluctant to show mine to Sabra; her regarding with favor any child picking hyacinths was beyond my imagining. But I tagged along behind Mamie
Holt, the first to enter the parlor, still hanging back waiting to see what would happen. And then, just as I had
expected, everybody began saying: "Naughty child!"
"The very idea, she might have known better," paying no
attention at all to Mamie's protests that Aunt Hannah
had told her she might. Unseen, I backed out into the
hall, not knowing exactly what to do next; and then in
came Willie Williamson. "Willie," I told him extending
my bunch, "you can have mine if you want to." Willie
asked no questions and gleefully added them to his own
sizable armful. But the storm of protests excited by
Mamie's hyacinths was nothing to what broke loose at
Willie's entrance. Mrs. Edwin Holt was so angry that
she could hardly speak, and all the other children coming with more hyacinths created such a hubbub that I
crept unnoticed into the yard, feeling thankful for my
presence of mind. No one had mentioned me, and I
thought I was now quite safe from discovery.

As I was walking back that evening with Sabra, she
said, "Mary Alves, did you pick any hyacinths?" Firmly
and unblushingly I answered, "No"; and there the matter rests till the Judgment Day.

v

When our visit to the Holts was ended we went to
Graham, where we had two first cousins: Cousin Sallie
King and Cousin Lizzie Graham. In those days a first
cousin was somebody you felt free to visit whenever you
wanted to. All you had to do was send word you were
coming. Graham was the town we went to when taking
the train to Hillsborough or Raleigh, and we always
spent the night with one of these two cousins, generally
Cousin Sallie, as she had lived at our house from the
time she was seven, when her mother died, until her

marriage to Tom King, and was just like their own sister to Sabra and my other sisters who had grown up with her. Miss Cattie drove us over in her beautiful new carriage, my soul expanding almost visibly with the delight of riding in an equipage of such style and elegance, just the kind suited for arrival at the Kings', who lived in a large, imposing-looking white house set way back from the street and distinguished from all others by one large very high sharp-pointed gable right in the middle of the roof. This "mansion" as I mentally dubbed it, remembering my favorite hymn:

> When I can read my title clear
> To mansions in the skies. . .

looked very grand to me; and the bedroom furniture painted a pale green with wreaths of pink flowers seemed ever so much prettier than our gloomy spool beds and mahogany four-posters. The young care little for antiques. That is an acquired taste.

Cousin Sallie was very pretty and wore beautiful clothes and hats which her husband always selected for her himself in Washington and Baltimore, where he often went. So sweet and lovely to me I loved her dearly; but I stood in awe of her husband, a big, handsome sort of man, albeit with rather coarse features, whom I always addressed as Mr. King instead of Cousin Tom.

I was a little afraid of his parents too, especially his mother, who had a way of shaking her head when put out, as she often was, though I am bound to say never with me. His father, a silent man who hardly ever spoke a word, it was whispered, had been a slave trader—something of which it seemed one should be much ashamed. It appeared that there were many niceties connected with the slave trade. One might buy and own slaves, and even give them away for wedding presents, but never, never sell them, nor whip them. One must be what the standards of the time considered a good master, or stand forever condemned in the eyes of one's fellowmen. A most remarkable epitaph in St. Michael's Church in Charleston, South Carolina, in its eulogistic catalogue of the man's virtues in the various relationships of life does not neglect to enumerate that he was also a good master.

One of our neighbors who, according to the darkies, had beaten a slave till he bled and then rubbed salt in the wounds was henceforth regarded with horror by the whole community.

Mr. King, himself an only child, disciplined their only child by proxy. He never corrected the boy himself, but would say: "Sallie, Tommy is wading in a mud puddle; go out and tell him to come into the house"; or even, sitting at the table with him, when Tommy would bang the silver about he'd say, "Sallie, tell Tommy to quit making that noise." And if there was any punishment, it was Cousin Sallie who meted it out.

VI

Tom King, destined to fail terribly as a husband, had already done so as a man, concerning which, of course, I knew nothing. When children came where people were talking of such things, somebody would speak of "little pitchers" and change the subject. Certainly there was then nothing wrong in his conduct in the home that a child would notice, and anyway I thought grown-ups always did right.

He was surely a good "provider." There seemed to be plenty of money for everything and lots of good things to eat. There was a silver ice pitcher just like the Holts' and a parlor full of fine furniture: no slippery haircloth on the chairs and sofas, but real velvet so soft to touch; a whatnot with lovely ornaments Tommy and I were not allowed to handle; a rosewood piano; and what I liked best, a kaleidoscope and a stereoscope—wonders I had never before seen.

Yes, Cousin Sallie had everything she wanted, including a fine horse and buggy, and seemed happy in spite of the fact that some of her relatives would have nothing to do with her. She was considered to have married beneath her in the first place; so when feeling already running high over Tom King's unsavory record as a member of the Ku Klux Klan was heightened by his turning Republican, either of which was enough to put him beyond the pale, ostracism became as inevitable as taxes.

Being a Ku Kluxer was not so bad, but when he and others were arrested and thrown into jail charged with hanging a Negro in Graham, he turned state's evidence, going scot-free while others were sentenced to prison; he was henceforth known as "Tom King the traitor." Joe Turner, one of those sentenced and a newspaper editor with a gift for satire, loved to lambast him and kept his infamy alive by constant lampoons. Perhaps after having sunk so low in popular esteem, it was only natural for him to seek prosperity by becoming a Republican and an officeholder. People have short memories, and nothing succeeds like success; so Tom King, after being a Federal Judge for many years, finally, his former infamies forgotten, died a respected man.

VII

As for Republicans, in those days there were no gradations as in the case of Reds, sometimes admittedly pink. It was always "Black Republican"—never gray or ash-colored. It is difficult now to understand the concentrated hate which Southerners felt for Republicans. But there it was—deep, intense, bitter as gall, the sort of feeling one has for deserters in time of war. These men, it was felt, had no longer any loyalty to the "Lost Cause," still as dear to the South in the day of defeat and humiliation as it ever had been in time of battle; and therefore they deserved to be treated as traitors who had sold themselves to the Republican party for pieces of silver. And some of them were.

Another cousin's husband, Rufus Barringer, a general in the Confederate army and a brother-in-law of Stonewall Jackson, after becoming a Republican had actually been refused communion in the First Presbyterian Church of Charlotte by another brother-in-law, D. H. Hill, also a prominent Confederate general, who, considering a Republican unfit to sit at the Lord's table, refused to pass him the bread and wine. This caused a split in the church, as my cousin's husband, a fine honorable man of great influence, left the First Church and started the Second Presbyterian Church, which equaled in importance the one from which it separated.

If you ask why such a man became a Republican, his apologists will tell you that it was because he hoped that if he and a good many other Southerners became Republicans, they would have influence enough to prevent the excesses that party was inflicting on the South.

Madison Leech, a Democratic politician of considerable influence, had made a speech quoted from Currituck to Cherokee in which he said: "The Ethiopian cannot change his skin, nor the leopard his spots, but by God, folks, how quick a white man becomes a nigger when he turns Republican." This speech was to become a terrible boomerang, for when he afterwards turned Republican and became a candidate for office, every newspaper made it a headline, and every orator in the campaign shouted it from the platform and pointed to Mad Leech as a horrible example of a white man becoming a nigger.

VIII

One fine day, we kissed Cousin Sallie good-by and went to visit Cousin Lizzie Graham, Uncle James Webb's eldest daughter, who was considered to have made a brilliant marriage when she wedded the rising young lawyer, Captain James Graham, the son of Governor Graham, whose praises father was always singing. During the war they had both been members of the Peace party, the idea being for the United States Government to end the war by buying and freeing all the slaves.

Governor Graham had given the young couple a pretty white house right next to the James Holts'. I greatly admired the back porch, which, enclosed in lattice work, was always cool and shady.

Here the event of the day which I enjoyed hugely was going with the colored nurse when she took baby James Augustus for his daily ride in the carriage, which I was allowed to help push. Usually we joined the nurse airing Dr. John Ruffin's children, Sterling and Allan, destined to be famous doctors. And very often joining other nurses, we would seek a shady spot and carry on a great confabulation. But once James's nurse took us to the jail, where she talked for a long time through the iron bars to a Negro man in the second story. Nothing very private about this conversation, which had to be shouted in order to be intelligible. On the way back I promised never to tell where we had been.

Cousin Lizzie had on her parlor table an exciting new book in large print with pictures called *Enoch Arden,* by Alfred Tennyson, which I read with many tears.

And then I spoiled all this fun by having sore eyes. Sabra had to bathe them in warm water every morning before I could open them, and I was obliged to stay in our room upstairs all day long, away from everybody and everything. Sabra knew me well enough to put all books out of reach. When my eyes were well Cousin Sallie came to drive us to the station a mile from the town as people objected to the noise of the trains, never thinking whether or not this would be good for business. Except for my sore eyes, it had been a lovely visit, but all regrets were forgotten in the excitement of riding on the train to Greensboro.

IX

Sister Annie, who was teaching in Greensboro, met
us at the station, and now I discovered that Sabra was
to stay at the Foulkeses' while I was to go with Sister
Annie to her boardinghouse. Here I became the pet of
the boarders, who laughed at everything I said. I suppose I was a precocious child; at any rate when I talked to
them about *Enoch Arden* and Poe's "Raven" or repeated
father's remarks about why there should be a hell, they
went off into fits of laughter. Captain and Mrs. Whaling
were among the boarders, and their sons, Thornton,
Horace, and Josh, were my playmates. Josh and I pulled
no punches, but once when we were struggling over
some trifle, the jacket of my dress flew open, revealing
my white underwaist; and Josh laughed. Deep mortification set in, making me wretched for days.

Nearly every afternoon Sister Annie, after putting
a clean dress on me, would take me downtown or go
visiting. Sometimes we would stop at Mr. Clark Porter's
drugstore, made famous by O. Henry, and get one of
those effervescent drinks that made such queer feelings
in my nose; and often we went to call on Miss Bertie
Sloan, whose real name was Mrs. Clark Porter. There
were Venetian blinds at her front door, making the
house inside look cool and pleasant.

The place I liked best was Mr. Cyrus Mendenhall's
big white house on Main Street opposite the McAdoo
Hotel. The Mendenhall house was set back in a yard
full of shrubbery and flowers, and tucked away under
overhanging vines was a summer house. It was fun
promenading down Main Street, cool and shady then
with great elm trees arching overhead; fun looking in
the shop windows; and fun watching ladies buggy riding with their beaux.

Mr. Mendenhall, a famous lawyer, tall and handsome,
with a close-cropped white beard, had been brought up
a Quaker together with his brothers, Junius and Nereus,

but was one no longer, having married outside the church. Sister Annie was great friends with his wife, a Miss Staples from Virginia, pretty, gay, and a very lively lady. She loved company, and evenings and especially Sunday afternoons it seemed as if the whole town came to play the piano and drink lemonade. Besides the piano there was a harp, a big golden affair belonging to Mary Mendenhall which I liked to go up and touch—"A harp within my hand."

Miss Mary Tate, the prettiest girl in town, arrayed in a froth of white muslin and lace with parasol and fan would come dashing up in a barouche drawn by two horses, Mr. Lionel Leversedge in white linen rushing to be the first to help her out and escort her into the house.

Lionel Leversedge! What a beautiful name, I thought, saying it over and over. There was a whole family of Leversedges, English people, who were finding it difficult to live in this strange new country where they had come to seek their fortunes. Mrs. Mendenhall had taken them under her wing, and Lionel, his sister Mary, and little Blanche, just right to be my playmate, were almost a part of the family.

In spite of all these excitements, I became very homesick; and Sabra, finding some of our neighbors uptown who were willing to take me back in their wagon, decided to send me home. They were to pick me up at Mr. Mendenhall's, where I was sent to meet them, carrying a large tin pail half full of oranges. When walking timidly up the path, I saw Mr. Mendenhall sitting on the porch surrounded by a group of his lawyer friends, I was completely overcome, not knowing what to do. Mr. Mendenhall came down the steps, and when I told him why I was there, he took me by the hand and, telling those distinguished-looking men that this was little Mary Alves Long, daughter of William J. Long, led me into the house to wait, saying he would call me when the wagon came. And when it did, taking me by one hand

and carrying my tin pail with the other, he took me out and lifted me into the shabby, rickety old wagon of which, little snob that I was, I felt deeply ashamed as I contrasted it with Cousin Sally King's and Mr. Banks Holt's equipages.

Anderson Moser, the owner, honest but poor, who had married Phoebe Ann Black, sat on the front seat with Bing Smith, son of that Adam who swore, and then beside me on the straw was Alice Jordan, whom I knew well and was truly rejoiced to see, feeling safe and happy to think I was going home. Alice, the daughter of Dr. Jordan, a traveling dentist who lived about four miles from us, was only about six years older than I was, but what a difference there was between us. She could saddle and bridle her own horse and, standing on the ground, put one foot into the stirrup and leap into the saddle. How she happened to go to Greensboro with Anderson Moser and Bing Smith no one ever explained; nor was I curious to know, as everything seemed to me natural and right as I am sure it was, since Sabra had given me into their care.

I spent the night at Alice's, sleeping in a bed decked with sheets, pillow cases, and counterpane made of gayly colored homespun woven by Mrs. Jordan.

The problem of getting me home next day, no one there knowing I was coming, was solved by Alice. After storing all my possessions away in saddlebags, placed carefully underneath the saddle, she mounted her horse, which I bestrode behind her, having both my arms clasped firmly about her waist.

"Hold on tight, now, Mary Alves," she said, as whipping up the horse we went galloping off home.

John saw us first, and gave a big whoop. "Here's Sis," he yelled, and everybody came running to welcome me back on my first homecoming.

x

Mother generally took me with her on those joyful occasions when she went to see her brothers in Hillsborough. My first recollection of these begins on the train where Mother and I were the only passengers, except for a Negro man sitting in the rear. I must have been very young, for I began a lively conversation with him, which was interrupted by Mother, who, calling me to her, whispering so as not to hurt his feelings, told me sternly that I was not to talk to strange Negro men, ever. So I had to content myself with looking out of the window—a dull prospect except at Haw River, where I always craned my neck for a look at the enchanting though distant view of Mr. Tom Holt's handsome big white house.

As a rule we stayed first with Uncle Tom, who lived next door to Mother's old home, still standing; but, since it was occupied by people we didn't know, I saw it only from the outside.

Mother had led a wonderful life in that old yellow house noted for the gracious hospitality dispensed by her parents. Grandfather Webb must have been a generous man, for besides his eight children and Aunty, there were his three orphan nephews, Hal, William P., and James D. Webb, all of whom went later to Alabama, where so many ambitious young men in North Carolina went to seek their fortunes.

It was a musical family, all gathering round Mother at the piano to sing part songs, their soprano, alto, bass, and tenor voices blending in one grand harmony. Sometimes Mother played the guitar, a beautiful instrument which her brothers had imported from Paris for her birthday gift. I used to marvel at its beauty and also at the contrast between the satinwood case with its narrow band of mother-of-pearl inlay and the plain pine of the sounding board. After Mother's death it became my most precious memento, which I did my best to preserve, but furnace-heated houses did not agree with its constitution, and finally, like the "one hoss shay," it lapsed into complete disintegration.

Here, growing up in this lively, prosperous, and carefree household, Mother had met and known all the distinguished people of the town and its many visitors, knowing nothing of the problems that bothered me. Wearing her own pretty clothes—no hand-me-downs—but bought specially for her with hat, gloves, and new shoes; going to school with other children, and to church and Sunday school, with money to put in the collection; never worrying over any scarcity in the family larder when company came, nor cows and bulls when sent on errands; and, being waited on by faithful, well-trained slaves, never performing any tasks more strenuous than sewing or knitting, Mother had led a life that compared with mine was a charmed existence.

However the hardships of her daily life at our house had left no mark on her, and she slipped back into life in Hillsborough as easily as into an old shoe. Of course, almost everyone being poor after the war, the difference was not so marked; townspeople often had to worry over food and fuel more even than Mother did.

There were the Heartts living next door to Uncle Tom in a very old house with practically no income except what Miss Alice and her widowed sister, Mrs. Bragg, earned by teaching a little school. Mrs. Heartt and their aunt, Miss Henrietta, wearing white caps, and bent almost double, seemed older than Grandma Long. When you went with Mother to visit the Heartts, you felt very quiet and subdued, speaking only when spoken to, and being very glad when it was time to say good-by.

Opposite Uncle Tom's was a tiny house with high steps which had once been Grandfather Webb's office. It was only a stone's throw from his house, but Mother said her cousin Hal was such a lazy boy he would always insist on riding horseback when coming or going.

At the foot of the unpaved street, very like a country road, there was a Negro church where white women from the North living in a little house next door taught a Negro school; their ostracism was absolute.

My cousin, Alves Webb, who was wearing aprons when I first remember him, as he sat beside me in front of the fire, tried to impress me by pushing a pin in and out of his apron to gather on it as much cloth as possible.

"You can't do that," he told me triumphantly. But being a girl, and a year older, I could and did.

Alves was fond of damson preserves. When sent to play in the yard, he would come in every few minutes to ask, "Mother, may I have some damson preserves?" "No, Alves, you can't," Aunt Rob would say. This would go on all the morning, Alves never giving up, and Aunt Rob never yielding.

Uncle Tom was a lawyer, and since court was in session he brought a number of his friends home to the four o'clock dinner, all leaving their high silk hats on the front porch, where we children awaited our call to the second table. Cousin Maggie started to put one on. "Don't touch it," Cousin John said. "He's a black Republican." And she dropped it like a hot potato. "What is a Republican?" I wanted to know. But nobody could explain except to say he was somebody not fit to wipe your shoes on.

Uncle James Webb lived over the river on a bluff bordered by the Dark Walk, two spots most alluring to my imaginative mind. Just inside the gate was an enormous beech tree bearing tiny but delicious nuts which, if ripe, I always stopped to eat in preparation for the steep climb to the house at the top of the hill.

Uncle James had married Miss Sarah Cheshire. One of Mother's favorite stories was about the journey to their wedding at Edenton. As there had been heavy rains the roads were almost impassable, the wheels of their carriage sinking in almost up to the hubs. As they must get there on time whether or no, they took many chances, crossing bridges over flooded streams when the planks were actually floating off underneath the horses' hoofs. Nor were they particular where they spent the night, staying at all sorts of queer places, just wherever they happened to be when night fell. Part of Mother's tale was this funny story of a man saying, "Oh Josiah, tell Hezekiah to tell Jeremiah to come in 'hyiah' and fix this 'fiah.' "

And Aunt Sarah, now stout and fat, was slender then with a waist so tiny you could span it with your two hands.

Unlike ours, Uncle James's yard was full of shrubbery and the most beautiful evergreen trees, all planted by Aunt Sarah's brother, the Reverend Joseph Cheshire, of Tarboro, who, wishing to escape the heat of the low country, always brought his family here for the summer. It was just like being in the country at Uncle James's, as there was not another house to be seen, only woods and fields in one of which was the famous mineral spring, making it a convenient place for picnics. Most exciting was the frequent and eventful passing of the train, a sight of never failing interest, far better in my opinion than having neighbors.

These, however, though unseen, were not far away. There were the Manlys, as the crow flies only about a block away on top of the next hill. At the bottom of this hill, growing on the Manly's side of the fence separating the two estates was a walnut tree, the cause of much dissension between my Cousin Maggie Webb and Sadie Manly. Whenever Maggie went to pick up the nuts falling on her side of the fence, Sadie would always violently protest, though never daring in the face of Maggie's equally violent claims to come over and pick them up.

On the opposite side of the house, not much farther off than the Manlys, was Poplar Grove, built by James

Hogg, where we often went to see my cousins, Anna and Lizzie Huske, who were much older than I. Here you had to keep very quiet as their grandmother, Cousin Annabel Norwood, was a very nervous person. Somebody was always saying "shush," and even when out of doors we spoke in whispers.

The Hazel Norwoods lived just beyond with their three little girls, and here you could be natural once more. Emily, the youngest, had a fine spirit. She had invited one of her rich schoolmates at the Misses Nash and Kollock's School to spend the afternoon. This little girl, who had expected to find Emily in surroundings suited to her appearance, began to make unkind remarks.

"Why, you live in a log house!" she said scornfully, "and you haven't got a silver ice pitcher. And you haven't got a Brussels carpet and no piano either."

"No," said Emily goaded beyond endurance, "we haven't, but we've got *manners*."

Very like ours was the size of Uncle James's family. Of his eleven children all were living at home with the exception of Cousin Lizzie Graham, and Cousin John Cox who had gone to Alabama. Then Uncle John also lived there, sleeping in "Kansas" as they called the little house where the overflow was accommodated; and Cousin Jim Fat, who had never shaken off the nickname acquired in babyhood though now tall, slim, and handsome, had brought his bride, Miss Rebecca Ruffin, home to live until times grew better; this making in all, I believe, a baker's dozen. But in those days, in spite of poverty and hard times, people still kept open house, and so they found somehow a bed and a place at the table for Mother and me.

And such a table! Aunt Sarah's dinners, noted for abundance, variety, and good cooking, were something to brag of. One of her specialties was stewed chicken and corn, a combination I never saw anywhere else, but the way she cooked it, something to lick your chops about. And so was her baked home-cured ham boiled in cider and, all sugared and spiced, roasted to a rich crusty brown. Aunt Sarah was famous for her pickles, too, especially her mangoes made by a recipe that claimed to make pickles seven years old in five hours. And her cake made with dried peaches instead of raisins and citron tasted almost as good as a regular fruit cake.

Cousin Jim was a hunter of renown, and when he went after partridges with his two bird dogs, the black and white pointer and the brown setter with perfectly marcelled coat, scampering eagerly along, he thought anything less than a hundred quail a poor bag.

These birds stewed in rich milk and butter, a dish much to Mother's liking, made a mighty good breakfast on cold frosty mornings. The topic everybody was discussing that year was whether it was possible to eat a partridge a day for thirty days in succession, the consensus of opinion being, "Of course—just give me a chance."

There was always plenty of rich milk, cream, and butter, as Uncle James kept a Jersey cow that produced more than all our cows put together. Aunt Sarah's fancy work when she came into the parlor after supper was "churning," not hard labor as practiced by Mary Shepherd and me; no, this was just like falling off a log. Sitting very daintily on the sofa with a big bowl of cream in her lap, Aunt Sarah, after making a few passes at the contents with a stout silver spoon, soon had a bowl full of firm golden butter.

"Why don't we churn like that?" I asked Mother.

"Because," she said, "we don't keep a Jersey cow."

Uncle John was always saying, "It's no disgrace to be poor, but it's powerful unhandy."

It was a very gay, happy family, full of jest and laughter with apparently no cares. Cousin Jim, in a state of newly wedded bliss, always went out to supper with his arm about his bride's waist, and I followed behind, full of thrills at beholding this romantic behavior. Cousin Annie, the beauty of the family, bent her charming head, crowned with a big chignon, over a piece of embroidery. Cousin Sarah did the same; but the other girls, all going to the Misses Nash and Kollock's School, had nothing to do except lessons.

These young girls gave me to understand that you had to be born in Hillsborough, that very wonderful place, in order to be a lady. When I went home and conveyed this sad news to my Cousin Eleanor Long, she laughed it to scorn, saying if that were true there would be very few ladies in the world.

My cousin Winder, being a boy a year younger than I, had no such ideas in his head; and together we roamed happily about the rocks above the Dark Walk gathering moss and lichens to decorate the graves in the cemetery for birds and cats, a joint project of Winder and his young sister. In our zeal we altered the original plan, for which we were severely scolded by her, who, putting everything back the way it was before, asked me how I, a perfect stranger, dared to change anything she had done. So then Winder and I began a brand new burying ground under a dogwood tree, the first interment being an old shoe the setter had dragged in.

The books I discovered on the shelves were all new and excitingly different. I liked the *Swiss Family Robinson* as much as *Robinson Crusoe;* and the *Old Mamzelle's Secret* and *The Dove in the Eagle's Nest,* my first experience with modern fiction, were even more thrilling than *The Vicar of Wakefield.*

It was in Hillsborough that I first began to notice that my clothes were strangely different. There were my gloves for instance—a pair donated by Cousin Mag—a bright Irish green, when everybody else was wearing black. I felt bare hands were less conspicuous, and carried my green gloves tightly crumpled in my hand. I became deeply conscious that my dresses were not in the prevailing fashion either, and this consciousness of being different made me shy and uncomfortable.

But once when we went to Uncle James's I had a dress that I thought was beautiful and right. Sister Annie had made it for me out of one of her old ones— a blue barége with a redingote trimmed with a picot edged ribbon to match.

Cousin Lizzie Graham was there with James Augustus, and my cousin Maggie was going to take him to see his grandmother, Mrs. Graham. Somehow it seemed very important for me to go, though not invited; and when Maggie was ready to start, there I was all dressed up in my blue barége with the firm intention of accompanying her. Though she said nothing, her looks as plainly as words told me that I was not wanted, though why I don't know. It was a very uneventful trip, of which nothing remains except a dim memory of Mrs. Graham. It was just one of the many things in Hillsborough which made me feel odd and out of my element.

Moments of unalloyed joy were those when I went with Aunt Sarah and Mother to Uncle James's store, where he, his two sons, and Uncle John spent most of their waking lives. This was no emporium, but just a plain country store. Behind it was a large wagon yard where the country people came to spend the night. This meant that instead of shutting up the store at night and going home till morning, somebody always had to be in the store ready to trade with them at all hours, a dog's life for any man. When Cousin Jim, years after, came to visit us in Minneapolis and saw men at home in the evenings with their families, watering the grass, or reading the newspaper, he said that was his idea of heaven. My brother Will clerked for a time in this store and often slept there all night with a Hillsborough boy named Fletcher Parks. A rusty old gun had been given them just in case there was a burglar. One night they were waked by a noise which seemed to be in the next room and, thinking to frighten the burglar away, fired off the gun through the transom. All was quiet except for a noise of dripping, drop by drop. Too frightened to investigate, they decided that the man they had shot was bleeding gradually to death. When daylight came the noise had stopped; and, finally going in, they discovered their victim to be a water bucket, now empty, standing on a shelf with a hole in its side.

These country stores are great money-makers, and this was no exception, all the sons including Winder becoming reasonably rich. Winder, who continued to live with his sisters in the old house, made many modern improvements, putting in central heat and a bathroom. He bought an automobile and wrote fairy tales to us about going to our old home and back in less than two hours. We couldn't believe it, remembering how long those painful journeys through mud and rain had been in days of yore. He loved Hillsborough and was well content to spend his life there, where often he was the only beau at the party in this town of girls, all depending on him to see them safely there and home again. For Hillsborough still had parties; beaux or no beaux, life must go on. And remembering how many women were happier because of him, who shall say his life was not well spent?

As for me, my memories are of sunshine and shadow. And one of the sunniest is when I returned, a girl of sixteen, wearing a blue cashmere dress made in the latest fashion and a white plush hat sporting a saucy ostrich feather.

5

SCHOOL DAYS

AFTER THE SURRENDER the only schools in our neighborhood within walking distance from us were "free" schools, which for many reasons Mary Shepherd and I were not allowed to attend—undesirable associations—poor teachers—of no educational value whatever. Pleasant Lodge Academy was where we longed to go, but even if there had been money enough, walking three miles twice a day was out of the question.

My sisters had been more fortunate, having gone to Smithwood under Mr. Thad Troy, a teacher whom they and everyone who knew him thought unsurpassed. Strict in discipline, tolerating no laxity in lessons or behavior, he nevertheless joked and played with his pupils during recess, making school so attractive that truancy and tardiness were practically nil. When Mr. Troy went on to wider fields, Father had employed various governesses, the one most talked of being Cousin Sue Webb, sister of "Old Sawney," whose renown as an educator was known and acclaimed all over the South and even at Yale and Princeton.

Governesses of course were now beyond us, and as my sisters themselves were teaching away from home, Mother undertook to teach Mary Shepherd and me. Mother had received the best education of her day and spoke of her teachers, Mrs. Robert Burwell and Miss Burke, daughter of Governor Burke, with the greatest respect and admiration. Besides being grounded in grammar and other branches considered essential, she had learned to paint on rice paper, to sing, and play extremely well on the piano and guitar, both by ear and by note. Mother was not one of those people who say when asked to sing or play, "Oh, I'm so sorry; I've left my music at home," for her extensive repertory was at her fingers' ends and after hearing a tune once she could come home, play it on the piano, and remember it forever. One of her pieces we asked for oftenest was "The Circus," so called because she had heard it played by a circus band. She had a beautiful voice that charmed all her listeners when she sang "Kathleen Mavourneen," "A Wet Sheet and a Flowing Sea," "Believe Me If All Those Endearing Young Charms," or "I Dreamt That I Dwelt in Marble Halls."

Mother's method was very simple. After breakfast when all our morning tasks were done, such as helping Aunty wash the dishes or claying the hearth, she would send us upstairs to study the lessons assigned the day before. Mother was thorough. She expected you to know your lesson, and if you didn't she kept on sending you back till you did. Grammar was her specialty. She was determined we should know grammar: declensions, conjugations, and parsing, and moreover that knowing it, we should speak correctly. Mother was as sensitive to bad grammar as she was to a false note in music; and no matter how many times a day her delicate ear was assailed by a double negative, or "I done it," "I seen it," "ain't," or "It's me, her, him, or us," she was always there, Johnny on the spot, to set us right. And if I ever said "me'n Mary Shepherd," her automatic response was invariably, "Why, you called her *mean*. You must say, 'Mary Shepherd and me,' if you want to be polite."

It's a wonder she made any headway, for between the Negroes and the many uneducated people in our neighborhood nobody could have been more exposed to bad

English. Daily we heard such atrocities as "yistiddy," "I would er went," "use to could," "ketch" or "cotch" for catch, "knowed," "gwine" for going, "ax" for ask, "hearn tell of" or "cain't." And how we laughed when Sue Martin, who had heard it was wrong to say the "pint" of a needle, came to borrow a "point" of vinegar.

I rather liked conjugations, especially the subjunctive. It was fun saying: I might, could, would, or should be, thou mightst, couldst, wouldst, or shouldst be, and so on in all three persons singular and plural. And irregular verbs were my meat. I knew the principal parts of every last one of them. Mother wasn't satisfied with our parsing the sentences in the grammar, but had us parse in Pollock's "Course of Time" and Young's "Night Thoughts." Sis Jane brought home a book with diagramming, which I adored and in which I excelled. I always knew where to put those straight or slanting marks, or those modifying phrases and clauses on ladder-like formations.

I liked geography, too, and learned every cape, north, east, south, and west, in all the continents. Also the principal cities of the world and all the capitals of the United States, which we not only named but located on rivers or bays. Mother would let me chant or sing them —Augusta on the Kennebec River, Concord on the Merrimac River, Newport on Narragansett Bay. That was easy to remember on account of the song:

> Toll, toll the bell
> At early dawn of day,
> For bright-eyed little Nell
> Of Narragansett Bay.

My sense of rhythm demanded a body of water for every town, and it bothered me that the map did not show Raleigh actually on a river; so mother said I might say "Raleigh near the Neuse." The capital of Florida was not on or near anything, but mother had a happy thought, and I sang rhythmically "Tallahassee inland."

Arithmetic we passed over lightly. Except for the multiplication table, all the weights and measures, multiplication, division, addition, and subtraction, and fractions including the vulgar variety, I knew practically nothing about it. Those a, b, and c sums were beyond me then—and now.

I learned geography, too, in our walks abroad. Our favorite walk was by the mill pond, where Mother would point out isthmuses, peninsulas, capes, or islands, and ask us to identify them. That was fun too.

As for spelling, it was duck soup. The method was to spell by syllables. From two syllables, B-A, bay, K-E-R, ker—baker, to polysyllables like *immateriality* at the back of the book. All that's out of fashion now, and so is good spelling. I never could understand why my pupils who could say "man" or "age" written separately couldn't when they were written together say "manage." I had never heard the term "visual," but I know now that I was a visualizer. Any word I had a mental picture of I could spell. Another thing that helped was that Will and John were forever asking me to spell words that stump most people.

"Sis, how do you spell *sassafras?*"

"Sis, I bet you, you can't spell *catarrh.*"

"If you spell *asafoetida* I'll let you have what's in my right hand."

Things like this made spelling seem a part of my daily life, for I knew what asafoetida was—something in a bag that you put in the chicken trough. And sassafras was a tree the roots of which had bark that you could sell. Everywhere you saw sassafras trees that had their roots dug up and the bark scraped off.

Among our textbooks, all old by the way, some dating back to Father's youth, were *Smith's Grammar, Webster's Spelling Book, Monteith's Geography, McGuffey's Reader;* and some elementary histories of the United States, Rome, and England—mostly stories such as "Alfred the Great and His Cakes," "Wolfe and Montcalm Climbing the Heights of Abraham," "Putnam Riding down the Steps," and "Romulus and Remus." Wolfe always seemed to me as much one of our patriots as Washington himself, and when I was shown his picture hanging on the walls of the State House in Toronto, I joyfully exclaimed, "Oh, he is one of our heroes, too," The guide sternly set me right. "An English hero, Madam," he assured me.

The textbook that influenced me most and has gone with me through life was the *National Fifth Reader*. Ours is the only copy I have ever seen. It was full of old standbys such as "Thanatopsis," Dryden's "Ode on Alexander's Feast," "The Raven," "Woodman Spare that Tree," and the one about the flag:

> When freedom from her mountain height
> Unfurled her standard to the air
> She tore the azure robe of night
> And set the stars of glory there.

The one that thrilled me most was Fitz-Greene Halleck's "Marco Bozzaris," which begins with a Turk dreaming of the hour "When Greece, her knee in suppliance bent, would tremble at his power." I was an early champion of Greece from reading this and Mrs. Hemans' and Byron's poems; and now that others are still dreaming the old dream of the Turk, everything that is within me rallies to the Greek cause; and I wish these enemies could hear Bozzaris cheer his band, as did the Turk, and fall back in defeat.

> Strike! for your altars and your fires,
> Strike! for the green graves of your sires,
> God, and your native land.

When Mother sent us upstairs to study, I did not always confine myself to the lessons assigned. Under the beds, which had long white counterpanes reaching to the floor, I had a secret cache of books that I could turn to when I got tired of study. I always studied flat on my stomach, and if I heard Mother coming, it was easy to slip one book under the bed and take out the other. One winter I read in this way practically all of Maria Edgeworth's novels and Moral Tales—and learned my lessons besides. At that time in my life I did not suffer from pangs of conscience. I read of such things in the Sunday school books, and wondered why I never felt like that.

I had found these books by accident one day when I was exploring the dark closet, quite on my own. They were in a big box which I managed to open and found to my joy to be full of books. The ones on top happened to be Maria Edgeworth's, bound in gray with gilt-edged leaves. I took several out, put the lid back, and carried the others to the hiding place under the bed. The first I read was *Castle Rackrent,* which set me against "absenteeism" for life. *Belinda* and *Ormond* followed in quick succession; about these I remember nothing except the titles, but the Moral Tales made a lasting impression. The one I remember best was the " 'Tis but—" story about two young couples who started their married life with exactly the same income, one being always prosperous and happy; the other always miserably in debt—all because of this " 'Tis but—" habit. If they saw anything they wanted, they would say " 'Tis but sixpence," " 'Tis but a shilling," " 'Tis but a pound," never denying themselves anything because it always seemed to cost so little. Result—misery.

The other couple budgeted their money, though they didn't call it that, but they knew that you must plan your expenditures and not buy other things just because they were cheap. Result—happiness, as Dickens points out in *David Copperfield.*

I always say Maria Edgeworth and Walter Scott brought me up. Their ideals became my ideals—not always lived up to, but there they were, a beacon to light my path. I cannot remember any moral instruc-

tions from my parents. Besides the Shorter Catechism,
I was taught the Ten Commandments, and I knew that
it was wrong to break them, but that was about all. I
had no idea what the Seventh Commandment meant,
and nobody ever offered to explain it. It remained for
Walter Scott's story of Rebecca ready to fling herself
from the battlements, or of Jeanie Deans, who could not
bring herself to tell a lie even to save her sister's life, to
bring home to me that a woman's honor was something
more precious than life itself.

Years afterward an unhappy event in a Western city
where I lived proved that the spirit of Rebecca was not
dead. A country girl coming to town in search of a
job went to an employment agency. The man in charge
took the girl to supper and afterwards offered to escort
her to a hotel which he had recommended. She went
with him unsuspectingly, discovering too late what his
intentions were. To save herself, she jumped out of the
window into the alley below, where she was found by
a policeman, badly but not fatally injured. It was a
cause célèbre, putting the girl on a pedestal and con-
signing the man to infamy.

II

And then the summer I was ten an astonishing thing
happened. Maybe it had something to do with my sister
Lizzie's engagement to marry Mr. Charles Stevens Porcher, formerly of Charleston, South Carolina, whom she
had met while on a visit to Cousin Helen Maria Gardner.

Father, having perfect confidence in the Gardners'
judgment, had written a letter giving his formal consent;
and preparations for Lizzie's marriage in October took
all the spare time of Mother, Aunty, and the bride-to-be.
I, however, choosing to be childishly intransigent, remained violently opposed, as it meant this favorite sister's
going away from home to live in Georgia. "That old
Shay," I called the future groom disrespectfully when,

on returning together from the post office, Lizzie, absorbed in her weekly love letter, paid no attention to me. Or maybe it was that Mary Shepherd was away on a visit with her sister Eleanor at the Banks Holts', and I was a very lonesome little girl.

At any rate, Miss Mary Hunter, Alice Smith's aunt, had opened a school at Smithwood, a one-room schoolhouse in the woods about a mile and a quarter from our house, and Mother decided to send me there. Nothing could have pleased me more, and I look back on that brief experience as the most perfect of my whole life. The only drawback was going and coming, but once I was there it was unalloyed bliss. At one point the road led through a wide open field where there were often stray cows of which I stood in mortal terror. One more hazard after that was Miss Suffy Smith's dog. Would he see me and come barking over the fence? Sometimes to avoid him I would go way out of my way around through the woods.

At school everything was perfect. For the first time in my life I was going to school with other children, and it seemed like heaven. Miss Hunter looked very pretty in a blue and white calico dress with a jet necklace and gold earrings; I adored her and I climbed to the top of the summer Pearmain apple tree to get the biggest red apple that ever was to lay on her desk.

The only furniture in the school was Miss Mary's table and the seats. Some of these were wooden benches with a board at the back. There was a pretty wide space between that and the seat, and one day little Johnny Amick rolled clear through and landed on the floor. It didn't hurt him any, and Miss Mary laughed with us. Some of the seats were just wooden slabs set against the walls as they had no backs. There was no blackboard, but as I had never seen a blackboard, its absence made no difference.

Smithwood had no well, and we children had to

bring all the water from Mr. Alex Euliss's spring, a quarter of a mile away down the road and over the fence past Henry Ellet's house. Taking the water bucket to the spring and back was one of the chief joys of the day, and sometimes Miss Mary would let Daisy Euliss and me do it twice. We never hurried on those trips—just took our time. Sometimes we would go in and visit with Mrs. Ellet—a dried-up, withered old woman with an enormous stomach that must have been due to a tumor, something Daisy and I had never heard of. There was a loom in the room, and her bed was covered with a white tufted spread with a beautiful white lace border reaching to the floor. The table was covered with a cloth having the same kind of a border. She had made all these borders herself, and there was nothing like them anywhere else in the neighborhood. I know now that it was rare handiwork, probably handed down from Germany.

The morning session was from eight o'clock to half past eleven, with a half-hour recess; and the afternoon from half past one to five, also with a half-hour recess; a very nice ratio—six hours of school and three for play. Miss Mary went home with Alice Smith to dinner, leaving the rest of us girls and boys to our own devices for two whole hours, something no one would now think of doing even in a city, much less in a lonesome spot like Smithwood. However, we did not betray the trust—not a word or an action from this group of backwoods children that would shock even my mother. Hen Johnson, the biggest boy in school, sometimes said, "Well, I'll be consarned," the nearest approach anyone made to profanity. This school, by the way, had no sanitary arrangements. The bushes took care of that, however, decently and in order.

There was nothing that could be construed as a playground, but we contrived to have running games of a sort like "I Spy" and "Honey in the Bee Ball." All of these games began with the same rhyme:

One's all, two's all
Zick's all, zan.
Bob tail, Dominicker
Ticktail tan.
Harum, scarum
Virgin Mary
Sinclum sanclum
Squashem, buck.

We found a place big enough to play "Round Town," a game faintly resembling baseball. Somebody hit a ball with a bat, and there was much running—how, where, or what to, I don't remember.

Riding saplings was another favorite sport. You pulled down a sapling big enough to hold your weight, and strong enough to resist it too, so that when you bestrode the sapling you would go up and down without going too close to the ground. The sapling had to be just right or it would throw you off like a bucking horse.

Then there was a tiny stream down in the woods, and somebody proposed building a dam. Never have I enjoyed anything as much in my whole life as building that dam. Everybody helped from the smallest to the biggest, bringing sticks, stones, and moss, and scooping up sand in the effort to make the water run over the dam, instead of under it and through it—an engineering feat that taxed all our skill. It was the last thing we looked at when we went home at night, and the first thing in the morning, to see if it was still there and to strengthen it if anything had gone wrong.

Our school was anything but graded; in fact the children were of such different ages and attainments that every child was practically in a class by himself. The only time I was in a class was when we stood up to spell. I had brought my textbooks from home and recited to Miss Mary just as I did to Mother, mainly reviews of what I had done before. The first day I was asked to give the capitals of the states I started singing them just as I had at home; "Augusta on the Kennebec River," and everybody began to laugh. So I didn't do that any more.

Our behavior was practically perfect—not a spitball thrown nor a note passed; and as for any impertinence to the teacher, such an idea never entered anybody's head.

Going and coming still weighed heavily on my mind, especially going home, as there were almost sure to be cows in the open field, and I would often go half a mile out of my way to avoid them.

So I made up my mind one afternoon that the next day I would go home by way of Grandma's, but said nothing about it to anybody. That day in school was a particularly happy one with nothing to fear. I would walk home with Caroline Miller and George Reitzel as far as their house; and then to Mr. Bain's store; and from there through the woods to Grandma's house. George's father owned a mill, and when we got to the mill branch it seemed a good idea to play about in it. My dress got wet almost to the waist and continued so all the way home. Grandma was much surprised to see me; and, noticing how wet my dress was, said I must go straight home and put on dry clothes. All this loitering along the way took a long time. When I finally reached home, tired, wet, and hungry, it was almost dark; and the family, not knowing where on earth I was, were simply frantic. My explanation was one of those things that didn't explain. It appeared that there were no extenuating circumstances, and I was all but whipped and sent supperless to bed. No kind words but one of the worst scoldings I ever got. And I had been so innocently happy going two miles out of my way all on account of Miss Suffy Smith's dog and some cows. A sad ending to an otherwise perfect day. It called to mind the night before the Battle of Waterloo—"Oh that on night so sweet such awful morn could rise!" Only this was in reverse from dawn to sunset.

My school days were over soon after that. I know

no more about the reason for the ending than for the beginning. Maybe because Mary Shepherd had come home. Mother sent word I couldn't come any longer, and Miss Mary came to collect the money. She figured it up with Mother and they found that I had been seventeen days, and the bill was seventy-five cents—such a little bit of money for such an awful lot of fun. I don't know that I had learned a single thing, but I had acquired a long, long string of never-dying memories.

6

OUR HOUSE

Our two-story frame house set on a hill was not a very big one, having besides dining room and parlor only six bedrooms. Double beds were in all rooms—in some cases two double beds, which might have been called quadruplet if we had ever heard the term twin beds. Mother's four-poster had a white frill all around it concealing the trundle bed big enough for two children; and there was also a low single bed that paid its double debt by being a sofa during the day. Even the big hair-cloth sofa in the parlor could be opened up, making room for two people; and out in Father's office there was another double bed where people who asked to stay all night were sometimes put. Father's boast was that he never turned anyone from his door. When the count was taken including my crib, we could sleep twenty-five people and one baby, besides an indefinite number for whom pallets could be spread.

The two double beds in the middle room upstairs were piled with feather beds and mattresses half way to the ceiling; and to arrange a pallet all you had to do was to lift one of these off, lay it on the floor, and spread it up. Of course it was not the guests but we children who slept on the pallets. Personally I thought pallets were fun, and no matter how hard, I would gladly have endured them the rest of my life for the sake of having company.

Our house faced east, and to this day whenever I wish to orient myself I mentally return, stand on the piazza, and, facing the old landmarks, discover "where I'm at." Straight through the house from east to west ran what we called a "passage," a place to hurry through in winter, but to spend the day in summer, it being the coolest place in the house. Since it was already partly furnished with two handsomely inlaid mahogany end tables and Father's secretary standing in the nook under the stairs, we had only to bring out all the comfortable chairs and put a bowl of flowers on the table to transform it into a sitting room. It was here I remember that my sister Jane assembled us one summer for "readings" aloud. *Guy Mannering* was the book she chose; and Meg Merrilies and Dominie Sampson became our daily companions. The Dominie tickled Father, who was always making fun of teachers by quoting, when one of them made any mistake, "Man is mortal and he's been a schoolmaster."

Jane had been having elocution lessons under Dr. Vance at the summer school in Chapel Hill, and her voice had taken on new cadences and intonations which thrilled me when she read the lines:

> Twist ye, twine ye, even so
> Mingle human joy and woe.

She had also acquired some new ways of pronouncing, and instructed us about the word God. Instead of saying Gaw-ud we must say Gäd with *a* as in father. Then there was the long *u* as in plume. We never said "Toosday" or "dook," but we did say "ploom," and henceforth it must be called ple-yume.

II

The downstairs room where we lived and moved and had our being most of the time was Mother's, the pleasantest in the house, crowded though it was with beds, sewing machine, bureau, tables, and chairs. In the winter room had to be made for the piano, as there was a fire in the parlor only when we had guests. Getting it moved was always an event. The legs were taken off, and then the Negroes would pick up the body; and with many directions: "Watch out for that door," "Lift it higher," "Turn it this way," the dogs barking and children getting underfoot, it was finally set up again. One very cold winter the dining room table was moved in for a while, all rejoicing over being able to eat without shivering, and without sausage gravy congealing on our plates. And, nobody being able to make butter come in a cold room, there was often a churn on the hearth. The butter from this churning, which was always white, we nicknamed "fireside" butter.

In summer Mary Shepherd and I churned out of doors under the big locust tree by the well and to keep off the flies tied a bunch of leaves to the dasher. We had no better sense than to think it was fun to jump up and down with the dasher, chanting "Come, butter, come," at the top of our lungs.

By day there was plenty of light in Mother's room. The east window was an especially large one, reaching almost to the floor; and the south windows, one on each side of the fireplace, were also comfortably large. When the sun shone straight, instead of slanting, through those windows, I knew it was noon without bothering to look at the clock on the mantelpiece.

At night on the small table by which Mother always sat with her workbasket there was one small kerosene lamp for everyone to see by. But remembering the candle it had so lately replaced, we didn't think it was dim. By comparison, it seemed as bright as the one-hundred watt bulb did when first seen.

III

Our parlor at the opposite end of the house was no sacrosanct place, and when winter was over it was one of my chosen haunts. Here on dog days when the Venetian

blinds were closed, I loved to cool my hot cheeks on the
haircloth sofa, taking care to avoid the ragged spots so
scratchy and also very mortifying. They couldn't be
mended, for nobody, not even Sabra could mend haircloth; and slipcovers were as yet unheard of. Here, too,
I loved to rock in my little black chair I had lugged in,
and admire to my heart's content the multicolored be-
flowered Brussels carpet, the marble-topped center table,
and the pictures hanging on the walls. "Shakespeare and
His Friends" hung over the mantelpiece, and over the
piano was the portrait of Uncle Edwin. I thought Uncle
Edwin the handsomest man in the world—his face clean
shaven except for sideburns, blue eyes, and a beautiful
red-lipped mouth. He had fought in the Seminole War
and had been stationed at Chicago when it was still called
Fort Dearborn; there he had bought a lot for a few
hundred dollars and, when transferred to another post,
had sold it for two thousand dollars. The tragedy of
this was that he had lived to see it sold for eighty thousand
dollars. He was a very religious man and kept a diary
of his daily meditations too deep for me to understand.
He decided to leave the Army and be a doctor, but his
finger became infected in the dissecting room and he
died in the prime of his life two years before my father
and mother were married.

Very special treasures were the tall handsome brass
andirons and the Pembroke table—the only thing in the
room still belonging to the family.

On the black mantelpiece besides a rather squatty
pair of silver candle-sticks, an old-fashioned pair of vases,
and a china lamb with rough, woolly coat, dear to my
heart, there was at each end an enormous conch shell
very knobby on the back but smooth as glass in its pink
interior. Never daring to lift these down myself, I was
always begging somebody to hold one to my ear and let
me listen to the roar of the sea.

Of the books on the marble-topped center table the

one I liked best was Aunt Agnes's scrapbook full of
poetry and steel engravings such as "The Valley Farm."
There was a carefully preserved valentine, beautifully
embossed, and bordered with lace paper and picturing a
bewhiskered gentleman, frock-coated and high-hatted,
and below two hands tightly clasped and the inscription
"To My Valentine."

Two poems made a lasting impression; one beginning

> Oh Fanny Foo Foo was a Japanese girl
> The child of the great Tycoon
> Her face was the color of lemon peel
> And the shape of a tablespoon

related a sad, sad story of young love. The other seemed
just made for me, addicted as I was to daydreaming:

> Of all amusements for the mind
> From logic down to fishing
> There isn't one that you can find
> So very cheap as wishing.
>
> A very choice diversion too
> If you but rightly use it,
> And not as some are apt to do
> Pervert it, and abuse it.

This solemn warning passed unheeded. Wishing
was already my chief diversion—almost a vice, my tend-
ency being to imagine glories and honors instead of
putting in hard licks to win them.

IV

Our dining room, long and narrow, with three west
windows, abounded in exits and entrances, opening out
to or into the parlor; middle room downstairs; passage;
platform, a kind of porch roofless but shaded by a damson tree with plums in easy reach; dining room closet;
pantry; and finally, the backstairs running up steeply
between walls, bang up against a wall at the top—no
landing place, and one had with a mighty effort to step
up at one side into the dirty-clothes closet, or at the other
into the passage in front of Aunty's room.

A large mahogany table capable of vast extension stood in the center of the room; a drop-leaf table in the corner next to the parlor; and the chairs stiffly against the side walls. Next to the staircase was the lumbering old claw-footed sideboard having storage space equal to a small closet, in its drawers for linen and silver, and on its shelves behind the center and side doors for Mother's best glass and china. On top, flanked by decanters, were Sabra's silver-wire cake basket and an old-fashioned castor which was a big help to Mary Shepherd and me in our table-setting. One fell swoop, and there were all the condiments in the middle of the table in everybody's reach.

Food and drink supposed to keep better in the dark were stored in the dining room closet under the staircase—a black hole if ever there was one. Once, when I was inside, the door blew shut. Could God really see me now? I wondered. Here were demijohns of cider and vinegar, stone jars of pickles and apple butter, blue and white ginger jars covered with a straw network, jugs of sorghum molasses, and bottles of Mother's blackberry wine.

In the pantry was the blue cupboard, in the top of which under lock and key Mother kept the sugar bowl, tea, cake, and cheese on the rare occasions when we had any. In the bottom part were scales, steelyards, mortars and pestles for beating spices, and the coffee grinder. In order to have it fresh, coffee was always ground just before breakfast—a privilege we children almost fought for.

The big safe had two compartments. In the top part behind doors of pierced tin, waiting for the next meal were the perishable left-overs: meat, bread, butter, or what have you. Not really a safe place at all, for here was where we children came looking for a snack. Maybe there would be a chicken leg, shavings of dried beef tasting mighty good with the heel of the loaf, or a dried-apple turnover—and sometimes, nothing at all. Once

I spied what I thought was a sweet-pickled peach and, though knowing I shouldn't, popped it into my mouth, and as quickly spit it out—a boiled onion.

Behind the wooden doors in the bottom part besides our dishes were all sorts of kitchen utensils, mostly baking tins of various shapes and sizes; jelly molds; cake cutters, my favorite the one that turned out a gingerbread man; and patty pans for a super deluxe delicacy called "chess" cake—a name I wondered about since it wasn't cake, and I saw no connection between it and our chessmen.

Opposite the sideboard was a fireplace, blocked up when I first remember it, the room being "supposedly" heated by a *coal* stove. Never having seen any coal I thought it was a *cold* stove, which in truth it was, all fires kindled there invariably dying out. Somebody having put in a shovel full of coals, some sticks of wood, and a little kindling, there would be a brief flare-up. Only that, and nothing more. By that time our black Maria was bringing in the coffee and hot biscuits which couldn't wait. "Taking two and buttering them while they were hot" became our chief concern, everybody forgetting about the stove.

V

One memorable winter the fireplace was opened up and a woodbox brought in. This was done to accommodate my cousin Wesley, who had made up his mind to be a doctor like his father and was staying with us that winter in the "middle room downstairs." As he was busy selling sewing machines all day, he would build a fire at four o'clock and settle down for three hours of study before breakfast. Father, always restless toward daybreak, moved in his chair and joined him. Hearing a door shut one morning, I went down to peek, and found them sitting there very happily, Wesley studying and Father lost in thought watching the fire. I went out, got

Mrs. George Mendenhall—"Aunt Delphina"

MOURNING PIECE—A CALDCLEUGH INHERITANCE

my little black rocking chair, and, nobody objecting, settled down beside them with a book.

At intervals Father would go outside to see how the dawn was coming along, I at his heels eager to share in the magic of the early frosty morning, as we stood together under the stars in a stillness broken only by the crowing of some neighbor's cock sure to be answered by other roosters in a sort of barnyard antiphony.

VI

Upstairs, the front room over Mother's belonged to my four sisters. Each spring the two bureaus and spool beds changed places, the bureaus being moved to the back and the beds to their summer quarters under the south windows on each side of the fireplace. The table under the east window remained stationary.

Over the mantelpiece hung an embroidered picture that had belonged to Aunt Agnes. The picture had composition. Besides the usual female figure in the foreground, leaning over a tomb under a weeping willow, there was in the background at the right a beautiful little church; and at the left, standing on a slope overlooking a lake, a stately pillared mansion. Who the artist was no one now knows, but the picture, still perfectly preserved, in its smooth perfection and easy grace would deserve to rank with those Chinese marvels of needlework.

VII

Father believed in closets—and the one next to my sisters' room was big enough not only for the washstand and tin tub but for bureaus and trunks. Beyond this was the "long closet" with a window at one end; but as this window opened into the "dark closet," it gave no light, unless the door of the "dark closet" happened to be open, which in my memory it never was. At the back there was a long row of hooks for hanging dresses. Going behind these one day, I discovered next to the dining room chimney a cubbyhole with enough light coming through the cracks in the roof for me to read by. This became my number-one hiding place; and here, with some forbidden book, I spent hours of stolen pleasure. I would hear people calling me, but I never answered—just kept right on reading until tired, when I would steal out of the house, and after some circuitous route suddenly appear in the midst of the family by way of the back door.

"Mary Alves, where on earth have you been?" they would chorus; and I would truthfully reply, "In the garden," or "In the orchard."

I never told anyone, not even Mary Shepherd or Will and John about my cubbyhole; it remained to the last—my dark secret.

VIII

The spot I loved best of all was the long piazza overlooking the front yard, shaded by tall elm trees and commanding a view of orchards, woods, and fields for more than a mile distant. The jagged blue line on the high horizon visible on very clear days was the Cane Creek Mountains, though foothills was a better name. There also a glimpse of the millpond against a back drop of the pond woods; and in the middle distance toward the left was a grove of pines spearheaded by one giant tree fit for a ship's mast. My passion for walking on a carpet of pine needles and listening to the strange sound of the wind in the branches made me late many times when sent to the Brown place for apples, as I always figured the shortest way there was through these pines.

Not a very wonderful view, but still a view which spoiled me entirely for living in hollows or rooms opening on light wells and narrow alleys. There weren't many days in the year when I didn't sit on this piazza, rocking and reading and dreaming. Or just gazing; sometimes at the spectacle of an approaching storm, while I shivered at the forked lightning and the rolling

of the corn wagons (the Negroes' name for thunder),
but sticking it out until the sheets of rain coming nearer
and nearer drove me inside.

As for the panorama of the scurrying clouds forming rapidly changing pictures of animals, people, and
castles—why that was my first movie. At night spooky
and beautiful to see the moon flying through clouds, hear
a screech owl in the orchard, or a whippoorwill lament-
ing from our roof top.

With all these things to keep me company, I was
never lonesome on the piazza.

IX

The life that went on in our backyard cabins, so
near and yet so far, was to us a separate and little understood existence. When I first remember these cabins,
they were still full of Negroes, not in our employ, but
to whose welfare we could not be indifferent. No forty
acres and a mule having been given them, these waifs
were left stranded on our premises by the ebbing tide of
Yankee promises. There was my beloved Aunt Hannah,
the only darkey I ever kissed, having forgotten in a burst
of affection that she was not kissable. That kiss left a
bad taste in my mouth and was never repeated. Aunt
Hannah was very religious, and if she got religion in the
middle of the night would wake us up shouting Hallelujahs under our windows. Nevertheless, her daughter
Caroline and Ike one night when we were all in the
parlor crept upstairs, stealing many valuables, including
a much prized blue silk dress.

There was Nat, brother of Ike, with his wife Bell
and their rapidly increasing family whom Mother helped
bring into the world. We noticed that winter a column
of smoke rising daily from the grove of pines. Will and
John investigated and found a still operated by Nat and
Ike, who had stolen the wheat they were distilling from
the storeroom behind father's office by crawling underneath and boring a hole in the floor.

Well, the only thing you can do with Negroes like that is to forgive them and start out afresh, hoping they will behave. Those few days Nat spent in jail Mother had to take care of Bell and the children; so when Nat returned, Mother was glad to see him. She handed him the key of the storeroom, telling him to get a bushel of wheat and have it ground at our mill to feed his family.

The Ku Klux Klan had begun operations in our neighborhood, frightening the Negroes and beating some of them brutally. Dressed in white, they would ride up to a cabin, ordering the Negroes when they came out to bring them a bucket of water, for they had just come from hell and were powerful thirsty. When the bucket came, they would pour it into a waterproof sack concealed under their robes and order another and another and another till the Negroes were sure they were the devil's own crew, as no mortal man could hold that much water. Mother thought it was outrageous, and I remember hearing her say so to some men who had come to warn her not to be scared if the Ku Klux came, as no harm would happen to any of us: "I cannot allow any of my Negroes to be whipped," she told them emphatically.

One night when I was sleeping in her room we were waked by a great commotion at the front gate—neighing of horses, bells, whistles, and those infernal noises heard at a bell-crowd or charivari. Mother raised the front window, but the only words she heard were said by a a drunken man asking, "Billy, where's my mule?"

"It's only the Ku Klux," she told father closing the window, unafraid while the Ku Klux, their noises dying away in the distance, passed on by.

When Maria failed to return Sunday night, as was her custom, accompanied by John I would go, proud of knowing how to use both hands, and milk the cows. Then before going to bed I would take some bread to her two children, half-white Lily and coal-black Babe. Since they were too little to put in the pin which fastened their door, I would do it for them, and then, climbing out the back window, return through the garden to the house.

Once one of Bell's babies died. Mr. Steel made the little pine coffin, and all the Negroes in the neighborhood came that night before the funeral, singing sad and doleful hymns till long after midnight.

But Negroes are a happy-go-lucky people and in spite of their miserable lot amused us all as they sang, danced hoedowns, and played the banjo, sometimes on one string only, till Mother was almost crazy. Their philosophy was better than ours for keeping spirits up. As Maria said, "I ain't got nuthin', I ain't never had nuthin', I don't never expect nuthin', and I don't worry."

X

Our house, never a mansion, was getting shabbier day by day. Cold in winter and very hot in summer, needing paint inside and out, and without a single modern convenience, yet it was still a home for us, and for those who had no other place to go. Here a welcome that never wore out awaited all who came—those who came for a meal, a night, or a summer; and those who came there to live.

Of these last, all except Aunty had been Father's wards, among them two sons of Uncle Edwin, who had married the fashionable beauty, Miss Phoebe Fitch, of Buffalo, New York. When they were married, they were said to be the handsomest couple who had ever walked down the aisle of that church. Helen Maria, the only daughter, had remained with her mother; but the boys, called to distinguish them from numerous others of that name, John O. and Jim Buffalo, lived for a time at our house.

There being very little money, Father decided to send John O. to West Point; and finding no one in North Carolina to appoint him, he went to Washington and secured his appointment from President Tyler himself.

Cousin Helen, going to visit him when he was stationed out West, met and married General Montgomery Gardner of Augusta, Georgia. The Gardner mansion, where Lafayette once spoke from the balcony, still stands in a fine state of preservation. After the surrender the Gardners made us a much-talked of visit, both being greatly admired. Besides the general admiration for Cousin Helen Maria, there was the sad story that when she came to unpack her trunk half her pretty clothes were ruined from the breaking of a jar of peach preserves. Moral: Never pack bottles containing liquids in with your clothes.

Sabra thought General Gardner the greatest man she had ever known, and was always quoting his famous remark that there were three things he didn't want to be: "A Negro, an army mule, and a private soldier."

XI

"It's not a home till it's planted" is the clever slogan of a nursery man in a Western city, and certainly planting had much to do with making our house a home though not done in the modern way, nothing being put near the house itself except a climbing rosebush. Our big front yard was enclosed by an ancient board fence with a five-barred gate at each end, and a little gate in the middle, excellent for swinging on. Pigs diabolically adept in finding weak places often broke through the fence.

"Pigs in the yard, Mary Alves. Run quick."

Pigs work fast, for before I could drive them out, they would have ruined many flowers and rooted up enough grass to spoil the looks of the yard for weeks. Father and old faithful Mum were the chief sufferers; Father couldn't bear to see the grass ruined, and Mum, to keep out intruders, was chained near the hole until it was repaired.

Mother, having come from Hillsborough, where everyone was a garden enthusiast, had done wonders for our yard. It is said that no one ever came to or left Hillsborough without bringing or taking a "slip." So Mother and Aunty between them had all the varieties adorning Hillsborough planted in our yard or garden. Across the front yard next to the fence was a wide border edged with jonquils and daffodils; and planted symmetrically on each side of the middle gate were crepe myrtles, pomegranates, spirea, boxwood, euonymus, roses, and flaming Japyrus Japonica. In between grew peonies, hollyhocks, and lavender, which Mother kept between the clean sheets in the blue press.

A slight hollow near the bottom of the yard was filled by an enormous Aurora rosebush growing around a big persimmon tree—a sight so beautiful when in full bloom that passers-by stopped to exclaim and admire. Scattered around here and there, planted in circles, were white hyacinths and dwarf cedars. On the south side of the yard, screening the rail fence, were osage oranges, and in front of them were althea bushes, a smoke tree, golden bells, and woodbine.

> Gone where the woodbine twineth
> And the Whangdoodle pineth

we used to say about something nobody could find.

There were only trees in the back yard, where flowering locusts sprinkled the ground with blossoms harboring bees for the bare feet of the unwary. Here were the Negro cabins at a proper distance, the smokehouse, the ashhopper, the dry kiln used for drying fruit, and the woodpile.

Like most Southern kitchens, ours was in the back yard, but nearer than most, having been moved close to the house. It was reached by a flight of steps descending from one platform to a lower and narrower one in front of the kitchen and storeroom adjoining. And a horrid hole it was, with two small windows, and when the door was shut, dark as a pocket. Once we tried whitewashing the soot-blackened walls; but soot and whitewash mingling, it was a sorry sight. The floor was so rough and uneven that sweeping it clean was impossible. Like heaven though for Mother to have it so near, as she had to be in and out all day long.

From this lower platform you entered our cellar, where in the summer we kept milk and butter in a trough with water which drained off through a pipe. But no sliding down our cellar door, which was upright just like other doors. Going down in this cellar was a venturesome and dreaded task, for I knew I might encounter a snake there. And once I did. I had got the pail of milk from the trough and was feeling pretty safe as I approached the steps, when I saw lying on the ground behind them an enormous black snake over which I must pass. I wasted no time, and was outside before that snake could say Jack Robinson. Will and John, armed with hoes to the rescue! Soon there was a dead snake.

The biggest outbuilding contained the corn crib, a shed for the carriage, and two stables used occasionally for the horses of guests arriving too late to go to the barn a long way off across the road. In the middle was the hen house, and over all the loft meant for hay but empty now except for odds and ends. Beyond this building came as an anticlimax the pigpen, placed far enough from the house not to be offensive, but not too far for carrying the kitchen slops.

Near by was the icehouse, with the roof falling in, but still with enough left for me to climb over and look down on the muddy hole underneath. The blacksmith shop next to the road was in much the same condition. The anvil and sledge hammer were still there, even the bellows, but no roar, and no flaming forge. Things were like that all over the South, falling to pieces, not ever to be restored.

XII

Our garden was separated from the back yard by a
row of Negro cabins and a tall paling, and had you flown
over it, would have looked very much like a quilt, its
squares of vegetables bordered by flower beds being nicely pieced together with strips of bright green grass. The
choicest of all the borders was just inside the gate guarded
there by a big silver leaf euonymus, and at the other end
by a Bartlett pear tree—my first objective August mornings when those pears, ripe and juicy, were lying on the
ground waiting to be picked up by the first comer. Taking one off the tree was strictly forbidden. Here, putting
on a big show every spring, were the big double hyacinths, white, pink, and blue, scenting the whole garden;
the white narcissus, favorite flower of my mother and
hers, snowdrops, yellow crocuses and "butter and eggs,"
violets and daffodils.

There too was the Persian iris, a tiny, lily-shaped
purple flower, not much to look at, but a perfect conversation piece, the question being, "Can you smell it?"
If you could, then you were an aristocrat; but if not,
just hoi polloi. Those who smelled nothing, being naturally suspicious of the proud aristocrats' claims, would
walk off loudly whispering to each other such remarks
as, "I bet she can't either."

Opposite the euonymus was an immense box, and
farther on rosebushes sheltering lilies of the valley and
cowslips. Other borders flaunted prince's feather, cocks-
comb, larkspur, and tiger lilies growing between box,
rose of Sharon, and crepe myrtle. A yellow Harrison rose,
lilacs, syringas, snowballs, and a gadding hop vine formed
a bower for the garden house. Not for worlds would
Mary Shepherd and I have let any of our brothers see us
on the way to this secret spot; and if we caught sight of
any of them in the garden, we would walk off as fast as
possible in the opposite direction and begin picking
flowers.

XIII

Mother's posies gratified our pride, but it was the vegetables and fruit in the garden that kept body and soul together. Besides every table vegetable known to Hillsborough, there were beds of thyme and mint and rows of sweet basil, sage, and marjoram. In one corner each child had his own row of popcorn that lived or died according to the care given by the owner. Once the corn didn't pop, because pollenized by a field of sweet corn planted too near. The melon patch abounded in cantaloupes, squash, cucumber, pumpkin, and watermelon. Greens! how to fill the pot with greens! Easy enough when cabbage, kale, and collards were plentiful, but in spring it became the problem of each day. Our Black Maria, taking me along to hold the basket, would add just enough lamb's quarter and wild mustard to make a mess of turnip greens big enough without spoiling its taste. You have to be born and "raised" in the South to understand the Southern passion for turnip greens, which has even found expression in a popular song. After the turnip greens were dished up, the darkies took over the pot liquor, dropping in corn meal dumplings, gobbled up with gusto in spite of their looking so green and greasy.

The asparagus bed was Mother's special care. She let no one but herself cut those tender succulent stalks.

Nothing was more popular than the peanuts. Even when they were first dug, hardly waiting to rub off their dirt, we began chewing up the soft, white, sweet shells.

Always a big patch of Irish potatoes well liked in hash, but which when served alone nobody really liked but me, everybody else preferring sweet potatoes of the variety that oozed candied juice all over the oven. But for a winter afternoon snack, give me a hot Irish potato roasted in the fireplace ashes and eaten with salt, burnt skin and all.

For molasses we planted a large patch of sorghum

which looked so much like the broomcorn growing next I had to look very carefully before cutting a cane to chew.

Small fruits had not been forgotten. There was a row of currant bushes in front of the Negro cabins, and not far off a strawberry bed and gooseberry bushes. Raspberries in three colors—red, black, and yellow—grew in the fence corners. Near the bottom of the garden was a grape arbor. The grapes climbing there were the Isabella. How I wished they were scuppernong or even Concord. There were at least a dozen Murillo cherry trees in the fence corners, and a row of fifty-seven blue plum trees which, beginning at the back of the long rectangle containing our house, yard, and garden, extended clear to the big front gate. Not far from the grape arbor was the May-apple tree—not just a tree but a lifesaver. The bloom had scarcely dropped before we began raiding the forbidden fruit, which, after the dull eating of a winter diet with almost no fresh vegetables or fruit, was just what our clogged systems needed. No use to threaten us with talk of dysentery or bloody flux! The craving was not to be denied. When the apples were ripe, our neighbors, knowing we had plenty to spare, came with their pails from far and near. Delightedly we would take them to the tree and help them fill baskets and buckets till they were running over.

Flowers, fruit, and vegetables! Together they made our garden a lovesome spot.

XIV

Kipling tells us that

> A garden is not made
> By singing, "Oh how beautiful,"
> And sitting in the shade.

Ours was no exception to this rule, and after the ploughing was done, there being no money to pay the Negroes, and very often no Negroes to pay, it devolved upon us

as a family to do the necessary planting, hoeing, weed-
ing, and harvesting.

Luckily we did not have to help on the plantation
which had been rented to a very good tenant farmer,
Mr. Andrew Keck. We furnished a house for him to
live in, the horses, wagons, plows, etc., in return for
which he was to give us a share of the crops, and also cut
and haul our firewood. The woodpile got pretty low,
sometimes down to the last log, and what a relief to see
Mr. Keck come driving through the gate with the load
we had been watching for. Getting the logs cut into
sticks for the fireplaces and kitchen stove was our responsibility. The Negroes living in the back yard were
supposed to do that in return for their cabins and firewood, but keeping them up to their bargain was next to
impossible. They made, moreover, frightful inroads on
the woodpile, as the cabin fireplaces were so large they
could burn half a log at a time; and even fence rails,
which had a way, like Rachel's children, of being *not*.
Fuel, in spite of acres and acres of woodland, remained
an ever-present problem. We had all the tools for
cutting: axe, sawhorse, handsaw, crosscut saw, and wedge
for splitting big logs before cutting them into lengths.
I learned early to use the axe as well as Will and John
did for cutting small sticks. Plenty of work at a woodpile
for children, all day long—picking up chips, carrying
baskets of trash for the smokehouse, and filling the
woodbox night and morning. I did them all and as long
as Will and John were there to boss me thought it was
fun. A phrase of woodpile philosophy has gone with
me through life: "Take off your coat, roll up your
sleeves, spit on your hands, and take a fresh 'holt.' "

But ours was no longer the big family it had been
the day I was born, it having gradually dwindled away.
Edwin, already far gone with consumption when he
came, was the first to go. The theory of contagion being
then unknown, no precautions were taken, and my sis-

ters were even allowed to nurse him. A guardian angel must have been hovering near, for nobody contracted the disease.

About the first of my memories was Cousin Annie Holt's wedding to her first cousin, Isaac Foust, which took place when I was about four. Still remembered are the cakes on the table, the bridal pair standing up together, and Lena Foust in a white dress with a pink sash—and Mother calling Mary Shepherd and me a few days later to give us the last of the wedding cake.

Cousin Sallie had already been married at her cousin's house in Graham, and Cousin Jim Holt had gone to seek and find his fortune in Florida; so now besides Aunty, Loraine, Alex, and Mary Shepherd there was just our own family, making altogether a baker's dozen. And to do the work we had only one servant now to cook, wash and iron, milk the cows, build the morning fires, do the chamber and other housework such as scrubbing floors—a full-time job for one pair of hands, for which besides her board she received fifty cents a week—an awful lot of money in those days of barter, and how Mother ever managed to raise it I can't imagine. If you took a dozen eggs or a pound of butter to the store, you didn't sell it for cash—you traded it for coffee, or kerosene oil, or some other commodity. Cash money was scarcer than hen's teeth. You had to have it for taxes, and raising that forty dollars each year took high financiering.

Under these circumstances it is easy to see that there was never any lack of tasks for children to do; and Mother, who believed that Satan finds mischief for idle hands, expected each child to do his share in the garden.

Though Mother had been waited on hand and foot before the war, she would undertake any task except washing and scrubbing, including setting out cabbage plants in the cool of the evening. It was a job for all hands: measuring off the distances, making the holes, putting in the plants, watering them, and lastly laying a big leaf—dock was the best—over each plant to protect it from the hot sun next morning. Doing it all together made it a sort of party.

Gathering vegetables for dinner such as tomatoes, cucumbers, corn, even grabbling for potatoes was a regular job lasting all summer. I was good at selecting young, tender ears of corn; the corn silk was the index—it mustn't be too green and pale, that meant the ear wasn't filled out—nor too dry and black—then the corn was too hard and tough. Peas and beans, I was an expert too at gathering these just right for table use and also in preparing them for the pot. At that job I was a natural born efficiency expert, everything having to be just right so that there were no unnecessary motions. Making long strings of red peppers was sort of fun. We hung ours in the closet, though many of our neighbors kept long garlands hanging on their front porches. No fun though in slicing and stringing okra—it was too sticky.

Once we were sent to pick a whole field of dried cow peas to be shelled and put away for winter use. I was pretty "uppity" that afternoon. I had become deeply interested in the English Royal Family through a picture in the *Chatterbox* of Princess Alexandra and her two sons dressed in sailor suits; and one in *Harper's Bazaar* of Queen Victoria and her whole family, including grandchildren. There was a key under this last, and I not only learned each one by name, but, imagining myself grown and wedded to the Duke of Clarence, felt I was one of the family; and with thoughts as wild and gay of wing as Eden's garden bird, I pictured myself wearing a blue silk dress with redingote and bustle returning with my two children to visit the family.

Filled with such ideas, I suddenly found picking peas a menial occupation and complained to my companions that if the Queen were to pass by she would not notice the little pea picker. That derisive nickname stuck to me a very long time.

XV

Almost equal to the work done in the garden was taking care of the fruit. Father had been a great planter, and, besides two large orchards devoted exclusively to apples and peaches of the finest varieties, there were quantities of cherries, pears, plums, quinces, damsons, and even a nectarine—a disappointingly tricky tree. It would bloom, produce large beautiful green nectarines which instead of ripening proceeded to rot. I watched them like a hawk but never a taste did I get; and the first nectarine I was ever to eat was a beautiful hothouse one bought at Harrod's in London. Delicious!

Besides Murillo and sugar cherries, there were ox-harts and black Tartarian, for which there was much competition between us and the birds. Plums too of many varieties—magnum bonum, greengage, a prune, and a New Orleans, biggest of all on the tiniest tree. Besides all these there were thickets of wild plums, yellow and red, excellent for eating when cooled in a pan of ice cold water from the well. What we didn't eat was left to rot.

Unfortunately there was no market for the fresh fruit, for everybody in the neighborhood either had his own or else was too poor to buy ours—which was anyone's for the asking, as we had so much more than we could possibly use. Once we piled a load of our choicest *ripe* peaches into the bottom of a wagon, and sent it to Greensboro, but after twenty miles of jolting over rough roads, the peaches were fit only for the garbage can. Even if we had known about and had had the material for wrapping the peaches separately in paper or putting them in crates or baskets, I doubt if there would have been enough of a market to make the venture pay.

Sugar was too scarce for much canning or preserving, but what little we did do was—according to the best Hillsborough standards—perfection. Mother's brandy peaches, kept for the choicest company, were tops and took days to make. For these we picked the finest clings. No knife ever marred their smooth perfection, Mother removing the fuzz by some process with lye. The next stage was letting them stand for days in a stone jar between layers of sugar doused with brandy. Mr. Andrew Smith's was the best. The cooking was done outdoors in Aunty's big copper preserving kettle, thoroughly cleaned with Jimson weed and vinegar to remove all green stains and prevent poisoning. There was much careful skimming of scum, given to us children as a reward for cleaning the kettle and bringing wood for the fire.

Before taking the kettle off the fire, Aunty was called for consultation; and if she said, "It's done," off came the kettle.

The winter apples were put away in barrels; but not being able to sell, preserve, or can our summer fruit, we had to dry it—a process completely lacking in poetry or interest. Pure drudgery. The only thing that made it at all endurable was that, since it was summer, my sisters were at home and the old cabin where we gathered for work, cool and comfortable, having practically no walls, was full of talk and laughter which nobody wanted to miss. Will and John, Mary Shepherd and I brought the fruit in, listening between loads with open mouths. It was ours too to take the fruit out and spread it in trays on a scaffold to dry in the sun, and also, to hasten the drying, to turn the fruit over every so often. A hot job if ever there was one, and one at which I once got a bad case of sunburn. My own fault, for I lingered too long admiring the effect of the sun on my bare arms. Sometimes it rained, and there was a mad rush to pile the trays on top of each other, covering the whole with an oilcloth. If the rain continued too long, the trays were put into the dry kiln and a fire built up. This was a great pity, as sun-dried fruit looks and tastes the best.

Some of this fruit was traded at the store, and the rest

put in sacks and stored away for winter use. Dried cherries were the most tasty and dried apples the least—especially those cut in quarters and dried with their skins on called "snitz." When boiled with jowl, the fattest part of a pig, it made a completely repulsive meal. Charles Lamb says the young hate fat. Mother never made us eat anything. She had two rules: "Eat anything you like." "Eat nothing you don't like." She seldom provided substitutes, and snitz and jowl was one of those one-dish meals when there was never anything else to eat. Dried apples even in turnovers failed to please. Some half forgotten lines come drifting through my mind:

> I loathe, abominate, despise
>
> .   .   .   .
>
> The meanest are dried apple pies.

On the other hand, Confederate fruit cake made with dried peaches was almost as good as one with raisins; and dried cherry dumpling with hard sauce tasted like more. Father used to say, "If you boil a rock with butter and sugar, the sauce will be good." Apple butter was pretty good, too, though made with sorghum. Making it was a supreme delight. Our crop of cane had to be taken to Mr. Alex Euliss's mill for grinding. A mule was hitched up walking round and round like the horses of a thrashing machine. The juice was boiled in a huge oblong iron kettle until it was the right consistency, after which most of it was poured into demijohns and a keg. In the meantime Mother had been busy peeling and slicing apples, and these were now poured into the residue left in the kettle and cooked until ready to be put in stone jars. By this time it was long after dark, and I was almost asleep after playing all day with Daisy and Irene Euliss.

I liked going to the Eulisses', for things there were so different. The front door was cut in half and the bottom part could be shut while the top part was left open just like a window shutter. Mr. Euliss, an ingenious sort of man, had rigged up a curious system of troughs running hither and yon for irrigating his fields. Nobody else had anything like it, and his garden was always fresh and green while everybody else's was drying up. He was a good neighbor too and saved Mike Shafner's life when the Ku Klux Klan had decided to kill him. Remembering how he and Mike Shafner had drunk from the same spring—a tie that could never be broken—he sent him word to ask no questions, but leave the country; and when the Ku Klux arrived, nobody was there.

XVI

December was a busy month. First there was hog-killing day, a long-looked-for event postponed until the weather was cold enough to keep the meat from becoming tainted. The Negroes, eager for their share of the spoils, were up before daybreak getting things ready; and by the time I arrived on the scene would have dragged the big iron pot down behind the barn and had a big fire going under it. This pot—the biggest I do believe in the whole world—holding untold gallons of water, did not hang between a triangle of slanting sticks, but stood on its own four feet. A barrel in which to scald the pigs was propped up firmly on its side near the pole where the pigs, all bristles removed, would be hung, white and shining, ready to be cut open and "de-entrailed."

I was not allowed to mingle with the crowd gathered here, but from my perch by the window in the loft I could watch one by one the sad procession of each struggling, squealing pig held up by its hind legs and propelled forward to its doom. I had carried them many a bucket of slop, knew each by name as they went past, and my heart was very pitiful.

Nothing was wasted. What we were too dainty to eat the Negroes devoured with delight—such things as the "lights" or lungs, the smelt, looking like a tongue, and

even the entrails, which they called "chitlings." Strange
smells issued from their cabins when "chitlings" were in
the pot, and we held our noses as we hurried past.

The small entrails were cleaned and used as casings
for link sausages. Making sausage was a tiresome business done down in the cellar, where we sat around
cutting up the meat, feeding it into the sausage grinder,
and putting it into bowls for mixing and seasoning.
Mother did the seasoning, most important job of all,
using a carefully prepared mixture of all the herbs in
the garden: thyme, sage, sweet basil, and marjoram.
Mother said things that didn't taste right weren't fit to
eat, and told us a story about two men whose business it
was to taste wine. After sampling a hogshead of sherry,
one said it tasted of leather, and the other of iron. When
it was emptied they found in the bottom an iron key
tied to a leather string.

Link sausages were made from the seasoned meat put
through the grinder a second time and forced into the
casing placed carefully over the spout. And a ticklish
job it was, too, requiring a slow grinder like Loraine,
and somebody with nimble fingers like Mary Shepherd
to hold up the casing, keep it in place as it filled, and
quickly pinch it into proper lengths.

Cutting up the lard into suitable pieces for trying
out was another cellar job, but the actual trying out
was done in a pot hung over a fire in the big kitchen and
carefully watched to prevent burning. The cracknels
left in the bottom of the pot made corn pone fit for a
king's table.

Two triumphs of Mother's skill, though very different from each other, were begun in the same pot.
After the jowls and brains were removed, the ears and
whatever else was left of the head were boiled together
with the pigs' feet in unsalted water. The pigs' feet were
put aside to be pickled or fried for a licking good breakfast; and the other meat, salted, spiced, and molded be-

came hogshead cheese, a delectable dish to serve unexpected company or to liven up an otherwise dull supper
for ourselves. It was often rendered superlative by being
pickled in vinegar, but we belittled it by calling it
"souse."

Every drop of the precious water freed from grease,
clarified with egg shells, strained through many cloths,
spiced, and sugared finally appeared at Christmas—a
quivering, delicate green delight known as pigs' foot
jelly. Garnished with syllabub, and eaten, with or without, fruitcake, it made an occasion of any meal.

Mary Shepherd and I had had a hand in the fruitcake, having pounded away every morning for days with
pestle and mortar on allspice, mace, cloves, and cinna-
mon till our eyes smarted. Stoning those sticky raisins
and slicing citron had compensations—occasional tasting
being winked at.

It took a grown-up to make "daily bread," a curious
Scotch cake, made by working some of our new, sweet
lard and sugar into flour until it could be rolled out flat
like pie crust and cut into cookies and "thimbles," made
with Mother's thimble, especially for us children. When
the big round cake-canister packed full of "daily bread"
was put on the shelf in the "locked closet," we knew that
now we were all ready for Christmas.

XVII

One of Mother's choice maxims was that all work
and no play makes Jack a dull boy. So she saw to it that
we were never too tired in the evenings to play "I Spy"
or "Prisoner's Base" and other running games, till it
was too dark to see. Mother admitted, or maybe boasted,
that she had been a tomboy when a girl, and one of her
stories concerned a sort of double header. Her best dress
was a rose-colored French challis which Grandfather had
bought for her in New York. She had worn this to a
party at which unexpectedly the guests began to play

a running game; and, to escape being caught, she had dashed into a rosebush, snagging the beautiful challis in many places. Going home she went to her room and, never telling a soul, raveled out the seams to get threads and darned it so expertly no one ever knew it had been torn.

We were all crazy about croquet, a brand new game Sister Annie had brought home. I would play it for hours all by myself with eight balls. Part of the fun was finding for these balls the kind of name that happened at that time to be my favorite. Once I triumphantly gave to each a name ending in "et" or "ette," calling myself Juliet.

Our croquet ground had as many hazards as a golf course, but they only added to the excitement, everybody gathering round to see if the ball actually behind one particular wicket was not only going to be knocked in position, but would actually roll right on down through the wicket. I was good at croquet. My foot hardly ever slipped when I croqueted a ball to kingdom come; and when I made a "split" roquet, both balls would generally go just where I wanted them to be. Also when I became a rover I often hit a ball near the opposite stake, getting two strokes and playing havoc with the enemy by separating their balls or putting them out of position. And, taught by Will and John, I became adept in strategy, being careful not to get "dead" on every ball, nor to neglect helping along a poor partner.

Somebody gave us "Authors," very popular and educational; and one of my Christmas presents was Parcheesi. Father never liked to see us playing cards, even such harmless games as Old Maid and Casino. To him every deck was a "greasy" deck and a device of Satan, but fortunately, instead of downright prohibition, he contented himself by merely looking on in disapproval.

Will and John played chess with the beautiful red and ivory set, a legacy from Cousin John O. when he stayed at our house after the surrender. He also left us *Webster's Unabridged Dictionary*, good for settling spelling disputes. The boys tried to teach me how to play chess, but I didn't have that kind of a mind, not even playing a good game of checkers. They were experts, even learning how to play double chess on the huge board that Cousin John O. made for this game which he had learned to play when in the Army.

All looked forward to winter nights behind the drawn blinds in Mother's room when we gathered round the hearth according to the usual pattern: Father and Aunty in opposite corners, snug in cushioned chairs. Mother, who always took the most uncomfortable chair, declaring she preferred it, sat busy sewing or knitting in the center of the circle by the kerosene lamp on the table, keeping a watchful eye on the rest of us tucked in here and there. When we asked her why she didn't rest, she always answered, "I cannot hold my hands."

These evenings were never dull, no two being just alike. All of us loved to play guessing games, especially "Twenty Questions." But we never stopped at twenty, keeping on and on till somebody guessed it or gave up. We ransacked our brains to choose the unguessable but seldom succeeded—John even guessing the crumbs that fell from the rich man's table, besides stumping the crowd with an eye from the tail of Juno's peacock. As we scorned to take any but historical or literary subjects, our fun and education danced happily along hand in hand. Too bad those two should ever be divorced.

Back in 1938 when classes in adult education were so numerous, my colored maid told me sadly that if she had had schooling she could get a job teaching "dull" education.

If Father wanted to read the two poems of Burns, he liked best—"The Twa Dogs" or "Tam O'Shanter"—somebody would poke up the fire or throw on a pine knot, so he wouldn't have to move from his corner. "The

Twa Dogs" was too deep for me, but I loved "Tam O'Shanter."

Napoleon was a frequent topic; the discourse always ending with the quotation: "Grand, gloomy, and peculiar, he sat upon the throne, a sceptered hermit rapt in the solitude of his own originality."

Very often he would read from a play by Shakespeare. Father had never studied elocution, but as he always read with deep feeling—the same perhaps that made everybody flock to the courtroom when William J. Long got up to speak—we always listened with rapt attention, moved to our innermost depths by such soul-shaking passages as the lines spoken by Othello gazing down at the lamp and the sleeping Desdemona:

> Put out the light and then put out the light,
> If I quench thee, thou flaming minister,
> I can again thy former light restore,
> Should I repent me; but once put out thy light,
> Thou cunning'st pattern of excelling nature,
> I know not where is that Promethean heat
> That can thy light relume.

But his mind reverted oftenest to old and perhaps bitter memories of secession days when in the spring of 1861 he was a member of the Secession Convention in Raleigh. Noted for his ability to "set the table in a roar" he was, I am told, in great demand as a dinner guest. For his own peace of mind and relaxation, though a Presbyterian elder, he said he always attended the Episcopal Church on Sundays, knowing that there he would not hear any talk of war.

He was bitterly opposed to the war, being convinced by his numerous visits to the North that an agricultural South versus an industrial North was bound to lose. Nevertheless, after Virginia seceded he signed the Ordinance of Secession as there seemed nothing else to do, everyone agreeing that otherwise North Carolina would become a battleground between that state and South Carolina.

His idea had been to stay in the Union and fight for our rights in Congress, and he blamed the hotheads of the South like Bob Toombs for bringing on the war, as he thought, from selfish motives. Twisting and untwisting his fingers, he would say in tones that set every fiber tingling: "There is, and there should be, a hell for men who seek to rise upon their Country's ruin."

He was very bitter too about the hanging of Mrs. Surrat, believing she had had nothing to do with Lincoln's assassination and was an innocent victim of a sort of mob violence. Lincoln's death, he declared, was the greatest calamity that could have befallen the South, since Lincoln, having proclaimed that it was impossible to leave the Union and therefore the South had never left it, would have prevented the horrors of Reconstruction.

XVIII

Mother could narrow off a heel or the toe of a stocking and talk at the same time, and having spent her youth in Hillsborough, she had plenty to talk about.

One night her mother, calling up the stair, had wakened her and her sister Anne: "Get up and look out of the window but don't be frightened. Wrap up before you come down, for it's turned very cold."

The sight they saw out of the window was the famous meteor shower of 1833. Immense showers of stars were coming down so thickly it seemed as if every one in the heavens were falling.

Hurrying down, they found everybody out in the back yard, the darkies greatly excited. Old Uncle Aleck, who was very religious and could read the Bible, was marching up and down shouting that the end of the world had come.

"Oh, Master, de Day of Judgment done come, jes like it say in de Bible. De sun and de moon shall turn to blood, and de yearth shall melt with fervent heat."

Grandfather never minced words. "You fool, you fool you," he interrupted, "don't you see how cold it's turning?"

The Oxford Webb book speaks of Grandfather as physician, merchant, and banker, but Mother spoke of him only as a doctor, repeating his maxims with the respect due the utterances of an oracle.

"Any doctor who never lost a patient never had any," he declared.

"Don't give coffee and tea to children. If it's good, it's bad for them; and slops aren't fit for anybody."

"Keep as good a table as you can afford. Better pay the butcher than the doctor."

"There's as much in the blood of people as there is in the blood of horses."

Once, awakened by a robber in the middle of the night, he rose and grappled with him but the thief got away.

At the trial of a suspect Grandfather testified that it was so dark you couldn't see your hand before your face, and that the intruder was a Negro.

"If it was as dark as that," asked the lawyer in cross-examination, "how do you know it was a Negro?"

"By the smell," he answered, and there being no objection, the testimony was allowed to stand.

Another of Mother's stories was about two sisters, one of whom had suddenly adopted views of extreme piety.

"Sarah Jane," Matty said, "you take off that hat, and I'll retrim it. It's wrong to wear flowers on a hat."

"But, Sister," Sarah Jane objected, "you wear feathers."

"Well," she answered, "you've got to draw the line somewhere, and I choose to draw it at feathers."

And one concerned a speech on the power of education.

"Just see," said the orator, "what education has done

for North Carolina. Once there wasn't a hill nor a river
in the whole state. Now look at the brawny rivers rolling to the ocean, and at them thar mountains higher'n
the clouds."

XIX

Those were red-letter days when our circle was wid-
ened to include travelers who asked to stay all night.
And a medley crew they were, stretching out through the
years like Banquo's children to the crack of doom:
humble folk like peddlers with their pack and its exciting contents; lawyers and judges going from one court
to another; Quakers from the west to attend quarterly
meeting, with tales of life in Ohio and Indiana; Captain
Julius Gray and other railroad magnates, who were
building the Cape Fear and Yadkin Valley Railroad to
run near us. We killed a sheep for them and ate it all
up in a day to keep it from spoiling. Others were cam-
paigners, who came to seek Father's advice and get some
of his funny stories. "Never defend yourself," he warned
them. "Always attack. Use satire and ridicule, laugh
your enemy out of court—that's the best way. And if
you wish to express scorn and contempt, keep your upper lip shaved."

Once when Governor Zebulon Vance came for a
consultation there was talk and laughter far far into the
night. I waked at midnight where I had fallen asleep
on Mother's bed, amazed to find them still talking.

Guests like these last had a hard time getting away
next morning. Father couldn't bear to see them go, and
just as they were ready to drive off he would put his foot
on the step of the carriage and start some new topic of
conversation, repeating this performance so often as they
progressed toward the gate that Mother would begin to
think that she would have to kill a chicken for dinner.

Among the Quakers who came was Cousin Milton
Lindley from Minneapolis, whose visit was to change
the course of all our lives. So different from all those

other solemn Quakers! He had brought me a beautiful brand-new story book with a bright blue cover, and I climbed right into his lap to look at the pictures and hear stories about his little girl.

Like many other Quakers, finding life difficult in the South at the approach of the Civil War, he had exchanged his lands in North Carolina for property near the Falls of St. Anthony, which, increasing in value with the growth of Minneapolis, had made him prosperous. Much taken with Sabra, he declared that she was too bright a woman to go on living in the South as it was then, and, offering to lend her the money, urged her to return home with him and become a teacher in the Minneapolis public schools.

We were used to partings, but it seemed like the end of the world when we saw them leave for that far country one cold spring day in 1872, and many tears were shed. Mine would stop and then suddenly burst forth afresh. Mother had to take me on her lap and sing "Beautiful Zion" to quiet me.

However, things didn't happen as expected, for Sabra, being unable to pass the examination, of course could not teach. What to do? When Moses said he was not able to lead the Israelites into the Promised Land, the Lord said to him, "What is in thine hand?" In Sabra's hand, it turned out to be a needle. Mother and Aunty had taught her all they knew, and she began to go out sewing by the day. Only a bare living in that; and so, her knowledge in drawing acquired at the Misses Nash and Kollock's School standing her in good stead, she took a course in drafting patterns for cutting out dresses and set up shop for herself. Her first location was on the top floor of a two-story wooden building on the corner of Nicollet Avenue and Fifth Street owned by Mr. Tom Skiles. One room she furnished as a bedroom, taking her meals at the Clark House on Hennepin and Fourth Street. With people like Mrs. Tom Skiles, Mrs.

Ed Barber, Miss Susie Sidle, Mrs. Moulton, and a host of others for her customers and friends it wasn't long before she became the town's leading dressmaker.

Presents began to arrive: silver napkin rings engraved with our names; beautiful though discarded garments of her wealthy customers, the like of which we had never seen, for Mary Shepherd and me. And on my twelfth birthday came—and I mean CAME—the diamond-back edition of Alfred Tennyson's poems, displacing in my affections Campbell, Hood, Longfellow, and even Scott and Byron. This little green book was the dawn of a new day which was to change me from a medievalist to a modern. I reveled in the beauty of the phrasing: "waves of shadow" going over the wheat which I had seen all my life; "immemorial elms"; and "the ringing plains of windy Troy."

Mary Shepherd said there were too many words and they didn't make sense, but I argued that if they were beautiful they didn't have to make sense; beauty was better than sense.

Nature took on a different aspect. When I heard the wind now it was blowing "in turret and tree" or "the windy tall elm"; when I looked at a wet moon, I saw "the flying boss of her own halo's dusky shield"; or at the reflection of the sun or moon in the millpond, it was "pillared light." Now with a host of new friends: Mariana in the moated grange; Maude whose feet had left the daisies rosy; Galahad with the strength of ten; Guinevere; the Lady of Shalott; Amy the shallow-hearted; and Lancelot and Elaine, I was living in a new world I loved with all my heart, and which in spite of those who now decry Tennyson, I still inhabit and adore.

Sometimes one of our visitors by night was a neighbor coming either to bring bad news, or to receive comfort, as in the case of Halley's Comet. "Does it mean the world is coming to an end?" And when Father said, "No, I'm sure it doesn't," the man went away feeling satisfied and safe.

There was that distressful night when Mr. Keck's son Kimsey returned to report on the wagon trip made to Greensboro.

"Mis' Long," he said, almost sobbing, "this morning I drug out old Charley. Last night he had the botts again terrible bad, and there wan't nothin' we could do to save him. He's dead, Mis' Long."

Old Charley dead! No team any more! Only old George now! We were bereft and stricken. Many times we had all gone out to the barnyard in deep distress to watch old Charlie in spasms of agony caused by the botts. And a terrible sight it was, as we sat on the top rail safe from his frantic heels, to see him plunging about, neighing horribly, or rolling on the ground in what appeared to be the throes of death. But he had always come out of it, and we had come to believe he always would. Old Charley dead! There was little sleep in the house that night.

When Uncle John heard of this calamity, he came to see us as soon as he could, bringing Mother the money to buy another horse. No wonder he was our favorite uncle!

XX

Summer was our gayest season when not only my sisters returned with tales of what they had done and seen but many cousins came flocking in from all directions—the more the merrier. Especially welcome was my beautiful Cousin Eleanor, this being her home since the death of Grandma Long. There was also my adorable double first cousin, Annie Long, for whose sake I climbed many trees daily for offerings of peaches and Seckel pears. There were many lovers in her train, one of whom, Cousin John Smith, came here to court her. I was his shadow, and they had to pry me out of his lap and almost lock me up to give him a chance to propose. But when he left, she was wearing his ring. And a happy marriage it was! One of the family jokes

was that the morning of their wedding in Concord,
Uncle Tom Webb and my Aunt Helen, who was her
mother, while waiting for the ceremony, were singing,
"How tedious and tasteless the hours."

Almost every mail brought news of arriving guests.
Mother was reading a letter from Cousin Mag Barringer, another double first, saying she and General Bar-
inger with Paul and Anna, his children by his first wife,
were coming soon. As usual when very happy I began
rocking violently, but being acutely conscious of larder
problems, I stopped short, struck by the dreadful
thought: "What in the world shall we give them to
eat?" Well, they came and delightful guests they were.
Paul and Anna, though living in a world of new shoes
and brand-new clothes so different from mine, gave me
no inferiority complex. Their

> Manners were not idle,
> But the fruit of loyal nature and of noble mind.

Paul with his fine two-bladed pocket knife—so unlike
Will's and John's old Barlow—carving his and my initials in the mimosa tree, all looking on in breathless
admiration, left behind a lasting memento of fun and
frolic. I could never pass that tree without stopping
to see if those initials were still there. The next time
I saw Paul he was the Chairman of the Faculty at the
University of Virginia in Charlottesville, where Mary
Shepherd and I had stopped off between trains to see
him and his wife.

When the Barringers left they took with them little
Alex, practically adopted by General Barringer, who
paid his board and sent him to school in Concord. Alex
made good, growing up to be that fine combination of
successful businessman and churchman honored and
respected by all who knew him. He never forgot us, always returning for a visit every summer to his beloved
Randolph.

GENERAL RUFUS BARRINGER

ANNIE HUSKE WEBB—MY BELOVED BENEFACTRESS
*Daughter of Dr. William Webb and Mary Castleman Webb
of St. Louis*

Very special visits were those made by Mr. Robert Caldcleugh, who with his older brother Emmet kept a confectionery store in Greensboro. They and their sister Mary, who kept house for them, were first cousins of Uncle James's children; and whenever any of them arrived in Greensboro on the way to our house, Mr. Robert would always drive them down, bringing boxes of wonderful candy and that strange new fruit called bananas. A handsome young man, he talked little but was a good listener, and we all hated to see him go.

Mary Shepherd, who always saw the comic side of things, made fun of Mr. Emmet, who annoyed her by continually pointing to some artificial flowers in the parlor and saying, "Look, Cousin Mary; we have flowers all the year round." He was also or thought he was a poet; and some of his poems, giving all manner of curious details—somewhat in the style of Walt Whitman, whose works I am sure he had never seen—were published by the Greensboro *Patriot,* because, being so extremely bad, they were funny. Only one line sticks in my memory, "The early rising kitchen girl."

Dinnertime with every leaf in the table to accommodate these summer visitors was always a riotous occasion. Forgotten now were the supreme efforts made to assemble a meal fit for a guest, and whatever we had was seasoned with fun and laughter. Father, seemingly without a care in the world, was always at his mirth-provoking best; and many is the time I've seen everybody—knives and forks laid down—holding both his sides, and begging, "Oh, Uncle William, please stop; we can't eat our dinner."

A shabby old house and getting shabbier, but with hospitality bright and shining as a newly minted coin.

XXI

But the most wonderful visit of all was the one made by our Sabra, the first since going to Minneapolis the

spring of 1872. It was the summer of 1876, and she came
home by Philadelphia, dazzling us with a trunkful of new
clothes and tales of the Centennial. Nothing had escaped her, and wherever she went everybody crowded
round listening open mouthed.

Full of new ideas that she had picked up in Minneapolis, she set about reforming our old-fashioned ways,
such as permitting flies in the house, especially in the
dining room. Not that we liked having flies—we hated
them, but knew nothing better to do about this plague
than to keep the blinds closed and to station little darkies
behind our chairs wielding flybrushes made from peacock feathers. Now in Minneapolis even the poorest
people had fly screens in the windows, and so must we.
Nothing daunted her indomitable spirit. Wire of course
was out of the question, but she sent to town for mos-
quito netting, and had old Mr. Steele, our miller, make
screens for every window. I verily believe ours was
the first house south of Mason and Dixon's line to have
fly screens in our windows. The sad thing was that nothing could be done about the doors except to keep them
closed as much as possible; but even so, these screens
were a decided improvement, filling my heart with sinful pride.

Mother's present, a blue and white ingrain carpet
for her room, was a star of the first magnitude, and even
though it was summer, laying it down brooked no delay.
Sabra was master of ceremonies, everybody coming to
look on, even the darkies and my kitty. As the carpet
had been made in Minneapolis according to Jane's meas-
urements, there was no doubt of its fitting the space.
Sabra's orders were sharp and to the point. First, a
layer of clean straw spread evenly on the floor, over
which Will and John unrolled strips of heavy paper,
smooth and straight. Then, amid ohs and ahs, came the
unrolling of the carpet, and after much stretching and

tacking Sabra announced that she didn't believe Folds and Griffiths could have done a better job.

Next she began making us all new dresses out of the beautiful materials she had brought. Sabra's motto was that the best is the cheapest; and she knew quality, her practiced forefinger's touch telling her all she wanted to know. If Sabra brought home a bargain, it never was a cheap article bought at a low price, but something really fine that had been marked down.

One of my new dresses was a white percale with green polka dots, made with two pockets on the skirt and trimmed with bands of green grasscloth. And the other was a pink and white plaid Scotch gingham having a basque buttoned in front and an overskirt looped up in the back to form a bustle. In either of these I felt ready to make my bow before the queen.

An invitation arrived to visit Uncle Tom's in Hillsborough, and it was finally decided that Sabra and Mother, with John driving, would go in the Jersey wagon and take me along. I was too excited to eat dinner the day we left, going by Saxapahaw and spending the night at Cousin James Newlin's. Before leaving next morning, Sabra cut out and basted new dresses for Cousins Em and Manie.

We had planned to visit every cousin on the line of march, and our next stop was at Cousin Adeline Webb's at Oaks, where we had dinner. Here we met Cousin Sue Webb, who had been my sisters' governess, Cousin Sam, and Cousin Addie, who had married her first Cousin Lee Webb and lived in Nashville. Cousin Adeline wouldn't let Addie go there to live for a long time, but one day she said, "Yes, you may go." And the whole family set to, trying to get her off before Cousin Adeline changed her mind. This was obedience of unusual order even in those days.

Cousin Sam, who had recently visited Cincinnati, had a tale of his own to tell about what he had seen in the stockyards.

"When Mother makes lard, she picks out the choicest pieces of fat, scouring 'em off and taking out every bristle; and even then the lard comes out looking a little dark. But there in Cincinnati they don't do any picking and choosing—just throw in the whole kit and caboodle, bristles and all. And when they finish, the lard comes out looking whiter'n the driven snow."

When we left there we went to the Binghams', finding among others there young William Bingham, whose father wrote *Bingham's Latin Grammar*. He was a handsome, brilliant boy of sixteen and, emboldened by my new percale, I found myself exchanging repartee with him. We had to stay there a long time, becoming waterbound because of a terrific rainfall; and there was nothing to do but wait till the creeks ran down. From there on, our progress was slow through the deep red mud of Orange County; and when we finally reached Uncle Tom's, they had about given us up for the night.

The day we went to dinner at Uncle James's there was a big crowd, including the whole Cheshire family from Tarboro and Miss Annie Roulhac. Sabra wore her best dress—a black silk, ruffled, shirred, piped, plaited to the nth degree; and of course a bustle. That Sabra from the despised Randolph County could in four years learn how to turn out such a marvel of handiwork seemed little short of a miracle.

As nobody had yet been to the Centennial, Sabra's story of all the wonderful things she had seen at Fairmount Park was listened to there, as everywhere else, with the same rapt attention probably given Columbus returning from the New World.

As for me, I became deeply aware of the pleasant feeling resulting from the consciousness of wearing the right clothes. I had felt it when talking to William Bingham; I felt it that day on meeting with looks of approval from Maggie Webb and Katie Cheshire; and I felt that powerful uplift again that week when, answering the door at Uncle Tom's, I saw before me the beautiful Miss Pauline Cameron standing there all smiles and graciousness, fashionably arrayed for a morning call in black silk with parasol and white gloves. Instead of wishing I could sink through the floor, I felt only the charm of this delightful contact as I asked her into the parlor and engaged her in conversation until the others came.

It is a humiliating confession, but unlike the Hillsborough ladies, who could look—and feel—superior in sackcloth and ashes, I never feel right unless my clothes feel right.

The end of that summer brought major changes in our household. When Sabra returned to Minneapolis, where my sister Annie was now teaching in the public schools, she was accompanied part way by Brother John, who hoped to find a job and live with Uncle William Webb's family in St. Louis; and my sister Jane and Cousin Eleanor, who were going to seek their fortunes in New York. They stopped over in Washington, Jane writing home that John got up and walked all over Washington before breakfast.

They all had a wonderful time at the Centennial, where they separated, John going to St. Louis and the others to New York, where Sabra would study the styles.

It was a lonesome winter that year at our house. Will was clerking in Uncle James's store in Hillsborough. Loraine was a governess in Mr. Tom Dixon's family down in Chatham; and Mary Shepherd had been invited by her sister Lizzie's employers to spend the winter at their house in Virginia and go to school with their daughters. As my sister Lizzie was married and living in Georgia, I was now the only child at home; and though I didn't know it, was the light of Aunty's and my parents' world.

Father would say to me, "Let's go and see if the old sow's pigs have come." At which Aunty, shocked to pieces, would bridle and grunt, while Father inexorably led me off in triumph.

Just for something to do, Father tried his hand at making what he called a mash for the cows, in the big pot used at hog-killing time. I was a big help in building the fire and keeping it going under the pot. Together we collected turnips, old cabbage stalks, Irish potatoes, onions, stirring in corn meal and scraps from the table. It was a wonderful mixture. The cows ate it, but I hesitate to add "and liked it." Anyway, there were no fatalities.

Mother let me read aloud to her *The Bride of Lammermoor,* a story so thrilling I just had to share it with somebody; and as we four sat around the fire, Father would read Burns or Shakespeare or just talk. Never before or since have I been of so much importance. Like Queen Esther, perhaps I had "come to the kingdom for such a time as this."

7

OUR NEIGHBORHOOD

Our neighborhood, including parts of Guilford, Randolph, Alamance, and Chatham counties, comprised, roughly speaking, a radius of five or six miles centered by an ancient landmark, namely, Grandpa Long's flour mill, from which had been derived our post-office address —"Long's Mills, Randolph County." As to the plural, that remains a mystery, there being only this one rickety old mill poised in slanting uncertainty aloof and alone.

Our house being almost in speaking distance, this decrepit mill, the millpond, and the house where our miller lived with his married daughter, Marthy Ann Black, were important factors in my life, as I was always being sent there on errands.

I thought the cascade over the milldam on the rocks below quite equal to the waters coming down at Lodore; and I never could resist detouring to visit and explore this charmed spot, keeping, while jumping from rock to rock over the foaming waters, a sharp lookout for snakes until I reached the bottom of the milldam at the top of the slope. And leaning out of the second story window of our house, whenever a freshet was in progress, I listened to the roar of the cataract, terrified lest the milldam might break—a catastrophe ranking in my eyes with Noah's flood.

The race in the miller's backyard was also a thing of thrills, as it speeded past faster than a horse could gallop to turn the big water wheel. There was a plank across the race which I never dared cross, as a fall into that swiftly rushing stream meant certain death.

Once Marthy Ann set my fishing pole in the race; and when I came next morning, there was a big catfish on the hook. We had never heard that catfish were scavengers, and so we ate them and the eels also with great satisfaction and safety, as our millpond seemed to be fed by unpolluted streams, though they were the headwaters of the creek called Stinking Quarter. According to the legend this name was given because the Indians had left the hindquarters of a deer to rot on the banks, and "stinking" of course was not descriptive of present conditions. We were not supposed to say "stink" ever, such a vulgar word being contrary to Hillsborough usage; and so we children took a guilty pleasure in emphasizing the first word when telling people we lived on the banks of *Stinking* Quarter.

Millers left alone with the grist and their consciences are popularly suspected of taking more than their lawful toll; and Father once heard a preacher in his funeral sermon for a miller declare that the deceased was as "honest as circumstances would permit." However, I never heard anyone express any doubts of our kind old Mr. Steele, enveloped in a saintly white floury aura, who was always ready to take time off to show Mary Shepherd and me the marvels of the mill, letting us peep into the hopper at the revolving millstones below, and also watch the bolting process, which, owing to some rifts in the bolting cloth, did not produce flour of that uniform fineness required for making good cake and bread.

As we had no money for repairs, the old mill was fast approaching a complete breakdown when fate intervened in the person of Mr. Tom Dixon, one of our Quaker neighbors from Snow Camp in Chatham. He made Father an offer of partnership, agreeing not only to repair the flour mill but also to install a sawmill, an

enterprise which would enable the people in our neighborhood to convert their timber, now standing idle in
the woods, into lumber that could be sold for cash—cash,
so badly needed, yet as unattainable as rubies. Father
'of course accepted the proposition, and Mr. Dixon arriving with a crew of workmen, money began to circulate
freely into unsuspected channels. The workmen would
sleep in the miller's house, but somebody must cook
for them. Here was a golden opportunity for poor Bell,
wife of that worthless Nat, then living in our backyard.
Would she be the cook for seventy-five cents per week?
She would indeed, not having seen seventy-five cents for
many a long day.

Then two of the other Negroes, Eli Black and Bud,
rescuer of our well bucket, were offered fifty cents apiece
to open up a sort of tunnel that carried off the water from
the waterwheel. This was really a horrid and even dan-
gerous job, as it meant crawling through a narrow place
where one might encounter such deadly snakes as the
pilot and copperhead. The lure of fifty cents was too
great to be refused, but when it came to a showdown,
Eli weakened, offering half his share to Bud for doing
part of his work. However at the pay off, when Eli received only twenty-five cents, and Bud seventy-five, he
thought there must be some mistake and complained to
Father that he was being cheated. The mathematics
were beyond poor Eli's understanding, but, having complete faith in Father's infallibility, he meekly accepted
the adverse verdict.

On completion of the sawmill, our post-office address
was now really and truly Long's "Mills." And there was
a sort of ceremony about sawing the first log. The tree
chosen for this occasion was a curly maple standing at
the head of our meadow, its huge round trunk bearing
many protuberances. Mr. Dixon planned to ride with
the sawyer on this initial trip and, seeing John and me
standing by, called to us to hop on too. To me, clinging

to each of them as we tore forward and backward until this monarch, guardian of our meadow, had become a pile of slabs, boards, and sawdust, it was a ride thrilling as Mazeppa's.

II

The new mill had a new miller, a young man who endeared himself to everybody by building a large flat-boat capable of holding about twenty people—though at the risk of their lives, as the top of the boat was then almost even with the water.

The miller asked me to name it, and as I had just been reading about Jason and the Golden Fleece I called it in my usual toploftical fashion the *Argonaut*.

On the advent of this leviathan our millpond suddenly became the "Newport" of the neighborhood, people flocking there, not to bathe, it is true, but to engage in boating. Now, instead of fishing from the bank they could row all about, casting their hooks anywhere they chose, an innovation resulting in a longer string of bigger fish.

Just boating was attraction enough for the young folks, and one summer John, Mary Shepherd, and I would often meet Dora Patterson and Will Goley, two youngsters I greatly admired, and after rowing to our hearts' content we would return to the bank for a game of "smut" or "casino," this being to my mind the perfect climax for a perfect boat ride.

To celebrate the launching of the first boat ever seen in those parts, somebody got up a picnic, held in the woods where the spring for the miller's house was situated. It was a perfect day in May, and people came from far and near, bringing their choicest viands, all displayed on one groaning table. No sandwiches at this picnic, but instead huge mounds of buttered biscuits, heaps of fried chicken, cold tongue, link sausages, and chipped beef, interspersed with hard boiled eggs, radishes, and cucumber pickles. Mrs. Palmer, noted for her cooking, had brought a roast chicken baked to such a tempting perfection of crisp brown that everybody wanted a piece. Mrs. Palmer complained that she herself never got a bite. Mother's choicest contribution was chess cake, these tiny little patties disappearing like magic along with huge wedges of custard, sweet potato, and molasses pies.

There were a few demijohns standing about, and though our neighbors, having no new-fangled ideas about temperance, were no strangers to hard liquor, my guess is that the contents were nothing stronger than persimmon beer, nobody wanting to be tipsy on this great day. Water from the excellent spring flowed freely, some man always standing by ready to pour a gourdful for all comers.

Both before and after dinner people took their turns at boating, making a complete circuit of the pond, mercifully with no accident in spite of crowding to the gunwales.

The picnic broke up at about five o'clock, people either going home or to the old Sellers house, now occupied by the Bakers, where a dance had been arranged to wind up the picnic with a grand flourish. Mary Shepherd and I, promising to come home early, were allowed to go and watch for the first time in our lives people dancing "Steal Partners" and the "Wild Irishmen" to the music of Lucine Fogleman's accordion.

But of all the voyages in this old scow, which I liked to think of as a galleon, the most enchanting was the one by the light of a full moon casting its usual spell of romance and mystery. This particular excursion we owed to Mr. Bascom Palmer, just returned from Trinity College, who had come to our house for supper, bringing his banjo. We had just taken our seats on the piazza ready for the musical, Bascom beginning to tune up, when the moon suddenly appeared big as a wagon wheel.

"Why don't we all go down and take a moonlight ride in the *Argonaut?*" Bascom asked. "I'd like to hear how my banjo sounds on the water."

Sis Lizzie enthusiastically agreeing, in less than no time we were sitting in the boat with John and Will at the oars. While Bascom, after singing such old standbys as "Shoo Fly" and "Listen to the Mocking Bird," delighted us with the latest hit songs of the day, winding up with "Silver Threads among the Gold," my romantic heart swelled almost to bursting as his voice rose to a crescendo with those words of unchanging love:

> Yes, my darling, you will be
> Always young and fair to me.

III

A funny story going the rounds ridiculing Southerners boasting of long descent and of prewar riches was about a man registering at a New York hotel who wrote after his name—S.F.V.P.B.W. These initials excited much curiosity, and the man, on being questioned, said they meant "Second Family of Virginia, Poor Before the War."

Well, there had never been any really rich people in our neighborhood before the war, and certainly none afterwards during those days of Reconstruction. However, there were many degrees of prosperity, ranging from people owning good-sized farms with comfortable houses, down to the landless living in wretched cabins who never had enough to eat and in the spring before the new harvest were practically beggars.

The women would come asking Mother to buy baskets of strawberries picked in our own fields—not as Mary Shepherd and I did, berry by berry, but by uprooting the whole plant bearing berries in all stages from dead ripe to green. A peck of such fruit might not yield a half pint. But Mother, knowing their desperate need, always found some sort of food to give them in exchange —a sack of corn meal, some eggs, or a piece of side meat from the smoke house. And as she knew they were tired and hungry from their long walk she would offer them biscuits or gingerbread with a drink of milk.

Others would come with empty hands, and Father would let them, under our supervision, shell a half bushel of corn from our crib; or give them an order on the mill. Old John Linton, noted for his laziness, insisted that we children should shell the corn, and Father, with rare understanding, had us humor him, explaining it was just the old man's way of showing his independent spirit.

Father owned a few hundred acres of land in Chatham where he allowed two families to live practically rent free. The head of one of these, Micajah Mann, was a shoemaker, and every fall if we had any leather on hand he would bring his workbench, lasts, and awl to our house and make shoes for us children. Nothing could have been clumsier or more uncomfortable than these badly fitting shoes full of wooden pegs that tore through our stockings into the soles of our feet, besides producing corns on our toes and blisters on our heels.

The other tenant, old Bill Mason, who occasionally came for a day's work on our flower beds, was, according to Father, wise in bird lore; but though I did my best, I never could get him to tell me anything new. Bill had a strong, buxom young daughter named Virgie, who came to work for us one summer during the fruit season; and like all the other white people of our neighborhood who went out for service expected to eat her meals with the family. Poor Virgie! She had BO to an extent not hitherto encountered, worse than a threshing machine crew or Negro harvest hands or any animal on the place. Even a whiff of Virgie, if she passed anywhere near, was enough to knock you down, and sitting at the table with her was very like eating in a pigsty. Something had to be done about it, or we should have to send her home. So Mother had Virgie move a couple of wash tubs into Father's office and fill them with hot water. Then, giving her some clean underwear, an old calico dress, a washrag, towels, soap, and some scented powder, she turned her loose for ablutions. And, believe it or not, she came out sweet-smelling as a baby.

Members of this lowest stratum were almost always of English extraction, though many women of German descent gladly eked out a bare subsistence by hiring out during rush seasons to work in the fields, binding up sheaves of wheat or raking hay. Theirs was a cheeseparing existence, saving shoe leather by walking barefooted to church on Sundays until reaching the branch nearest the church, they would sit down on a log to wash their feet and put on the shoes and stockings they had been carrying.

IV

One of the finest examples of these hardworking "Dutch" women as they called themselves was the wife of our tenant farmer, Mrs. Andrew Keck. I was always glad when Mother sent me and Mary Shepherd to the Kecks', being ever hopeful that Mrs. Keck would offer us bread and honey. If she didn't do this, I would always ask for it, a practice strongly condemned by Mary Shepherd, who on the way there would lecture me on its evils, extracting my solemn promise not to beg. So easy to give, so hard to keep. When we had said good-by and started to go and still no mention of bread and honey, I always turned back, saying shamelessly, "Please, Mrs. Keck, may we have some bread and honey?" And on the way home Mary Shepherd mumbled reproofs between bites; but I munched happily away, my mouth too full for talk, and listened unrepentant and unashamed.

The Kecks' house, though only a one-room log cabin, with chinks daubed with mud, was a place full of interest to me. For one thing there was the papering on the chimney done, not with wallpaper, but with the advertisements of an Atlanta hospital, picturing before and after operations such horrid deformities as feet turned backward and harelips. Since in those days these people practically never took a newspaper, the only source of supply, their humble homes were as bare of this modern household necessity as Mother Hubbard's cupboard was of bones.

Another feature of this charming house was the "pit" in front of the hearth where vegetables and other foods were stored during the winter. The door of the pit was a part of the floor, some of the planks having been sawed off and put on hinges; and cunningly inserted in one of the planks so that nobody could stumble over it was an iron ring serving as a handle.

It was always a big moment when Mrs. Keck, lifting up this door, would climb down the ladder into the pit in search of a gift for Mother of yams or a mess of sauerkraut—"so handy," she said "for frying when company dropped in unexpectedly."

The Kecks had no stove of course, but there could be no smells more tantalizing than those issuing from their immense fireplace, sometimes from a pot swung over the fire where in a savory stew known as "Brunswick" squirrels simmered in a delicious hodgepodge of tomatoes, corn, okra, red peppers, or anything else fancy might suggest; sometimes from the big iron oven on the hearth baking a huge loaf of salt-rising bread tasting as good as it smelled when spread with butter and honey; sometimes from the skillet, where slices of salt pork and a rabbit cut in pieces like a chicken were slowly but surely becoming ready to melt in your mouth. Tularemia and bubonic germs not being in our dictionary, there was nothing to prevent smacking our lips over these Southern dishes, so rich and tasty that they might have been filched from the table of the gods.

As to the furniture, that was the sort one might expect in a one-room log cabin. There were no comfortable seats in which to rest from one's labors—just a few split-bottom chairs with backs as uncompromising as predestination. The rest of the furniture consisted of one all-purpose table, a cupboard, bench with bucket and basin over which hung a towel and looking glass, a chest of drawers, and in each of the rear corners of the room a big double bed for Bobbrellen and her parents. A ladder led to the loft where Kimsey, only son and heir, shivered in winter and sweated in summer.

Not exactly furniture, but taking up most of the room in the center of the house, was an immense loom on which Bobbrellen and her mother wove most of the cloth needed by the family, cotton, woolen, and even a little linen. To see the loom in action was a very special joy, and Mary Shepherd and I felt very lucky when we found Mrs. Keck sitting at the loom throwing the shuttle backwards and forwards and making an appalling racket, shaking the whole cabin when she pressed the pedals down.

The cloth woven on this loom was a home product from start to finish. Cotton had to be planted, cultivated, picked, seeded, carded, and spun; flax soaked and heckled; wool must have the cockleburs removed—a hateful task I often had to do, for Mother too had learned to card and spin, skillfully turning out those rolls, white and fleecy as the waves looking soft as carded wool where the Hesperus went down.

Homemade, too, were the dyes coloring the "homespun" used for dresses, shirts, and even sheets and pillow cases.

Rag carpets were another product of her loom, and many were the rugs, big and little, Mrs. Keck wove from the rags we children sewed together and wound into balls.

Though perfect in every homely task, Mrs. Keck had little if any book learning. When Uncle Wesley rode up to her front door the day after her wedding and said, "Mrs. Keck, I congratulate you," she asked, "And what do you mean by that?" However, for the needs of her family her skill in household arts was more important.

Her butter was better than any we could make—firm and golden and so free from buttermilk that it brought top price in Greensboro.

And all this perfection was accomplished with much hard work and no conveniences whatever. Milk and butter, to prevent spoiling, had to be kept in a box in the spring branch at the bottom of a rather steep hill up which every drop of water for household purposes had to be carried. No wonder the backs of such women grew stooped and bent long before their time.

The Kecks while with us prospered in every way. Their bees, chickens, pigs, and cows thrived and multiplied under their care, the hens always laying and their cows not going dry for the longest time. Mr. Keck was the prize hog caller of the neighborhood, and in the late fall all of us stopped to listen every morning while he summoned his pigs to a corn breakfast. Up till then they had been mast fed but of course had to be corn fed to make them fit for killing.

Their only horse was a silver gray stallion named Ranger, beautiful to look at with heavy mane and tail, but a terror to us all. Whenever we stole in the barn for a peek, there would be much snapping at us with bared teeth, snorting, and pawing the ground. It was hard to get by on our way to the Kecks' without going in for a look, as Ranger was the nearest thing we had to a circus, and mornings and evenings when Kimsey rode him to the spring for water, standing at a safe distance behind fences, we watched Ranger rearing on his hind legs, neighing, prancing, or curvetting and finally bounding off at a swift gallop.

When their great-aunt, Miss Suffy Smith, died, she left them her house, which, although bowed with age, must have seemed like a palace with its many rooms and its wonderful Dutch oven built into the chimney with niches for baking bread or keeping things hot in some remarkable manner too complicated for me to remember.

There was a great catalpa tree in the front yard, and here, under its protective shade, the Kecks, except Kimsey, who had moved to Indiana, gladly came to end their days in the peace and quiet of their own home.

v

But the errand of top priority to Mary Shepherd and me was going twice a week to the post office kept by Mrs. Sellers. Wednesday was the big day, for our postman, starting his weekly trip at Graham, brought us our letters, newspapers, and magazines then; while Friday, on returning from Asheville, he merely collected our letters and parcels to be posted in Graham.

It was only a quarter of a mile to the Sellerses', most of the way being through our home field, a big forty-acre rectangle, into which was inserted the tiny oblong containing our house, yard, and garden. Even if alone, I always felt perfectly safe in this field, enclosed by a high rail fence which no bull or cow could possibly jump, or hog penetrate.

On Wednesdays Mary Shepherd and I, hardly taking time to eat our dinner, set off for the Sellerses'. Climbing over the fence at the Balm of Gilead tree, we hastened along the path through tall broomsedge, past deep red gullies I loved to explore, not pausing even to pick blackberries, old field plums, or persimmons. It was not the mail we were hurrying for. No indeed! We were hoping the postman would be late. Our idea was to get there as soon as possible for our usual glorious games with the Sellers children while waiting for the postman.

When we reached the fence in a strip of woods, perched on the top rail, we surveyed the open tract of woodland where there might be and often were stray cows. If there were any we avoided this hazard by crossing the creek on stepping stones, and sticking close to the fence of the Sellerses' orchard.

If no cows appeared, we went boldly on past the big

still-house owned and operated by Dr. Sellers. People hauled their apples and peaches here to be distilled, paying for the process with part of the brandy. When in operation, the still-house was a pleasant and friendly spot to which we might flee from dogs or cows; but in winter or spring when shut down it was forbidding and awesome, as all empty places were to me, and I gave it a wide berth.

Just beyond, we crossed the creek on a log which had a fence on one side to hold to if the water was high or the log slippery. I loved crossing logs, my head never swimming nor my feet slipping. Nothing more to fear now, for we were well acquainted with the Sellerses' dog, and their gate was only a step farther.

Here was our childhood's Earthly Paradise. A weeping willow under whose green shade we played marbles and mumble peg or built doll houses lent its enchantment to the spot, as did the peacocks strutting before us with tails outspread. Compared to these lordly birds how commonplace were our old Muscovy duck, gander, and even our turkey gobbler.

Having a creek in one's backyard was like something in a fairy tale almost equal to a tree bearing golden apples. Here in this creek the Sellers children might go wading in January if they liked, while we had to wait until May. For there were no prohibitions in this heavenly place. Perhaps when you have eleven children you get a little careless. At any rate, Mrs. Sellers showed unbounded confidence in the discretion of her offspring, letting them do whatever they liked.

Most enjoyable of all to us was the fact that they were allowed to build a fire where they actually cooked. Nothing ever tasted better than the potatoes or green corn roasted in the embers, or the sausages toasted at the end of a long stick. Once when Ben and Tom, the two oldest boys, returned with a long string of sunfish caught in our millpond, we actually had a fish fry.

Ben and Tom, devoted friends of Will and John, were, like them, always spoken of as one, and so were Eliza and Annie, about the age of Mary Shepherd and me and our special playmates at dolls.

When it came to running games, all old enough to walk took part. The Sellerses' yard was just made for running games, with plenty of places to hide when playing "I Spy." And since there were chinks in the underpinnings, you could look under the house and discover what your adversaries were doing on the other side. And their kitchen was just the right height to play "Antony Over."

The big rambling white house had many porches, the one on the front being just my idea of a portico. It wasn't very big, but it had beautiful lattice-work pillars. These offered a perpetual temptation to my climbing disposition, but one to which there was no chance of my ever yielding, for the solitude so necessary for such a feat was unknown at the Sellerses'.

One of the large rooms downstairs was a schoolroom presided over by their governess, who taught them among other things to play on the piano. Poor Miss O'Connor! Somehow you always felt so sorry for her, a pale, cowering creature, though I think nobody was ever rude or unkind. Perhaps this shrinking was caused by her having a sore ear, which she always kept covered, a mystery to which no one ever referred. Where she spent her vacations was a mystery, too, but she always disappeared in the summer and returned in the fall. Having a governess put the Sellers children quite out of our class, but I never coveted Miss O'Connor, being sure that Mother knew a million times more.

When Augusta, the eldest daughter, was twenty, her parents invited all their friends to come and spend the day. Mary Shepherd and I were invited, too, by Eliza and Annie to a quilting party they were having in the schoolroom at the same time. The quilt of course was

only for a doll, but it had been stretched on a frame all
ready for quilting just like a big one, only as it was so
small you didn't have to roll it up, for everyone could
reach across. For our private refreshments Eliza and
Annie made peach leather over the coals in the fireplace
—a confection rightly named, since eating it required
much mastication.

The dinner table was set up on the side porch picnic
fashion with plenty of fried chicken, cold ham, pickles,
and custard pie. And out in the yard eggnog was lavishly
dispensed from a huge tub. Afterwards, the table having
been removed, there was dancing on the porch with
music furnished by what was very like an orchestra—
Lucine Fogleman playing the accordion, Bascom Palmer
the banjo, George the fiddle, and Miss O'Connor the
piano.

It was a party for grown-ups; and standing there on
the side lines, sipping eggnog for the first time in my
life, I felt grown-up myself. Strangely enough I felt old
when I was young, and now when I am old I feel young.
Do the old ever feel old? I wonder. In Hillsborough
when everyone was gossiping about young and beautiful
Sue Nash marrying old Mr. Burgwyn, Aunt Rob told
us a joke on her husband, then over sixty: "Tom says Mr.
Burgwyn isn't old, for he went to school with him."

Yes, the Sellerses' was our Earthly Paradise, and after
the mail had been distributed, Mary Shepherd and I,
hating to leave, lingered as long as we dared. When we
finally left, Eliza and Annie would always walk "a piece"
with us, sometimes as far as our fence; and then, still being loath to part, we would walk "a piece" back with
them. The family would meantime become wildly impatient over this delay, and often on our way back we
would meet a searching party full of reproaches.

Dr. Sellers, whom I remember as always riding horseback, was a benevolent-looking man with spectacles and
white locks curling up under his stiff black hat. It was

whispered that he was a "radical," a word that meant nothing to me, anymore than "conservative" did. When somebody tauntingly told me that Father was a "conservative," I denied it indignantly and fled for consolation to Mother, who told me it was true but nothing to be ashamed of, as it was only another word for Democrat.

Calling himself a Democrat, by the way, was a bitter pill to Father, who had been a Whig before the war and hated all Democrats, particularly Andrew Jackson, who he said had ruined many people with his notions about banks making it difficult to borrow money. Father's idea was that without credit business would come to a standstill, and that if you had to pay as you went, you wouldn't go very far. A favorite anecdote of his concerned a man who, wishing to borrow money, was told that money was very scarce. On returning from the bank empty-handed, he said money wasn't scarce—there was plenty of money. What was scarce was collateral. If he had only had collateral, he could have got all the money he wanted.

Dr. Sellers was a man who had many irons in the fire; and when Eliza and Annie told us one day that he was going into business at Company Shops and move the family there, Mary Shepherd and I were stunned and stricken. Life without the Sellerses just didn't seem possible.

To comfort us, Mother proposed that we have a farewell picnic in honor of Eliza and Annie and invite Decie and Dora Palmer, who, next to the Sellerses, were our best friends. All I remember about the picnic, which was held at the miller's spring, is that we had a wonderful time connected somehow with mussels; but a thing or two occurred on the way home that fixed the day forever in my memory. We had of course stopped for a look at the millpond when some daring spirit proposed that we take off all our clothes and go in wading up to our waists. All agreed except Dora Palmer and Mary Shepherd, who tried in vain to hold me back. Undressing in a convenient thicket, we had waded boldly in ankle deep when a derisive yell from a group of small boys concealed near by in another thicket put an end to the frolic, as overcome with shame we rushed to cover in the thicket, dressing ourselves as quickly as possible.

Other things were in store to make this day memorable. Just as, once more clothed, I started across the road to climb the fence into our field, I heard a cry: "There's Dr. Black's bull." And there he was sure enough, grazing in the fence corner. Too terrified to move, I stopped in my tracks; but Mary Shepherd, with her usual presence of mind, dragged me safely to the fence.

But a happy ending was in store. When we got home there was an unexpected guest, our beloved Uncle John; and sitting happily on his knee eating French candy, I forgot all my troubles.

VI

No one or anything ever filled the blank left in our lives by the departure of the Sellers family; though the Palmers might have done so had they not lived three long miles away; for surely there was never a family more interesting than the Palmers. It was a big family with originally seventeen children; but the war and sickness had taken heavy toll, and now there were only nine children, ranging from my sister Sabra's age down to mine— all living at home except Aleck, the oldest, who was married and lived in some far-off place near Egypt and the Gulf.

All of the Palmers, from parents down to Connie, the youngest boy, believed in having a good time. Money might be scarce, but there was always enough to buy the latest song, for it was a musical family, everybody singing or playing some sort of instrument. Mr. Palmer, whose name was Orrin, was always ready to drive his daughters anywhere they wanted to go, whether to church or to a dance. Naturally they adored him and were very proud of his ancestry, telling us his mother was an Alston and had kept her youthful looks so long that when her son escorted her anywhere, strangers thought she was his sister.

Mrs. Palmer, named Sylvina, belonged to one of the German families in the neighborhood, and her fried chicken and pigs' feet were equally famous. Company, of which there was much too much, always came away singing her praises, no matter what the nationality of the dish. Every Saturday afternoon one could observe tied to the Palmers' palings a long line of horses belonging to the girls' beaux who had come from far and near, even from Graham, for over Sunday—or maybe longer— wearing Mrs. Palmer's patience very thin.

"What can a body do," she asked our black Maria, "to make boys go home?" Maria's advice was sound, though drastic. "I done tole her, 'Mis' Palmer, you feeds 'em too high. Stid 'er givin' 'em fried chicken, batter cakes, and honey, jes set 'em down Monday mornin' to fat back, cornpone, and sorghum, an' I know dey'll all git on dey horses right after dey done et an' streak it off home.' "

Not only did the Palmers lead a gay existence at home, they were the life of the neighborhood.

When there was a commencement at Smithwood, there were the Palmers to furnish the music, Bascom and George accompanying with fiddle and banjo, their sisters singing a popular ditty of the time about "my darling Daisy Dean" and "meadows fresh and green, fresh and green."

When the Methodists of Liberty Grove announced they were going to have tableaux at night to raise money for hymn books, who could strike an attitude better than the Palmers! Nobody could ever forget them in that tableau entitled *The Drunkard's Family*: Bascom as father with uplifted chair, Helen, the mother, shrinking back in horror, one hand uplifted to ward off the blow and the other reaching toward the affrighted children: Decie, Dora, and Connie, cowering at her feet.

Tableaux all by themselves were wonderful enough but to have them at night—simply stupendous. For one thing there were no lights in the church. And getting there in the dark—how could one do that? Would Father let us go? Mother told me to ask him. An emphatic "No" at first, but finally it was settled that Mary Shepherd and I might go in the Jersey wagon driven by our faithful Bud. And as for the lights, there were myriads. A row of candles served as footlights, and practically every kerosene lamp in the neighborhood, with chimney polished clean and bright, cast its rays into this floodlight, one enormous hanging lamp miraculously suspended from the ceiling, as dazzling as sun, moon, and stars.

Again it was the Palmer boys who got up the tournaments, a choice diversion very few neighborhoods could boast of; and these tournaments, directed by the Palmers, attracted crowds of spectators from all four counties. The first one was held near the Palmers' home, but the site for the next one was near Liberty Grove, where there was a long stretch of straight road through a wide open space suitable for parking buggies and wagons. As all our family except Father were going, we borrowed for the occasion Grandma Long's great four-horse wagon and two extra horses. Chairs were set on the straw-covered floor, and as there was more than a hint of frost in the air, to warm our feet, there were plenty of hot bricks wrapped in old pieces of carpet, besides an elegant little foot-warmer holding live coals, belonging to Aunty.

Bud, cracking his whip over the horses, drew up with a flourish, and as we were early, picked a choice spot for our wagon commanding a fine view of the "course" and also of the platform draped in bunting where the queen and her ladies in waiting would sit, these of course to be

chosen by the winners of the tournament. Connie
Palmer had sent me word that if Donna Brown didn't
come and if he won the tournament, he would crown
me queen. It was what Mr. Roosevelt would have called
an "iffy" proposition; nevertheless, it gave me a hope,
and I looked anxiously about to see if Connie was among
the gayly caparisoned knights dashing about, and practicing for the event by tilting for the ring; and sure
enough there he was with lance in hand madly dashing
for the ring—and missing it. Poor Connie! Neither he
nor anyone else had any chance, for of course that handsome daredevil of a Bascom was certain to be victor.

Having been crowned king, Bascom, with the crown
for the queen—a gay little affair of flowers and ribbon,
on the tip of his lance—rode up and down the lists inspecting the maidens in his search for a queen, everybody wondering who the lucky girl would be; finally he
reined up short in front of my sister Lizzie. She, however, was obliged to decline, as the queen must attend
the ball given that night at Dr. Black's, a place too far
from home for her to think of going. Bascom dashed
angrily off to choose another, and finally the queen and
the maids of honor all being selected, the coronation was
accomplished with much ceremony and éclat.

And now through the Palmers, romance began to
seep secondhand into my life and Mary Shepherd's.
As the saying goes, we were very near the rose. Sweet-
tempered Dora, our special friend, though the youngest
of the Palmers, was the first to wed. She had chosen for
her life partner a handsome stranger from Durham whom
she had met at a distant church not far from Saxapahaw.
She was attracted by his "pretty pants"; it was a case of
love at first sight. He had a pretty name too—Rosemond
—suited well to such fine apparel. I wanted to know
what he said when proposing, but Dora, blushing deeply,
very properly refused; that, she said, was sacred.

Religion and romance in those days went hand in

glove. Sports on Sunday being then unheard of, young men would ride miles to attend church, looking forward, of course, to meeting the pretty girls afterward at the "spring," or picnic dinner spread on a white cloth. If marriages are really made in heaven, at what better place could they begin than a church?

Dora's wedding, the first in the neighborhood we had ever attended, was in the morning, Dora being a lovely bride in her traveling dress and hat. Mrs. Palmer had done her utmost, the *pièce de résistance* being a pig roasted whole, beautifully browned, with an apple in his mouth. I had never tasted anything better. The guests, sitting at tables, were served by the young men, one of whom, putting the head of the pig on a plate, set it in front of Helen Palmer, intending it for a joke. Everybody laughed but Helen, who took it as an affront and roundly told him off.

She was the quick-tempered member of the family, given to flaring up and speaking her mind; and her encounter with old Mrs. Coltrane was a neighborhood classic. Both had lost teeth and each was wearing a plate. Helen's best beau having taken her for a buggy ride, they happened to pass the house belonging to Mrs. Coltrane, who hailed them from her front porch.

"Stop! Stop!" she called, and they stopped.

Rushing down to the gate, she said, "Helen, show me your false teeth. I want to see if they look like mine," and taking hers out, held them up for inspection.

Helen was never speechless.

"Mrs. Coltrane, it's perfectly disgusting showing your plate like that, and I'll have you to know, Mrs. Coltrane, that my teeth are never on exhibition. Good-by."

When Annie Palmer was married to Mr. George Rogers (who lived near Graham), Wesley, Mary Shepherd, and I were all invited to the morning wedding. After the breakfast, Annie took us to one side and told us that the wedding party were all driving to Mr. Rogers's home for the "infare" that night, and as there were several extra seats, we were all invited to go. They would pass our house on the way and would stop to see if we were allowed to go. On our way home Wesley declared his intention of declining, as the invitation was plainly a second thought, and if he couldn't be corn, he wouldn't be shucks. Mary Shepherd and I had no such scruples, and permission being given, we were "saddled and bridled and ready to ride" when the procession halted at our gate, Mary Shepherd being assigned to Mike Fox's buggy while I was put in with Charlie Curtis, a neighbor of Mr. Rogers. Poor Charlie! A nice, handsome, very polite young man, he hadn't expected anything like me to be wished on him. I was just thirteen and this was my first buggy ride with a beau. I could think of nothing to talk about except how bad the roads were, and how good the weather, topics I felt were not the sort usually discussed during buggy rides. "Tedious and tasteless" were the hours for us both, my only thrill being an occasional glimpse of the bride's head reposing on the bridegroom's shoulder.

At the Rogers farmhouse all was bustle and commotion, guests arriving from Haw River, Graham, and Company Shops, among them, to my great delight Eliza Sellers, now eighteen, who, full of smiles, came bursting into the room where we were dressing, looking citified and grown-up in a long, handsome, dark green dress. It was the first time I had seen her since the family had moved, but gone was the old familiar footing I remembered between us, though she and Mary Shepherd fell into each other's arms like long-lost friends.

The dress I had brought to wear in the evening, sent from Minneapolis, was a pretty red and black checked white bunting trimmed with mother-of-pearl fishscales, buttoned up the back, and of course short. I had thought it the last word until I saw that all the other girls, even the bride, were wearing long, dark dresses; then I sud-

denly felt awkward and conspicuous. Anyway I thought
my hair was all right, Sister Lizzie having pinned on a
frizzled bang, which with my long hair in two plaits
wound round my head something like a coronet gave
me what I fancied was a grown-up look.

Everyone exclaimed over the long supper table with
platters of fried chicken, turkey, ham, hot biscuits, jellies
and preserves, pumpkin and custard pies, and a tall iced
cake in the center. What struck my fancy most was the
butter, which looked like large golden pineapples, an
effect achieved, I was told, by squeezing the butter
through a stocking.

And then came the dance—nothing pale and anemic
like "Steal Partners." No, this was the real thing with
square dances where you sacheted and swung your partners, winding up with the grand right and left. An expert did the calling, not one word of which I could
understand. What sounded like "gentiswakes" was really
"Cheat or swing."

To my surprise partners were plentiful and kind in
guiding my steps aright, especially tall, handsome Mr.
Patton, with whom I chattered like a magpie. And between dances there were promenades on the porch to
cool off. Towards midnight as we were walking there
deep in conversation about *Ivanhoe* suddenly a crowd
of strange figures stole around the corner, and then—
pandemonium. Of all the horrible, hideous, indescribable noises, these were surely the worst. Scared to death,
I clung to Mr. Patton, who told me there was nothing
to be afraid of as this was only a charivari come to sere-
nade the bridal couple. "Shivaree" was the way he pronounced it, quite correctly too, I think, as it surely made
me shiver. But our North Carolina charivari was nothing like the one in *Green Grow the Lilacs*, this one ending happily enough with the crowd being invited in for
cakes and cider.

The dance was supposed to last all night, it being impossible to provide beds for all these people; and I had thought it was going to be fun to sit up all night; but when five o'clock came, all savor had departed. As I nodded uncomfortably in my chair by the fire, one of the Rogers girls led me upstairs, and there, sandwiched in, lying crosswise on the bed, supremely conscious of having had the time of my life, I fell into deep and happy slumber.

VII

No other amusement in our neighborhood could compare of course with a tournament, and so the people of this impoverished and hard-working community had to content themselves with anything that brought them together: church commencements, sales, roof-raisings, corn-shuckings, and even funerals.

What I liked about funerals was the customary lamentations. It wasn't what the mourners said but how they said it. There is certainly nothing hair-raising about the statement, "Pappy went to bed at twelve o'clock and next morning he was dead"; but when shouted by a devoted daughter over and over again with sobs and tears, somehow it gave me a decadent, though pleasurable thrill.

Father, it seems, had been addicted to sales, his purchases being apparently without rhyme or reason. Tucked away in an old cabin were eight-day clocks with painted faces, showing the moon, all busily falling to pieces. These works of art had probably been brought over from Germany. Another specialty was Bibles—huge family Bibles in the German language printed in excessively black type. I often wonder had these Bibles been preserved if they would now possess a museum value.

One result of these sales was an anecdote that gave our family an oft repeated byword. It seems that the widow was privileged to bid in anything up to a certain figure, and at one sale after all the cows had been sold, this right having been exercised by bidding in five barrels of whiskey, a man complained that she had exceeded the limit. A neighbor came to her defense exclaiming: "What's five barrels of whiskey in a family where there's no milk?"

While church was never spoken of as recreation, nevertheless much more went on at those weekly get-togethers than listening to a sermon. Here boy brought, or met, girl; and men swapped news and jokes while their wives exchanged confidences, recipes, or patterns, and saw with their own eyes the latest style in hats or dresses.

The month of August after the corn was "laid by" and fall crops not yet ready for gathering was the time for camp meetings. At Mount Pleasant, to make attendance in hot weather as attractive as possible, an arbor was set up in front of the church, the seats being backless benches; and tents were erected at a safe distance, where families were encamped for the duration.

To camp in a tent, eating under a tree three times a day, and going to church at night—that was my childhood ambition, unattainable as the moon, for we were not even Methodists. But daytime attendance provided considerable excitement, especially at the mourner's bench. What a thrill when in response to the preacher's ardent appeal to come forward, one or more women would suddenly rush down the aisle to the bench directly at the foot of the pulpit and, falling on their knees, weep and bewail their sins, and when "converted," would rise and, shouting "Hallelujahs!" tell the world they had got religion.

Hellfire and damnation was the doctrine preached then. One memorable preacher made hell seem very near and heaven very far, as he walked up and down the long platform outdoors shouting over and over again, "You cannot sit at the Lord's table and the devil's banquet both; which will you choose?" Thinking fearfully of the "worm that dieth not"—and how I did hate worms from caterpillars to those horned tobacco worms—when listening to such appeals I always made silent vows of repentance, my Presbyterian inhibitions never permitting even a thought of public confession at the mourners' bench.

Soon forgotten were these gloomy thoughts when during the noon intermission we joined the crowd arranging their picnic dinners in tempting fashion under some sheltering tree. I liked inspecting the viands spread for these delectable banquets, casting a wishful eye at the pink heart of a watermelon, or my favorite, custard pie. That refrain:

> And may you live on custard pie
> And go to hebben when you die.

aptly described the destiny of my choice.

One never knew how long meetings would last, for that depended on the daily stream of mourners; and it was whispered that many girls, not wanting their good times to end so soon, would prolong the meetings by just pretending to be mourners.

The Baptists always drew a big crowd at their baptizings done at some millpond, no country church of course possessing a pool. People went early, for latecomers had no chance of getting a good view. The candidates, wearing their worst clothes, were a sorry-looking lot while waiting their turn, and even worse after being "dipped." When they came out looking so bedraggled and forlorn, I felt thankful to be a Presbyterian and to have had my baptism done tidily by "sprinkling" when I was a baby.

The solemnity of one baptism came to a sudden end when one candidate, coming to the surface after being dipped under, suddenly began reaching out to grab the green apples bobbing up and down that had floated out of his pockets.

But the great religious event of the year, throwing every other in the shade, was the Rocky River Quarterly Meeting of the Quakers, attended not only by local members and their neighbors of all beliefs, but also by many Quakers from the West in Indiana, Ohio, and even Minnesota. This event was always the second Sunday in May, and though a long way off down in Chatham, all roads led that day to Rocky River; people being glad to shed winter thoughts and garments and sally forth in spring apparel to meet old friends and perhaps make new ones.

Yes, it was a great day. Once I remember, just before we got there, seeing a long cavalcade of fifty horsemen enter the road just ahead of us—a sight so impressive to behold that we were almost glad to take their dust.

There were always two places of worship provided, one the church itself and the other an arbor where I longed to sit with the other young people right in the midst of things and watch the crowds arriving and getting the horses unhitched and tied, and also see the never-ending stream of people milling up and down the road to the spring. Churchgoing seemed always to make people very thirsty. Mother, however, led us inside the church, where everything was quiet and solemn as always at a Quaker meeting. No pulpit here, but a long platform where both men and women in Quaker costume were sitting quietly, speaking only when the spirit moved them. All was peace and quiet—no mention of everlasting torment and no appeals to come forward and be saved—a time apparently for meditation.

What a relief, when it was all over, and we went out to eat fried chicken and the inevitable custard pie with our neighbors. That, and the walk to the spring, were to me and many others the really high moments of the day.

VIII

When the Sellerses moved away, no one could be found able or willing to be postmistress; and so, finally yielding to pressure, Mother consented to serve, taking over enough space in father's desk for keeping the stamps and all other paraphernalia. To Mary Shepherd and me it appeared as compensation for losing the Sellerses. Now instead of our going for the mail, people would come here. Like the Palmers! What fun to have them come once or even twice a week, maybe getting a new song which they would try out on Mother's piano, letting us be the first to hear it. And so it proved, we hearing such gems as "Goodbye Charlie," "Beautiful Mabel Clare," "My Jockey Cap and Feather," and "The Jolliest Girl That's Out":

> And if my partner squeeze my hand,
> I neither frown nor pout;
> It pleases him, it don't hurt me,
> I'm the jolliest girl that's out.

"That's just how I'm going to act," I told myself.

Our postman was due at three o'clock, and every Wednesday I'd sit in my black rocking chair on the piazza to look for his coming, keeping a watchful eye on the shadow cast by the house, as it moved up the trunk of the big elm tree, knowing just where it would be at three o'clock. I wasn't equal to telling time by the sun the way the Kecks did, just squinting at that orb and saying, "Sun's an hour high," "Half an hour before sundown," " 'Bout four o'clock," and getting it right too; but this shadow on the elm tree was as good as a clock.

Having the post office was in a way a liberal education as we got to know almost everybody in our neighborhood, and something of what they believed and thought, and their ways of doing things. All planting, for instance, was according to the phases of the moon as recorded in the almanac.

The oddest person was old Hammerleg Kivett, as everybody called him. He always rode his horse up to the front gate and, not wishing to come any further, would "holler." Instead of saying "Howdy," his old country greeting was, "How do you rise today?" Mary Shepherd and I, not knowing exactly how we rose, always giggled over answering, but wishing to be polite, contributed some information about the state of our health. Which they tell me by modern standards is a mistake, people saying that "How do you do?" is not an inquiry about health at all, but merely a greeting like "Good morning."

One of my friends said her husband told her on his return home, "Well, I asked Mr. Smith today how he was, and the darn fool went and told me."

IX

When Mother had come from Hillsborough as a bride, bringing her piano, to live with Father's parents for a time, our neighborhood impressed her as "a negative place, neither good nor evil," but as the years went on, she felt there was more good than evil. Life and property were pretty safe, nothing of much value ever being stolen, and nobody getting murdered. North Carolina's law making housebreaking a capital offense made people think twice before breaking a lock. Most of the time, at our house, they would have found no necessity for breaking locks, as nobody but me ever thought of locking doors before going to bed.

Once when I was very little, there being a great disturbance at the hen house, Mother roused us all, and, just as we were, all in our night clothes, the little procession followed Mother, carrying a candle, to see what all this noise was about. What would have happened had we been confronted by an intruder, we'll never know. Finding nothing and nobody, we decided it must have been a weasel.

But one summer, after the Centennial, we began to hear reports of various outrages. People complained of their smokehouses and springhouses being robbed; and a band of masked men was said to have gone at night to lone, lorn Miss Katy Graves and forced her to give them all the money she had in the house.

However, with three protectors, Cousin Osmond, Will, and John all sleeping in the house, I felt no fears. Will, after his experience in Uncle James's store, had decided to open a store for himself in a brand new house just across the road from the mill—a fine location, as people coming to the mill found it a convenient place to do their shopping.

What really worried me that summer was that old fear of the Judgment Day, suddenly revived, and ever present. The darkies, worried too, had told me that a child at Greensboro, born deaf and dumb, had spoken for the first time in its life, declaring that the Judgment Day was coming on the Fourth of July. And now every red streak in the sky put me in a panic, and there was no sleeping at night, unless Mother was my bedfellow.

One night Mary Shepherd and I were sleeping upstairs over Mother's room. I heard the dogs barking, and wondered why. Then presently I heard Bud's voice. What on earth was he doing here in the middle of the night? Then Mother called, telling us to get up and look out of the window, but not to be scared. The sight I saw was what I had been dreading to see all summer— a world on fire! There was the sky reddened with flames leaping high in the air and clouds of smoke and fire rolling to overwhelm us. But I wasn't scared, now that the Judgment Day had really come. I just sat there, still and frozen; and awaited my fate, calm and tearless. Perhaps that's how we'll all feel on Judgment Day.

Then Mother came up and told us that what we saw was a real sure-enough fire burning up Will's store. As there had been absolutely nothing on the premises to cause a fire, somebody had undoubtedly robbed the store, and, to conceal the crime, set the store on fire. Poor Will! I came to life again, and feeling this minor tragedy acutely, wept bitter tears.

X

The day of the commencement at Pleasant Lodge Academy, to which I had long looked forward, dawning bright and clear, everything seemed auspicious for a happy outing. After breakfast Mother helped me braid my hair, tying it with a brand new ribbon. My dress was a black and white percale made with overskirt and basque, both being cut out in battlements bound with black. Of course had it been buttoned in front, it would have seemed more grown up, but when mother pinned on an embroidered white collar with a jabot, that seemed a minor matter. And my hat—that was the crowning splendor—for it was the white chip with pink roses, given me by that dear Loraine. Mother had put up a nice lunch, and as my handsome Cousin Wes was taking me in his buggy, my cup seemed not only full, but running over.

All went well until we passed a neighbor's house, just as a mother and daughter came out expecting to walk to the Academy. Wes stopped—and, could I believe my ears?—he was offering them a ride. This was his sewing-machine buggy, and as there was no room on the front seat, he opened up the back where the machines were kept and seated them on the floor with their legs hanging down. And amid peals of laughter from everybody but me, off we went. All my pleasure in our equipage gone, I sat unnoticed, stricken and silent, while the others talked and laughed.

On reaching the Academy, we separated, our companions joining some friends, and I sitting with a pretty girl never met before, whose easy friendly manners made me feel grown up and sophisticated and restored me to good humor. It was a long day, the Commencement exercises ending late in the afternoon, following which several other people and I went to Mr. Peter Smith's to spend the interval before the evening meeting. This, the climax of the day, was to be a grand promenade, with lemonade for refreshments! something unheard of before in our neighborhood.

All the girls sat on benches ranged against the wall, waiting for the boys' invitations to promenade. I, never having attended the school, knew only one boy, Charlie Crutchfield, who walked me up and down quite a while. Wes came up to ask me if I would have some lemonade, but knowing his slender resources, though longing to partake of this delicious drink, I couldn't think of having him spend any money on me and told a very white lie. I said I wasn't thirsty. Not cheered by seeing Wes treat several other girls to lemonade, I found it on the whole a dismal evening, with no partners and no lemonade.

Imagine my feelings when I learned the next day that Father had given Wes a whole dollar, especially to buy me lemonade!

XI

Father was rich in lore of horse and mule flesh; and how he loved to discourse on both! He was very particular about taking proper care of them, insisting that all harness be removed during the noon hour, which, he said, refreshed a horse as much as food and drink. He was also very careful about having them shod properly. "A horse," he used to say, "is no better than his hoofs." And I've often thought, apropos of corns and chilblains, or a day of sight-seeing, how very true that was of folks. The neighbors thought Father was a wizard, because he could look in a horse's mouth and tell how old he was. He had deep affection and admiration for fine horses, and declared that the most beautiful sight in the world was a beautiful woman on a beautiful horse.

Father had a deep respect for mules, insisting they were more cautious than horses, always trying out unfamiliar ground before putting their feet down hard. Incurably suspicious, they were sure to shy away from the newfangled and unaccustomed. The old-time fashions were good enough for them.

I had always felt more or less puffed up about living where four counties rubbed elbows. And though our barn, located across the road, at least two city blocks from the house where it could be neither seen nor smelled, looked just like any other, in my opinion the fact that the dividing line between Randolph and Guilford ran right through the middle, with Alamance and Chatham to the right and left just around the corner, set it apart from all other barns. And then something happened that put our four corners in the limelight.

One well-remembered June morning old Uncle Mose came with a long face to tell us that a big hog had died the night before and the turkey buzzards were already hovering over the back yard. This was sad news, for it meant a lot less hog with our hominy the coming winter; but no use crying over spilt milk; so Uncle Mose was told to get busy and drag off the carcass before the buzzards actually swooped down.

Darkies have a natural affinity for mules; and so Uncle Mose brought a big black mule named Jim Crow to do the job. He tied a chain around the hog, fastening it securely to a singletree harnessed to Jim Crow. Everything was proceeding according to plan, as the military say, and Uncle Mose was about to say "Gidup" when, Jim Crow turning his head to see what was going on, the little wafting June breezes upset all plans.

One whiff was enough for Jim Crow. No use to say "Gidup" now, for, with one bound, he started as if catapulted forth, jerking the reins from Uncle Mose's hand. I caught a glimpse as he passed the house, the hog bounding high in the air, and I rushed out on the porch to see Jim Crow running like the wind, everybody in pursuit yelling "Whoa," and the chickens squawking as they scattered to cover. Jim Crow cleared the five-barred gate, the hog standing out straight behind, and running across the road similarly cleared the gate to the barnyard, jumping from Randolph into Guilford. He ran through the barnyard, down the long lane, past the spring, jumped the bars there, and, running through the woods a couple of miles, leaped a rail fence from Guilford into Alamance. Here somebody tried to stop him, but he turned around and, jumping from Alamance back into Guilford, proceeded back the way he had come, and leaped from Guilford back into Randolph. We had heard the pounding of his hoofs and ran out to stop him; but Jim Crow eluded each outstretched hand as he tore down the road out of sight, fleeing from that body of death, in part, at least, still attached to the singletree, bounding now high, now low.

Assault would have been winded long before old Jim Crow finally stopped of his own accord, eight miles away in Chatham. The battered singletree was still there, but no trace of the hog. Four counties claimed its remains, as impartially and equally distributed as if they had been cremated and scattered on the winds.

Down in those four counties, they tell me, there are still people who repeat the saga of Jim Crow's run-away race, with death at his heels.

BOOK TWO

Crossing New Frontiers

1

THE SPRING OF HOPE

TO MARY SHEPHERD and me, the summer of 1878 seemed just like any other summer. We had observed, it is true, a perpetual conclave, lapsing into silence whenever we appeared; still, we thought nothing of it, and when the big news broke that we were going to boarding school that fall, at Peace Institute in Raleigh, it was a bolt from the blue.

This remarkable event had come about through our sisters Jane and Eleanor having sought their fortunes in New York—Jane wanting to be a teacher in the public schools, and Eleanor, an artist. Neither had wholly achieved her ambition, but, nevertheless, much had come of this venture; and both, besides supporting themselves in New York, had acquired money, enough to send us to Peace. The tuition and board was then two hundred and forty dollars per annum, besides such extras as ten dollars a year for washing and pew rent, each fifty cents a month. An enormous sum! This ten dollars was given to me at the beginning of the year for this purpose, and, to my everlasting credit, though I had no allowance for pocket money, I spent every penny each month just as intended.

Jane had earned her money partly by substituting in the New York Public Schools and partly by doing all sorts of odd jobs such as being a bookkeeper for a dressmaker who instructed her among other things al-

ways to make out the stub before making out the check.
Important information passed on to me, and, though
many years elapsed before I owned a checkbook, I remembered and followed this advice.

Sewing by the day was not despised, one of her pa-
trons being the wife of a prominent magazine editor and
poet, Richard Watson Gilder. Belonging to the aristocracy of kind hearts, the Gilders treated Jane like one
of the family, having her sit at the table with them instead of sending her a tray. He presented Jane with a
volume of his poems which I vainly tried to read—so
dry they reminded me of the lines in Father's joke book:

> If there should be another flood,
> For refuge, hither fly;
> Though all the world should be submerged,
> This book would still be dry.

Jane had won the wife's heart by her impulsive
Southern fashion of springing to her aid in any little
difficulty such as buttoning her shoes—something she
told Jane she dared not ask of any servant.

II

Getting us outfitted became the order of the day,
and a big job it was for all hands. Aunty and Mother
made our underclothes, plain and simple, but nothing to
hang our heads for, with much fine handiwork of her-
ringbone and featherstitching and even a little Ham-
burg edging. Jane and Eleanor, fresh from New York,
made our dresses, Eleanor bossing the job, as she could
do anything with a needle. Together they made all of
Mary Shepherd's dresses, but only my everyday ones,
for Sabra was going to send my Sunday and second best
from Minneapolis. The dress I was to travel in, a dark
gray-green worsted with a polonaise, buttoned down the
back and edged with a plaited frill, made me strut a
little. And even the two calico dresses with basques
buttoned up in front were quite to my liking, being

just as good as any calico dress could possibly be. Eleanor, as good a milliner as she was a dressmaker, trimmed our straw hats with a ribbon bow and a pert quill sticking up on one side. Our winter hats we were to buy in Raleigh.

All this new finery was to be packed, together with the required new rubbers, raincoat, sheets, and pillow cases into two brand-new Saratoga trunks, a fitting climax to a wardrobe which, though modest, was yet beyond all our expectations.

III

One important question Mary Shepherd and I were allowed to decide for ourselves, namely, what names we should henceforth be called by. Neither of us wished to go on being called "Mayshepherd" and "Mryalves," and the question was, who should be called what? "Shepherd" didn't seem suitable for a first name; and so, too young and careless to think whether or not this would hurt Mother's feelings, we finally agreed that she should be "Mary"; and I, after considering Alma, Annabel, Amelia, Adelaide, etc., etc., decided to keep my own name of Alves. My signature I concluded to part in the middle and began diligently practicing the writing of "M. Alves Long" over and over just to see how it would look. I kept this signature for many years, but being by nature averse to waste motions, I finally dropped the M., and became Alves only. If Mother was hurt she gave no sign, but it is the regret of a lifetime that I didn't leave my name just as it was, in the good old Southern fashion. "Alves" being an unusual name, even close friends have never learned how to spell it, and have invented as many variations as Cohen possesses, writing it: Alice, Aves, Alvis, Avis, or Alvez. And sometimes calling me "Alveze." For "Alves" I have fought, bled, and almost died.

IV

Father took entire charge of the trip to Raleigh sixty miles away, decreeing that instead of our going to Graham and taking the train there to Raleigh, we should drive the whole way via Saxapahaw and Chapel Hill. Wesley would take us in the Jersey wagon, and Osmond would go along in the covered wagon carrying our trunks and also a load of flour to be sold in Raleigh—this, by the way, being the justification for the caravan. It was all very like the Irishman who had accidentally dropped a nickel through a hole in the sidewalk. It seemed silly to take up the sidewalk for only a nickel; so, to make it worth his while, he dropped in a dollar.

The real reason of course was Father's fixed determination to have us go by and visit the University, the Alma Mater of himself and all of his brothers except Uncle Edwin. Chapel Hill was now the daily theme of his conversation, with much talk of the two literary societies: the Dialectic and the Philanthropian, the members of which for the sake of brevity were called Di's and Phi's.

There were many anecdotes, the most popular being the one about Professor Elias Mitchell's famous outwitting of the whole student body. Chapel attendance at the University was then compulsory, and the students, thinking the Scripture readings much too long, removed the Bible from its cover, leaving in its place a pile of some old newspapers. But the merry ha ha expected never came; for when Professor Mitchell opened the cover, he showed no surprise, and made no comment, but, closing the cover, calmly recited the 119th Psalm, which everybody knows is by far the longest chapter in the Bible. Next day the Bible was back.

Another story was about the boy who convulsed the class by pronouncing the phrase "Scipio waging war in Africa" as "Skipio wagging war in Afryca."

As an example of perseverance being rewarded,

Father told how Uncle James, arriving late to choose a partner for the grand march during commencement, had gone down the line of girls sitting in a row, getting "No" for an answer until he reached the bottom, where the most beautiful girl of all, sitting there, said, "Yes."

One tale, not so pleasant, concerned a student accused of robbing his roommate and expelled on what Father considered insufficient evidence.

Long years afterward the University sought to bestow an honorary degree upon this boy who had gone West and become a national figure of great renown. In rejecting the honor he showed what Father called "the proper spirit."

Father, an acknowledged expert in disjointing a fowl or carving a ham or any kind of roast, always making it go round, had acquired this art at his boardinghouse in Chapel Hill. He would stick in his fork and never move it, and when he had finished serving the others, the only piece left for him was the one into which he had stuck his fork.

v

We were to spend the first night at the home of Cousin James Newlin, who kept open house on a scale that required no previous notice. All you had to do was to drive up and say you had come, and there was always poundcake and fried chicken, and a glad-handed welcome from Cousin Eliza and the children: Em, Mamie, and Mike, whom I secretly adored. A handsome fellow he was, something of a dandy, and his delicately striped pantaloons, spotless linen, and shined shoes were beyond everything. Cousin James himself was a big, silent man who never took any notice, but everybody else made up for that.

Father, to whom it never occurred that it might not always be convenient to have guests, had written Mrs. Harris that we would spend the second night with her at Chapel Hill and had received a very cordial reply.

She was almost a blood relation, the sister of Isaac Foust, who had married Cousin Annie Holt, and besides, an intimate friend of my sisters. Her husband, who was a doctor, had taken her to Paris on their honeymoon and had spent a year there studying, a most unusual event in those days.

Lena Foust, whom I remembered in white dress and pink sash at her brother's wedding, lived with her sister and was always being held up to me as a shining example in manners. "Mary Alves, take your elbows off the table. Lena Foust never puts hers on. Eat slowly, the way Lena Foust does." I loved putting my elbows on the table. Somehow it made me feel elegant and at ease, and these admonitions made me dread meeting her again. But my fears were groundless, for that night at supper, charming and cordial, she made a pretty picture laughing and talking, with both elbows on the table.

The next morning bright and early Jim Ruffin, at the request of my brother Will, came to show us round the campus. He was the son of Colonel Thomas Ruffin, a great friend of Father's, and I had often seen him in Hillsborough and knew him as a little girl knows a big boy, which is to say, not at all.

That day I recognized for the first time that the three years difference in our ages had put Mary Shepherd and me into separate worlds. Now seventeen, with the gift of beauty and a year's experience at Greensboro Female College, she was a young lady attracting beaux as honey does flies, but I was still a little girl, and a plain one too, with no airs or graces.

Jim Ruffin, who met her for the first time, "fell" for her at once; and after a casual "howdy do" to me, addressed all his remarks thereafter exclusively to her; and when other boys appeared, he introduced them with all the airs of proprietorship. Luckily I didn't mind, being highly pleased with the whole performance and very proud of the attention Mary Shepherd was receiving.

The best thing I know about myself is that neither then nor afterwards was I ever jealous of Mary Shepherd's beauty or her beaux.

To speed us on the last lap of our journey, Mrs. Harris gave us an early dinner. The horse was fresh, and Wesley drove off at a rattling pace, there still being thirty miles to go. It rained that afternoon, and nothing could have been more dismal. Do what we could, our clothes and spirits were both dampened. We overtook Osmond, who had had an early start, just as we reached the gate at Peace Institute after dark. How thankful I felt that since the rain had made us late everybody was at supper and there was no one to witness our bedraggled, unimpressive arrival, or to see us on the way to our room.

We freshened up as best we could, and I remember passing through a hall crowded with chattering girls walking up and down with their arms around each other's waists and casting curious looks at us as we were taken down to an empty dining room for a late supper. I ate little, for homesickness had swept over me like a tidal wave.

VI

The bright spot of that first bewildering day as, feeling strange and deflated, I sat in the Assembly Room, waiting to be classified, was Maggie Merrimon, daughter of Senator Merrimon, who lived opposite in a big yellow house. Wherever Maggie Merrimon was, her whole life through, there was sweetness and light. That morning she amused herself and us by pointing out distinguished personalities as they came and went. The bearded man carrying a palmetto fan which, she said, was as much a part of him as his beard, was Professor Baumann, the idolized music teacher, regarded in his little community as highly as Paderewski ever was. That lively blonde talking with him was Sallie Marsh from Salisbury, who claimed to be an infidel; and the tall, pale girl with her was Linda

Rumple, daughter of a Presbyterian preacher in Salisbury. These two, friends and roommates, were Professor Baumann's prize pupils, and nobody knew which was better, but most people thought it was Sallie. At concerts when she sat at the piano everybody held his breath. Linda's mother had made her practice with heavy weights tied to her wrists; and that was why she could strike those deep bass notes with such force.

The two tall girls wearing calico frocks with long trains and looking exactly alike were the twins, George and Edwina Johnson, from Virginia. They always wore different hair ribbons, and if you noticed which was which as they sat in the regular seats at breakfast, then you could tell them apart the rest of the day. The dashing looking brunette was Fannie Baker from Florida, considered the prettiest girl in school, and the most popular.

The tall, stern, handsome man was our Principal, Mr. John Burwell, always called, "Mr. Johnny." Everyone stood in awe of him, and being sent to his office for an "interview" was a much dreaded ordeal. The severe-looking lady in black was our Lady Principal, Mrs. Drury Lacy, who had charge of the Assembly Room and held all her classes on the platform or stage, keeping order and teaching at the same time, a difficult job at which she was highly successful.

The handsome woman with the wide, pleasant mouth, and slightly darkened upper lip, was Miss Mary Heffelman, the new teacher of mathematics and science, from Chambersburg, Pennsylvania. "A Yankee?" I asked with bated breath, never having seen one before.

"Yes, of course," said Maggie, "and many other teachers are also Yankees. They are nice though, and if it wasn't for their accent, you wouldn't know it."

At this point one of the new girls, Mary Wilson from Morganton, broke in saying, "I haven't had such a good time since my grandma died." A new, and to me, a shocking remark, but I laughed with the rest.

Mary was a great talker, and she proceded to tell us about her father, a civil engineer, who had built a railroad track up Round Knob with sixteen or maybe seventeen hairpin curves. He was a jolly father, fond of joking with his children and had the intriguing custom whenever he had taken his bath, of standing in the door, and shouting, "Bring me my Afghanistan to cover my Baluchistan." That, I thought, was the acme of wit.

All the Wilson girls, and there were four of them, had a "line" which never failed to amuse. Mary, who had few inhibitions, was destined to get me into my first scrape. It was a bold but harmless incident resulting in a summons to Mr. Johnny's office. "What do you mean," he asked me, "by promenading next to the fence across the front yard and talking to the boys on the other side?" Not knowing what I had meant, I said nothing. And after a few more questions of that sort, to none of which I answered a word, he gave up, and cautioning me against a repetition of the offense, sent me back to my class, relieved, but not crushed to earth. In fact, I no longer felt afraid of Mr. Johnny.

The general effect of that first day's "bull session" was to depress me further, for, though I had racked my brain, I had not been able to think of a single thing to say. These girls, all brought up in towns, used to pretty clothes and parties, lived in a world I had never known, and I had nothing of interest to tell them. Deep in my heart I felt that I would never belong. It was the beginning of an inferiority complex that would embitter many years.

VII

Peace Institute itself, a four-storied building with imposing white columns and extensive grounds threaded with walks adorned here and there with latticed arches and bordered with flowers, seemed palatial to me. Situated on the edge of town, with cotton fields at the rear, it overlooked in front, on opposite sides of Wilmington Street, the residences of Senator Merrimon and of beautiful Miss Mary Lewis, whom we were always craning our necks to catch a glimpse of whenever she issued forth, dressed for a party in silks, satin, or some ravishing creation of lace and white organdy, just the kind of thing that makes a Southern girl irresistible.

On the unimportant little street on the west side near a few insignificant small houses in one of which the Baumanns lived rose the mansion of my dreams. Surely there never was a house with so many bay windows, a more magnificent portal rich with carving and a glittering brass knocker, or a more intriguing cupola resplendent with colored glass and offering a view towards all four quarters of the earth.

I could survey all this magnificence from my third-story window, and this became "my house," the scene of all my dreams and vain imaginings.

In great contrast to this and the elegant houses in front were the wretched hovels in the squalid alley bounding our domain on the east. These miserable dwellings were inhabited by a curious looking people I thought were mulattoes, but instead were those rare creatures—albino Negroes.

"So nigh was grandeur" to their dust, but, being used to such sights, we girls never gave it a thought. We were not concerned about the "forgotten man," because we didn't know he had been forgotten. And even now, there are still those as ignorant as we. Speaking recently to a group of young people I said something about "the forgotten man," and after I had left the room, somebody who could hardly speak for laughing came rushing out to tell me that one of the girls had asked, "Who *is* the forgotten man?"

Those magnificent front porches of Peace behind lofty white pillars became my chosen haunts, each from top to bottom having its own special memory enshrined in my heart. The lowest one, paved with brick, held the water bucket and coconut dipper, the Mecca on week-days of hasty pilgrimages between classes and on hot Sundays the lodestone to which we made a beeline on returning from church. Unhygienic? Yes, but as we didn't know it, no evil consequence ever happened. And when I lay in the infirmary, parched with thirst and forbidden to drink water, how my heart turned with longing to that old bucket.

And the first story porch, approached from each side by a circular staircase—why that was where I first saw sweet Shellie Smith, dearest idol of my heart.

She was a "new" girl from Madison, Florida, a town I came to know well from her descriptions. Bewitchingly dressed in a cream-colored lace bunting and wearing jet bracelets, the kind I had long wanted, she was returning from her first shopping expedition downtown; and as she went about, offering with the sweetest smile in the world her bag of candy to every girl, whether she knew her or not, she won all hearts. From that time forward I had a "crush" on Shellie Smith.

As for the other two porches, they were where I watched crimson sunsets blazing behind tall, windy oaks; or where I tiptoed to on early mornings when everyone else was asleep and, sitting on a hard wooden bench, "crammed" for examinations with my head as clear as a bell in that cool sweet air. Here I learned whole pages of dates, geometry problems, algebraic formulas, and one day, the whole of our natural history book.

The grounds at the rear excited no interest, being devoted to such prosaic things as outbuildings and kitchen gardens. Far different was the yard at the side of the west wing, for this was a recreation center provided with a swing, a flying Jenny, and an enormous rocker with seats high up in the air at each end, facing each other, with room for several girls. As it could be operated by one girl, it was almost as good as my little black rocking chair; and many were the happy hours it sweetened for me perched up there alone with a book.

As the Burwell apartments were located at the front of the east wing, this west yard was naturally the place chosen by the boys for their serenades. No sweeter moment than when wakened by midnight songs beneath your window! Sooner or later Mr. Johnny was sure to interrupt, but in the meantime there was opportunity for the more daring girls to lower notes in their shoes and draw up replies, or even exchange a little lively conversation. Lucky me, that first year, to have a room on the west side! Even when Mr. Johnny came, those dauntless midnight minstrels never neglected, while taking to their heels, to sing those parting strains:

> Good night, ladies, we're going to leave you now.
> Merrily we roll along, roll along—
> We're going to leave you now.

VIII

Peace on the inside even to my unpracticed eye was anything but palatial. Here were no marble halls, but plain plaster and wood. Our bedrooms, containing only the necessary articles of furniture: bed, bureau, two straight chairs, and washstand, were downright ugly, and remained so, as the custom of bringing decorations from home was then entirely unknown.

The teachers' rooms were no better, and poor Madame Fromm, our German teacher, who occupied a tiny hall bedroom containing a big double bed, used to say so pathetically, "My room is nothing than bed."

There were no bathrooms, our washstand equipment being the only provision for baths! but on each floor there was hot and cold water plentiful enough for all requirements. We could fill our pitchers as often as we liked. And greatest luxury of all was the central heating system, the first I had ever seen. It made taking a bath in winter as pleasant as in summer.

PEACE INSTITUTE DURING THE BURWELL DAYS

JANE TAYLOR LONG, TEACHER AT PEACE INSTITUTE
She made learning interesting and easy

The entrance hall was not in the least imposing, and the small reception room and parlor beyond, furnished very simply, contained nothing that I remember.

The Assembly Room, two stories in height, entirely bare of decoration, had a stage at one end containing, besides a table and grand piano, many chairs for the pupils of our Lady Principal.

When I look at the beautiful library now at Peace College with its many well-stacked alcoves, card indexes, magazines, files of newspapers, and reading tables, I smile, remembering the little bare room of my day with chairs ranged against the wall, a table, and two small bookcases mounted on chests of drawers. No provision having been made for reading matter, there were, of course, no reading tables. Incidentally, during the years I was at Peace, I never saw a magazine, or a newspaper. Dickens's works were on a top shelf, but, had I been allowed to browse, I would have become a Dickens enthusiast before I grew up. As it was I read only the two I had heard recommended, *Oliver Twist* and *A Tale of Two Cities.*

Other books were some large volumes of bound magazines which I used to take out Saturdays, thinking they would last over Sunday. They lasted all right, most of the articles being either dull or beyond my comprehension.

There were many books of the Sunday school variety, the most popular being the "Pansy" books and *Hitherto,* by Mrs. A. D. T. Whitney.

One of Pansy's made a lasting impression. It was the story of a religious rich girl who, becoming impoverished, went to live in a cheap boardinghouse where she met the hero, a young streetcar conductor, very ungrammatical, with no knowledge of table etiquette or religion. After being converted by the rich girl, he showed immediate and remarkable improvement in his speech and table manners, no longer saying, "I done it," and no

longer eating peas with a knife. Hitherto I had believed
that conversion to Christianity was for the betterment of
my morals; but now I pondered wishfully this breath-
taking notion that it could improve almost automatically
my speech and manners. A little skeptical though, as
I recalled many Christians in our neighborhood who
with similar bad habits had as yet suffered no change.

Of *Hitherto,* read again and again, I remember
only two passages, one, that "men always expect their
babies will be safely born," and the other concerning
a little girl who on returning from a party confessed she
had eaten four pieces of cake; upon her mother's slight
reproof she said, "Why not? There was plenty." To
which the mother replied, "But suppose everybody had
eaten four pieces of cake!"

Far better equipped than the library was the gym-
nasium at the top of the building, which was also the
art gallery by day, the hours for gym being from nine
to ten at night. Here the easels, pictures, and statues
all being pushed to one side, we repaired the first three
nights in the week to exercise "free hand," and also with
dumbbells, rings, and wands. Even a little dancing was
thrown in, one intricate number called the "Andalu-
sian," done with many twists, bows, and turns, as we
went round in a huge circle taking in the whole room.
The schottische and polka were also taught, and what
fun we had chanting "Heel and toe, and away we go"
as we dashed enthusiastically about the room. Everybody
was crazy about gym. It was the custom those first three
days when dressing for the afternoon to don our gym
suits of bright blue flannel made with perody waists, and
trimmed with red braid. There were bloomers of course,
making this a sweltering costume on warm autumn and
spring afternoons and evenings. But we didn't mind;
anything connected with gym was fun.

At the close of gym we were supposed to go directly
to our rooms, but, ingenious little pests that we were,

we prolonged this period by kissing each other good
night, wandering from door to door upstairs and downstairs, doing our level best to get as far as possible from
our own doors until finally we had instituted a sort of
"sit up" strike. To remedy this state of affairs, the kissing bell was devised. Ten minutes was allowed for kissing, at the end of which a bell rang, and woe betide the
girl who was not in her room when the teacher made
her rounds.

IX

Our day's long routine of exercise, study, and classes,
lasting from out of bed into bed, began with a rising
bell at seven o'clock, followed twenty-five minutes later
by a warning bell, prelude to the breakfast bell at seven-
thirty. Many girls would always wait for the second bell
and, jumping into their clothes with the speed of fire-
men, race madly downstairs, frantically buttoning as
they went, in their efforts to get in under the wire.

Waking was always a sad time for me, for homesickness rushed over me like high tide. There is no remedy
for homesickness but to go home, and so each morning
I woke with that same sorrowing dread that gives to
Michelangelo's statue of Day that look of divine despair.

The idea of waking without grief became a sort of
obsession with me, and I read with delight all expres-
sions of the idea in literature, a favorite passage being
Ellen's song to James FitzJames:

> Soldier rest, thy warfare o'er,
> Sleep the sleep that knows no waking
> Morn of toil, nor night of waking.

I often thought sentimentally of dying and decided
on an epitaph for my tombstone:

> Asleep in Jesus, blessed sleep
> From which none ever wake to weep.

Not that I ever wept. Never a tear did I shed, though
there were plenty of homesick girls who did. One just

couldn't stop and had to be sent home. No, mine was a stony-hearted grief too deep for tears, unflinchingly and proudly concealed even from Mary Shepherd, who, by the way, had found a most intimate friend in Minnie Faucette and was happy as a lark. I learned how to live with loneliness, and as a result developed fortitude to an amazing degree.

After breakfast, weather permitting, all the girls were sent into the grounds for a twenty-minute period of exercise. This they did in couples, walking in a fond embrace furiously up and down the paths. It was the custom to make engagements for these promenades ahead of time, popular girls like Fannie Baker being engaged weeks ahead. This exercise period was to me a terrible ordeal. The truth was that, just as I feared, I was a rank outsider; for, being only fourteen, I was too young in years and interests to make friends with older girls, who were much interested in beaux, while the only lovers I cared anything about, such as Ravenswood and Ivanhoe, lived only in books. And so, feeling I had nothing to talk about, I was too timid to ask anyone to promenade with me; and as nobody ever asked me, I was on the spot, compelled to wander about like a lost sheep, feeling myself an object of scorn or derision.

Many were the subterfuges I employed to shorten the time or to keep out of sight. As often as I dared I would ask permission to go upstairs for something which I truthfully phrased as "left," instead of "forgotten"; and a terrible time I took to find it. Then I would repair to the lavatory, concealing myself there till I could stand it no longer, after which I would swing a little, or sit on the joggling board, or watch the girls whirling up and down on the flying Jenny, something I longed to do, but never could. As a last resort I would visit the water bucket and be at the door ready to pop inside the minute the bell began to ring. Anything to avoid promenading alone in plain sight. If God had paid the least attention to my prayers, there would have been rain enough for another deluge, and breakfast would always have been twenty minutes late.

Nine o'clock always found us seated in the Assembly Hall for roll call and a brief devotional led by Mr. Johnny, after which we went to classes or remained in the hall for study until three o'clock except for the welcome interlude of dinner and freedom until the afternoon session beginning at two o'clock.

At three the whole school assembled for roll call, the reply to which was not "present" but "perfect" or "imperfect." Perfect, if during the day while passing from one class to another, you had not whispered or spoken a single word to anyone—a really superhuman feat; and imperfect if you had, which meant getting demerits, a very serious business if you got too many, indicating you were incorrigible and liable to expulsion. Were we always strictly truthful? I really believe most of us were. At any rate, there were few who replied "imperfect"; and though there were a few snickers when some flagrant offender answered "perfect" in loud, firm tones, such a one never really lost caste. As for myself, I will say that when I yielded to temptation whispering the "im" to myself and speaking loudly the "perfect," my conscience never felt a single pang.

The hour from three to four was divided between exercising again in the yard and dressing for the afternoon. On no account were we to wear the same dress all day. After a study hour from four to five we had free time until supper.

Playing croquet then was what I liked best, and as I was to my astonishment much the best player in school, I was actually in demand as a partner. The croquet ground being just about as rough and uneven as the one at home, even with the addition of acorns, I found little difficulty in overcoming all obstructions. My skill at croquet and my exploits as a rover would have won me an

Oscar, had there been such a thing. How I hated to hear the ringing of that supper bell at six o'clock!

There was about an hour and a half of free time between supper and the study hour at eight o'clock, which had to be spent in the entrance and adjoining hall, since we were not allowed to go to our rooms. There seemed to be a determined effort to keep us out of our own or other girls' rooms; why, I never discovered. But there was little opportunity for visiting. And if you were caught in another girl's room after bedtime, you were sent to Mr. Johnny the next day. There being no amusement provided for this period, I used to sit on one of the couches listening to the girls discussing such topics as "Is it possible for a girl to be engaged to a boy and not kiss him?" Betty Hawkins, a pretty red-haired girl, maintained that it was, for she had been engaged to several boys, even two at one time, and had never kissed a single one.

The only other diversion was to pay a visit to saintly old Dr. Drury Lacy, the husband of our Lady Principal. All the girls liked Dr. Lacy, and he liked all the girls. He was the first person you looked up on returning from vacation, and most of the girls paid their respects to him every evening, generally kissing him good-night. I adored him, but loathed kissing those abundant white whiskers yellowed about the mouth and tasting of tobacco. So I had contrived a fine technique to avoid all kisses, by stealing in and out when he was surrounded by other girls. It was the same method I used to dodge kissing girls with bad complexions, it being an unwritten law that when you met any girl for the first time upon returning to school after vacation, you must exchange kisses with her. So I would carefully arrange this first meeting to occur at some place like the dinner table, where kisses were not allowed.

In spite of age and whispers, Dr. Lacy was a most romantic figure, being the hero of *Alone,* a novel by his cousin Mrs. Terhune, who wrote under the nom de plume of Marion Harland.

"Did you get on your knees when you proposed to the heroine?" I asked him.

"No," he roared indignantly, "I never got on my knees to anybody but my Maker."

Dr. Lacy's son Ben was also a romantic figure to us girls, as he was known to be courting pretty Miss Mary Burwell, Mr. Johnny's eldest daughter. It was rumored that there was some opposition, but we girls were all on his side. Our wisdom was justified, because there never could have been a more successful marriage than theirs turned out to be.

There was another old man I made friends with, the Reverend Dr. Robert Burwell, the first President of Peace, and the father of Mr. Johnny. Dr. Burwell, now retired, occupied a suite of rooms on the ground floor of the west wing near the science laboratory and the rooms filled with pianos where lessons and practicing went on from morn to dewy eve. Here in these surroundings he lived a life apart from all school activities. No girls ever came trooping into his room with laughter and kisses, and I do not remember any girl except myself ever paying him a visit, which I had done, very timidly at first, to deliver a message from Mother, once a pupil of his wife, considered the finest woman teacher of North Carolina. He had married my parents and liked to talk about old times and show me some of his treasured books and pictures. He told me that Father had the strange power of hypnotizing people, something I had never heard of before; and that when he was courting Mother, who was rather small, people used to tease him by saying,

> Man wants but *little* here below
> But wants that *little*, Long.

X

Saturday and Sunday, of course, had each its special routine. The barbarous custom of having school on Saturday not having then raised its ugly head, we were free during the day except for two hours in the morning, one a study hour, and the other devoted to letter writing, everybody being supposed to write home once a week.

Discipline was relaxed during this hour, and we might sit with other girls, whispering about anything we pleased. Autograph albums were circulated freely at this time, containing besides such sentiments as

> Roses are red, and violets blue,
> Sugar is sweet and so are you.

witty specimens as

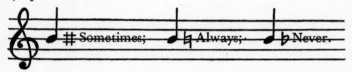

Another favorite was to say "I love you" in the four languages, English, French, Spanish, and Latin. I had no album myself, but loved to write in others my special piece of advice:

> Better trust all and be deceived,
> And rue that trust and that deceiving,
> Than doubt one heart that if believed
> Had blessed that trust, and that believing.

A memorable event of the letter writing period was a joint composition of myself and Shellie Smith—sweet Shellie Smith who wore a number thirteen shoe and could even wear a number twelve, and to whom no male human being could remain indifferent.

On her way to Peace, Shellie had visited her uncle in Bennettsville, South Carolina, where she had become engaged to Julius Dudley, a distant cousin of mine whom I had never met. Julius had stopped to see Shellie on his way to Military School in Charlotte and had given her his ring, and they now exchanged a weekly letter. Subsequently at a Christmas party she had met and become engaged to Sam Dick in Greensboro, a student in

the same school with Julius Dudley, and they too exchanged a weekly letter. All went well until the following spring, when the boys compared notes and each dis-
patched a blistering letter charging Shellie with high
crimes and misdemeanors.

In this crisis Shellie came to me for help, and together we concocted an epistle we considered a fine
example of satire liberally sprinkled with all the ses-
quipedalian words I could think of, and sent a copy to
each boy. A joint reply of studied insult came by return
mail accusing Shellie of having swallowed the dictionary.

Saturday night was prayer meeting night, and there
were two prayer meetings, nicknamed the "Saints" and
the "Sinners."

The Saints, which only members of the church could
attend, met at Professor Baumann's house, and was presided over by Mrs. Baumann's sister, Miss Bettie Penick.

The Sinners, led by our Lady Principal, Mrs. Lacy,
was conducted in the library, where, sitting on uncomfortable chairs, we felt as solemn as if in church. The
meeting was opened and closed with prayers and there
was also Scripture reading. There being nothing dis-
tinctive about the exercises, I remember only that they
were extremely boring, and that everybody was very
glad when they were over.

It was very different at the Saints. In the first place it
was nice to go across the street and relax on comfortable
chairs and couches in a real home. And then Miss Betty
was one of those extraordinary persons who overcome
all handicaps. Though very, very homely, she was not
at all self-conscious. Lively, genial, and gracious, she
made everyone feel at home and, moreover, important
and necessary to the scheme of things. Everybody went
with the liveliest anticipations and returned feeling they
had been realized. There were earnest prayers and Scripture reading, but there was also an opportunity for self-
expression, everyone being given an opportunity to ex-

press her opinion regarding those seemingly trivial matters that school girls think important.

For instance, what should one do when asked, "How
do you like my new dress or hat?" Said hat and dress
being as you thought very ugly. For this Miss Betty laid
down two principles not to be transgressed: First, tell
no lies; second, hurt no feelings. This opened the flood-
gates, and a "free for all" followed, Miss Betty guiding
with a skilful hand so that only one person spoke at a
time. "How could you tell disagreeable truths without
hurting one's feelings?" somebody asked. The conclu-
sion finally reached was to speak only of something you
did admire saying: "What a pretty color," "It fits like
a glove," "That shade of blue is so becoming to you,"
thus telling pleasant truths, which, of course, hurt no
feelings.

And finally there were cakes and—figuratively speaking—ale. Schoolgirls never forget they have stomachs,
and the sweet taste lingering in our mouths as we went
back no doubt sweetened our souls, in accordance with
Browning's doctrine that "body helps soul as much as
soul helps body."

Sunday was, on the whole, a dull day, and, had it
not been for going to church, could never have been
survived. For the march there, we were lined up in
couples, each girl with her roommate; and the monitor
for the morning made the rounds of the rooms listing
the names of the girls and, if anyone was sick, finding
someone to pair off with her roommate. All the girls
going assembled in the entrance hall and, as the monitor
read the names, took their places in line.

Being monitor Sunday morning was a much-coveted
honor, which came my way but seldom. As nearly every
girl in school was a Presbyterian, that was the church
most of us attended, always going and coming through
Capital Square. We sat upstairs in the gallery on the
right side facing the pulpit, the gallery opposite on the

left being reserved for Negroes. Here we had an excellent view of the choir, our chosen idol there being the tenor, handsome Mr. Leo Heartt, adored in spite of his having a wife and several children.

Down below, after the Sunday clothes of the congregation, the cynosure attracting us was the Governor and his wife. There were two governors in my day: Governor Jarvis with bald head and red beard very like a whisk broom and Governor Fowle, who in spite of being slightly bald, looked, I thought, handsome and stately, as a governor should.

We were all very fond of our preacher, Dr. Watkins, whose sermons, though now in the limbo of forgotten things, kept us wide awake.

As we came out of church there was always a crowd of boys waiting to stare at us, all of whom as we started to take the short cut through the Capital Square took to their heels, racing madly to lean over the railing at the National Hotel as we passed it on our way home, for all of us a big moment.

After Sunday dinner, enlivened by dessert, we went to our rooms for a deadly afternoon unless we had secreted a forbidden book. I had now reached the stage where I would read novels on Sunday, those dear forbidden books smuggled in by the day scholars. Popular books of that day were *Phillis* and *Molly Bawn* by the Duchess, *Lucile* by Owen Meredith, and *Moths* by Ouida, this last being the *Forever Amber* of our time. Another thriller was *Saint Elmo* by Augusta J. Evans. No harm in any of these, nor any good. As for *Moths* the only thing I remember is a bit of wisdom every woman ought to know, contributed by a worldly woman to her debutante daughter: "Make your dress of a horse blanket, if you will, but make it fit!"

Far better than these were the old timers brought in: *Children of the Abbey, Jane Eyre,* and *Thaddeus of*

Warsaw. I almost lost my eyesight over *Thaddeus of Warsaw* through weeping copiously over his misfortunes while confined to my room with sore eyes and forbidden to read anything. A pleasing result was that I was not allowed to study at night for the rest of that year.

Campbell's line, "And Freedom shrieked when Kosciusko fell," had already awakened my sympathy with Poland, heightened now by Inez McCall's reciting in tones that curdled my blood a poem beginning:

> Whence come those shrieks so wild and shrill
> That like an arrow cleave the air?

the answer being of course "from yon temple" where a Polish mother strove vainly to protect her son from the Russians. Truly there is nothing new under the sun! I still have to be sorry for the Poles, and hate the Russians.

Going to church at night was about the same as in the morning except you could choose your partner, and we sat downstairs in the Amen corner, a secluded spot where we could see nothing of interest, nor ourselves be seen or heard. Shellie Smith and I were always in a merry mood, narrowly escaping convulsions as we tried to choke off a giggle.

On the way home there was always a chance that something excitingly different might happen as the long line of girls headed and footed by only one teacher at each end offered a shining mark to the venturesome, as the darkness made it easy for boys to edge their way into our ranks. When this happened our swift grapevine warning meant, "Talk as loud as you can, and drown them out," this making it easy for the boys to accompany us even to the front gate itself, where, unseen and unsuspected, they vanished into the night.

XI

The big event of that first and every other year was the State Fair occurring in October. The cadets of the

Bingham Military School at Mebanesville came in a body parading at the Fair, and also on Wednesday afternoons at Peace. Little Rob Bingham, looking very cute in his uniform, was the darling of all the girls. His mother, Cousin Dell Bingham, held court in the front hall, all the girls being taken up and introduced. I of course felt very proud of these new cousins, whom I now met for the first time. We had admired the cadets at a distance, but that evening we were to meet them face to face at the annual reception given by Peace in their honor. I was all ready for this occasion, my two dresses having arrived from Minneapolis. My Sunday best, a beautiful light blue cashmere made with an overskirt and a basque with a blue silk vest ornamented with large Dresden China buttons, was the prettiest dress in school.

Even with this dress, I felt timid and bashful as these strange boys led me off on a promenade up and down the corridors, finally returning to the starting place for an exchange of partners. Conversation lagged with all but one, who told of raids made on cornfields and henhouses and the finesse necessary lest a chicken squawk and bring the farmer after them with shotgun and dogs. In return I told him about my pictures of the royal family of England, and Queen Alexandra with her two sons, even repeating Tennyson's lines of welcome:

> Sea king's daughter from over the sea, Alexandra,
> Saxon and Norman and Dane are we
> But all of us Danes in our welcome to thee, Alexandra.

He told me he had never met a girl who knew so much history.

The next day we went in buses to the Fair, and after viewing the fancy livestock, jellies, and quilts, we were taken to the top of the grandstand, where girls from all over the state were promenading with their beaux. Ella Holt, Mr. Tom Holt's daughter, was there in a red silk dress with a train sweeping up the floor. In my second best dress of gray cloth with black silk plaited frills, and vest with brass buttons, in spite of wearing a bedroom slipper on my sore foot, I had a comfortable feeling of being fashionable and chic.

The aftermath of this meeting with the Bingham Cadets was the widespread desire to distinguish ourselves by some sort of an exploit that we could brag about. The only thing we could think of was a raid on the turnip patch in the back yard. And so, one dark night about eleven o'clock, we gathered at the back door on the third floor and stole cautiously down the long staircase. Just as the last girl reached the bottom step, there was a strange noise, which sent us scurrying back up the stairs, tiptoeing ignominiously into our rooms, and so to bed, feeling very thankful to arrive safe and undiscovered, but alas! with nothing to boast of. We were very like two girls I knew who, tired of humdrum living, racked their brains while planning their vacations, to think of something startling they might do to shock everybody. All to no avail, and Lyda remarked disgustedly, "Well, Susan, it seems no matter what we do, we'll still be respectable."

This year a new and interesting occasion was added to the repertory of events. Mr. Johnny one morning at the end of his devotional announced that an invitation had arrived from Senator and Mrs. Merrimon to the marriage ceremony of their daughter Mary to Mr. Lee Slater Overman that afternoon at the Presbyterian Church at half past four o'clock. All girls wishing to attend would go to their rooms to dress at the close of school and be in the entrance hall ready to leave at half past three. As all the "old" girls had known the bride when she was a student at Peace, and both new and old girls were glad to skip study hour in favor of a wedding, there was almost universal acceptance. Of the remnant who remained besides myself, staying on account of a sore foot, I remember only Mary Wilson left behind as a punishment for some misdemeanor.

When the bridal party came out on the Merrimon porch to get in the carriages taking them to the church, there was naturally much craning of necks by all but Mary Wilson, who boldly stationed herself at the window where, all of us glorying in her spunk, she remained arguing with the teacher in charge until the last carriage departed.

Of course the modern way would have been to avoid the stress and strain of possible disobedience by sending all of us to the window to see what we could.

"Sit down," thundered a teacher to a boy standing up.

"I won't," said the boy.

"Then stand up," said the teacher; "I will be obeyed."

Thanksgiving was always celebrated by a visit to the State Insane Asylum, a strange place for a holiday outing. The bus ride to the other side of town and back was part of the fun. Once on arriving, we were greeted by yells from the barred windows above, so terrifying that we started to climb back into the buses. One man shouted a request to tell his daughter Margaret Fraley in Salisbury to come to see him. Once inside things were as usual. We were taken to the wards, where the women were sewing, and through the kitchen, where cabbage and fat pork were boiling in huge kettles; into the dining room, where the tables were set with tin plates and cups; once into the men's ward and shown a strait jacket, and allowed to converse with a man who knew more history than we did. Finally we were shown into an immense parlor, where, sitting on the red velvet sofas and chairs, we ate cake and drank wine. Somehow it didn't taste right in that terrifying, gloomy building with strange close smells where unhappy people lived in misery and despair.

Dr. Grissom, a portly, benevolent, and pompous-looking man, always made us a little speech inviting us to come again. At the moment I wished only to depart, and when I stepped out into the cool November air, I climbed into the bus with happy anticipation of a Thanksgiving dinner. I also felt a deep sense of escape.

XII

Life in the classroom was much to my liking. As I not only felt a deep responsibility toward Jane, who was making such a sacrifice to pay for my education, but was also naturally ambitious and desirous of getting the highest marks in all my studies, I did my level best to be perfect in each day's lessons.

Mathematics came near being my Waterloo. I was put in the beginners' class in arithmetic, where Kate Fuller, a tiny little girl compared to my five feet seven inches, completely outshone me in fractions, always getting the answer before I did, and getting it right. However, I soon mastered the mechanical processes. I already knew perfectly the multiplication table, and also the tables of weights and measures. I could paper the walls of a room and carpet the floor, but not having a mathematical mind could not solve problems that required thought. However, I could and did memorize the solution of all problems in the book, which practically made me letter perfect in recitation and examinations. This was why so many people wanted to sit beside me in the classroom. I saw no harm in giving help, but being always surrounded by the incompetent, I was never tempted to ask it for myself.

Once fate played me a shabby trick. I had memorized every problem in the algebra except one, which, being all worked out and explained, I thought would never be given; but our clever teacher thinking otherwise, my mark was reduced by ten.

I was an apt pupil in all my other studies. Mother, my only teacher, had grounded me in grammar; hence Latin presented no difficulty. I learned quickly the de-

clension of all nouns and pronouns, being much pleased
with *hic, haec, hoc.* Conjugations were just as easy both
in Latin and in French, their peculiar spelling being
easily memorized.

Being a visualizer I was good in English spelling too,
and beat Julia Creech in two matches winning on the
words *belligerent* and *embarrassed.* Our spelling book
at Peace was Swinton's *One Hundred Words,* which, containing all the catches in the English language was as
devilish a book as could have been devised. I learned
them all: *villain, villein; pneumatic, numismatics; religious, sacrilegious;* etc.

History, with whole pages of Egyptian dates now
happily forgotten, bothered me not at all.

Being naturally meek and timid, and in my desire
to get high marks always attentive to the teacher, I conducted myself during lessons, except for giving aid during examinations, practically perfectly. Only once did I
stage a rebellion so violent and outrageous that I went
unpunished.

Not having a mathematical mind, I found algebra
very difficult; but this month, working my head off to
equal my rival, Dixie Leach, I made as I thought a
perfect record, never missing a single question or failing
at the blackboard, and confidently expected one hundred. When Miss Heffelman, my most loved and admired teacher, read the marks, giving Dixie one hundred
and me ninety-eight, I saw red.

"That's not fair," I accused, "you're cheating me. I
haven't made a single mistake this whole month and I
deserve one hundred just as much as Dixie."

Poor Miss Heffelman! With a powerful personality
she was the finest disciplinarian in school, equal to Mr.
Johnny. But the more she argued and commanded, the
more I answered back, completely beside myself; and
seeing she could do nothing with me, she went on with
the lesson, leaving me to sob out my grief and anger un-

noticed. She did not give me demerits or report me to Mr. Johnny, nor did she raise my mark.

The other pupils had sat petrified with astonishment, being a little scared, as if a pet dog had suddenly gone mad. "Beware the fury of a patient man." I think we all have secret springs that when touched set off an explosion. This had been no tantrum, but the same kind of rebellion felt by Patrick Henry crying: "Give me liberty, or give me death."

As a matter of fact, discipline presented no problem at Peace, there being no impertinence, no open disobedience, nor any disorder in the class room. Even though there were infractions of the impossible rule of not speaking to anyone while passing to classes, yet it may be said to have worked, as everyone whispering spoke in such low tones that the quiet demanded appeared to be forthcoming.

One girl, it is true, was expelled, but for conduct said to have occurred elsewhere; and one girl was discovered to be a thief. She, however, though publicly exposed was given another chance. Though morally weak, she had character of a sort enabling her to endure for the remaining years before graduation an ostracism so cruelly complete it was enough to break a stoic.

"Let me write the songs of a nation," said Napoleon, wishing to make his country patriotic. But I, wishing to make the rising generation virtuous would ask to write the slang; no one can tell how much subtle undermining of character had been accomplished by that detestable phrase—"It's all right if you can get by with it." Though I had never heard this phrase, it expressed my unconscious philosophy, leading me into devious paths of lawlessness. I found the long study hours in the Assembly Room terribly boring, and to escape the monotony I would turn the card hanging on the door signifying a visit to the lavatory, and go instead to my room and read a forbidden book.

THE SPRING OF HOPE

I even got bold enough to go into the library and take from the bookcase drawer that interesting novel by the Baroness Tautphoeus called *The Initials,* which Miss Emma Mattoon, after the weekly reading every Friday night, had deposited there for safe-keeping during the intervening week. This proved a fatal error on my part, for one day as I sat in my room completely absorbed in the story Miss Emma opened the door and took the book out of my hand. She didn't spare me. I listened in silence, feeling disgraced for life in her eyes and my own. Like everyone else, I loved and admired her, but after this could not bear to be in her presence. I don't know that my character was improved by this experience, but my conduct was; hereafter I turned the card only for the purpose originally intended.

The most popular subject in school was elocution. Our teacher, Mrs. Bristow, had us memorize long poems which with appropriate gestures we recited together. Nowadays they call them "Verse Choirs"—then known as "Concert Recitations," new to Raleigh, and extremely popular both with performers and audience.

In "Darius Green" and his flying machine we flapped our arms like the wings of the eagle; and in "High Tide on the Coast of Lincolnshire," we hauled away with all our might at imaginary ropes as we recited the old mayor's appeal:

> Pull as ye never pulled before;
> Good ringers, pull your best. . . .

"Aux Italiens" was the most thrilling of these, as in this, instead of merely reciting, we actually sang those impassioned words from Verdi's *Trovatore,* "Non ti scordar di me."

Another elocution teacher, Miss Lucia Vail, pretty and petite, exquisitely dressed, with not a hair in her curly locks ever out of place, horrified by our "slovenly Southern speech," tried to make us pronounce our *r's* by having us trill them in "Around the rough and rugged rocks the ragged rascals ran." At trilling I was a total failure. Miss Vail harped on our careless elisions such as "j'ever" for "did you ever," and required us to bring in lists of those we overheard. We were very diligent about this, and Mrs. Watkins, our preacher's wife, spoke with pleasure of how attentive Peace girls had become to her husband's sermons, not suspecting the real reason to be that his sermons abounded in these errors and also those curious Virginia pronunciations: imme*j*itly, *cyar*pet, and *gyar*den.

A great acquisition to the Faculty was a new Latin teacher, Miss Jennie Faison, who introduced the new Roman pronunciation which was sweeping the country. Now instead of saying Julius Caesar and veni, vidi, vici (*c,* as in *city*), we said Yoolyoose Kysar and wani, wedi, weki (*i* as in *machine*). Father's joke about Skipio wagging war in Afryca had lost something of its savor, Skipio now being the correct pronunciation.

We all liked Miss Jennie, and this new way of pronouncing made us feel learned and up-to-date.

She also required us to put English into Latin—not so easy. On examination one of the questions was an English translation of a passage in Sallust which we had to restore to the original form written by Sallust. Imagine that!

Another new teacher, Miss Fannie Arrington, was also very popular. Tall, stately, and handsome and always wearing pretty clothes, she was much admired. On Sundays when she appeared at the head of our line in rustling black silk, wearing the heavy gold chain and cross then so fashionable, we gloried in her looks.

Another thing we liked about Miss Fannie was the personal interest she showed in us by noticing, and commenting, always favorably, upon our looks, remarking: "You have a pretty hand with those long taper fingers," or "White even teeth," or "Those arched eyebrows give you an intellectual look." On being told Miss Fannie

had said of me that I had a free, graceful walk, I ascended
straightway into the seventh heaven.

XIII

Perhaps there never was a boarding school with no
complaint about food, but when Miss Antoinette Mor-
ton was housekeeper there was certainly little cause and
very little complaint, though a few jokes.

A rather complimentary one inquired, "Why are our
desserts like our dentist?" The ungrammatical answer
being: "Because they are ever *et*." Our dentist's name
being, as you have doubtless guessed, *Everett*.

The breakfast hash, nicknamed "mystery," poured
over hot biscuits was also "ever et"; and the potato cakes
fried to a rich brown crisp were so popular that nobody
wanted to serve them, plates coming back so fast for a
second helping that the one serving had difficulty in
saving even one for herself, it being an unwritten law
that she must not help herself until everyone else had
been served.

We had desserts twice during the week, Saturday's
always being two gingersnaps and an apple, which according to custom was always taken to our rooms.

One dessert, a delicious boiled custard served during
the Christmas holidays, was blamed for the epidemic that
followed, thirty girls and some of the teachers being
taken ill the same day. No explanation was ever given
us, but all sorts of rumors were afloat, the one most
generally accepted being that Miss Antoinette had mis-
takenly used Prussic acid as a flavor instead of vanilla.
The infirmary being filled to overflowing, most of us
remained in our rooms, Miss Agnes Lacy and Miss
Emma Mattoon making the rounds together and ad-
ministering a horrid, sweetish, pink medicine.

"Do you feel better?" they asked me after a dose.

"Yes," I feebly admitted, "but it won't last."

And it didn't, but my answer they considered a huge

joke, and it was a long time before I heard the last of it.

Mrs. John Burwell died during this epidemic, but as she was already ill, we never knew whether or not the custard had anything to do with her death.

We girls had greatly admired her beauty and grace and sincerely mourned her passing, but were glad that Miss Mary, the eldest daughter, whom we all liked, was there to take her mother's place as the head of the household.

After Miss Antoinette left, the food under the new regime being none too plentiful, a very sarcastic conundrum was hailed with delight. Marcellus, our faithful factotum, had a custom of ringing the dinner bell enthusiastically up and down the halls and even out of doors, making a racket so resounding that we thought the conundrum a fine example of poetic justice:

"Which of Shakespeare's plays does our dinner bell remind you of?"

Answer: "Much Ado About Nothing."

Rarely did one get a second helping; and the morning Miss Pitt put an extra sausage on my plate, I was tragically not hungry. Taking food from the table was strictly forbidden, but this was an emergency. Carefully slipping my sausage into a biscuit, and then by a little sleight of hand transferring the biscuit to my pocket, I finally had it safely secreted in my desk. Watchfully biding my time until I was really hungry, I managed at last by sticking my head under the desk to consume unseen, to the last crumb, what I still remember as the most delicious morsel of a lifetime.

During Christmas holidays the "boxes" received by the girls remaining at school were the chief point of interest. That first Christmas the girls were allowed to have these boxes in their rooms, but afterwards they were all sent to one room where the girls took their friends to share in the goodies.

I thought Shellie Smith's box the most wonderful

in the world. Practically everybody in Madison, whom Shellie had talked of until they seemed like my friends and neighbors, had sent her something. Charlie Dickenson had sent her raisins; Dixie Beggs, who was redheaded and a Baptist, a box of candy; Peck and Tebo, her twin brothers, a quantity of nuts; Daisy Paramore, her best friend, with a foot almost as small as Shellie's own, a box of taffy pulled by herself; Walter Bunting, a very special friend, a very special box of French candy. Besides a quantity of oranges, larger, sweeter, and juicier than any we had ever before seen, there were shaddocks, a fruit strange to all of us, looking and tasting very like grapefruit. Other Florida specialties were kumquats, sugar cane, and guava jelly. Darling, generous Shellie! She had more fun dispensing these goodies than we did in devouring them.

Another box that lingers in my memory was one belonging to Kerr Morehead of Leaksville, a granddaughter of Governor Morehead. We used to say that titian-haired Kerr Morehead had everything: beauty, brains, charm, character, sweet disposition, riches, and a pedigree. Certainly this box had everything. Kerr kept it in her room, and it was fun to dash in when no teacher was looking, and when Kerr pulled it out from under the bed, stick in your thumb and pull out some of its many "plums." Besides fruitcake, candy, mince pies, cheese, raisins, dried figs, brandy peaches, and dates, there was a whole turkey, a baked ham, quantities of fried chicken, crisp little link sausages, Dixie biscuit, and quail, stuffed and roasted whole!

XIV

Peace, I believe, was the first boarding school in North Carolina to open a kindergarten, pretty Margie Busbee being a star pupil. Though only six, she had become for a brief period our youngest boarder, and of course, everybody's pet. I remember her as a pretty little girl dressed in white, with long brown curls, and a small mouth, the kind described as "rosebud." Even at such a tender age she had begun to write, her poems ranking in the eyes of our little community as the works of a genius.

The teacher at the head of the kindergarten was Mrs. Foster, a widow with two grown sons, Robert and Omega, with whom she lived in a house not far from Peace. Romance again touched our lives, it being rumored that she was courted by Mr. Johnny; and there was great excitement when he married this fascinating lady and departed on a wedding tour.

And still more when on their return these two young men came to live in the Burwell suite. There had always been a determined effort to keep young men away from the girls, but these two were were now established in our midst, on a friendly and familiar footing, pleasing to all parties concerned as the boys themselves never took the slightest advantage of the situation.

During the absence of the bridal pair, Dr. Robert Burwell was left in charge, much to my delight as I found it easy to inveigle him on Thursday and Friday afternoons, when there was no gym, to take us into the country for a walk. Returning from one of these excursions, and finding ourselves at the door of the Penitentiary, we persuaded Dr. Burwell to take us inside. The authorities, deeply impressed by the honor, gave us a warm welcome, showing us everything supposed to be "seeable," the result being that we were late for supper, something unheard of and positively scandalous. Much shaking of heads and caustic comment: Going to the Penitentiary, the very idea! What could Dr. Burwell be thinking of! Mr. Johnny ought to be told of such goings on!

For my part I couldn't see that it was any worse than a visit to the Insane Asylum, besides being much pleasanter. Convicts working away in their stripes were a much less painful sight than those unhappy creatures shut up in wards with nothing to do.

XV

When I was about fifteen, the Presbyterian church conducted revival meetings at Peace, and I became deeply concerned about my soul's salvation. Fright had a good deal to do with the matter, as the theme of these meetings was: "The soul that sinneth, it shall die." I developed a conscience and along with several other girls decided to join the church.

The Saturday before Easter we were all taken down to the church to be examined separately by the members of the session. One of the elders interviewing me asked this question: "If God called you to be a missionary to Africa, would you go?"

That was a poser. I did not want to go. Of that much I was certain. But if I said I wouldn't go, maybe they would disgrace me by not letting me join the church. That would be terrible. On the other hand, I mustn't tell a lie in order to join. I was certain of that too. Suddenly I remembered he had said "*if* God called you," and I remembered how God had called Samuel, and I thought if I heard him calling, as Samuel did, I would also answer, "Here am I." So I said, "Yes," and I hope it was the truth.

After joining the church I felt a new and deep responsibility for my conduct and honestly tried to behave as a church member should. And then came a great temptation. I didn't like my cloak. Though it was of handsome broadcloth with a silk vest and beautiful jet buttons, the cut was different, and there were no pockets with the grass trimming then so popular. When I went home that summer I decided to hide my cloak where it would never be found. Near my old cubbyhole there was just such a place. But when I thought of all the lies I would have to tell, I didn't do it, wearing it again the next winter, and the next. And a sore trial it was!

To my surprise, after joining the church, I was still haunted by dreams of the Judgment Day. So I talked the matter over with Alice McRae from Virginia, who had the most beautiful red hair in the world, and her intimate friend, Laura McCants, a dark-haired beauty from Winnsboro, South Carolina. These two often amused themselves by drawing me out on the subject of "true love," laughing when I quoted Shakespeare, declaring that "Love is not love which alters when it alteration finds."

They laughed now at my fears of the Judgment Day.

"Do you believe that you will die?" asked Alice.

"Why of course I do."

"Then that will be the Judgment Day for you. Don't you see? It's bound to come, so why not stop worrying about when?"

And the miracle was that I did stop, never giving it a second thought from that day to this.

XVI

Mary Shepherd did not return the second year, Eleanor's money being exhausted, and I went back alone with a heavy heart, wondering who would be my roommate. No one suitable being found, I roomed alone, feeling lonesome and bereft; and then I was told the joyful news that Mary Shepherd was coming back.

This was how it happened. She had made a deep impression on Mr. Johnny by her scholarship and other qualities which marked her as far above the average. And, as he now needed, not a teacher, but a girl who could take charge of two little orphan sisters attending the kindergarten and who could also be a helper for Mrs. Campbell, the cooking teacher, he offered Mary her board and tuition if she would undertake both of these tasks. And a happy day it was for me when we were all installed in a large room with two double beds.

By having a cooking teacher, Peace again demonstrated that it was truly a progressive school. Mrs. Campbell had classes not only for the girls attending Peace, but also for the ladies of Raleigh, who flocked to learn how to bone a ham and what to do with the cold chicken left from the Sunday dinner. One matron acidly remarked that Mrs. Campbell had showed them twenty ways to serve the chicken, but everybody knew that cold sliced was the best.

The circumstance that occasioned most comment was the fact that Mrs. Campbell wore no apron, demonstrating that a skilful cook could beat up a cake, fry, boil, and stew, and still remain immaculate.

XVII

The first two years were the hardest; during them I had tried my best to become more like other girls, though with indifferent success. But in spite of this, life the third year began to seem very like a fairy tale.

Most marvelous to begin with was my sister Jane's becoming one of the faculty at Peace, having taken Miss Emma Mattoon's place as a teacher of English. This appointment was a natural consequence of the happiest event of Jane's professional career, namely, being asked to teach a Model School for Children during the summer session of the University of North Carolina. There she had become great friends with the popular professor of elocution, Dr. James J. Vance of Canada, who had electrified everyone by his insistence on the long "u" in words like plume, and on accenting the first syllable in li'brary and lit'erary. Both these apostles of something new in education were the shining lights of the season, and both were invited to teach the next summer at the University of South Carolina. The climax for Jane was Mr. Burwell's offer, which she joyfully accepted.

To have one's sister a member of the faculty is more likely than not to be a cause for embarrassment, but not so in this case. Jane's popularity was immediate and widespread, shedding on me a little reflected glory. The girls used to come crowding into her room, sitting on the floor, to listen to her tales of life in New York, as

well as her views on morals, manners, and life itself.
Many of the girls became her lifelong friends, including
Addie Bagley, afterwards Mrs. Josephus Daniels; Kerr
and Lily Morehead; and our cousins Sadie and Mary
Kerr Bingham.

As I was often included in the invitations Jane received from Mrs. Bagley and our cousin Mr. Thomas
Hogg, life became more interesting on Saturdays. It was
fun going to see the Bagleys, who lived with the Reeds,
just off the main shopping street in a house behind the
bank, and eat chicken and brandy peaches, food being
then one of the important interests of my life. Addie,
with her long dark curls, I thought the prettiest little
girl I had ever seen. I found going to the Hoggs' for
Saturday dinner equally delightful and listened open-
mouthed to Cousin Thomas's tales of travel. One story
was about a night in a Jerusalem hotel when the lights
went out during the very poor dinner. As they sat there
in the darkness, somebody remarked that this must be
the worst hotel in the world. "Stranger," said a voice,
"have you ever been to the Yarborough Hotel in Raleigh, North Carolina?"

Next in importance to Jane's advent was my new
roommate. Mary Shepherd, becoming a teacher herself,
had not returned with Jane and me, and I had many
doubts about my roommate, who to my great joy turned
out to be Bessie Yates, a little, dark-haired girl from
Greensboro, who, though endowed with all the qualities
that make a girl popular, became quite inexplicably my
devoted friend. It seemed a miracle to have an intimate
friend like Bess. I couldn't believe it would last; but
it did, as long as she lived.

Now at last I was one of the crowd, and a wonderful
crowd it was, a galaxy of bright and shining stars like
Jessie Gray, Kerr Morehead, Nanny Anderson, and
Alice Wilson, all new girls—and of course Shellie Smith.

Bess and I made a great team in croquet, being practically invincible. Her split roquet was even better than mine, and with unerring aim she seldom missed hitting a ball, no matter how distant. We loved walks into the country, liked the same books, and adored poetry.

Very popular with the boys, she had many stories to tell of these affairs, and feeling almost as thrilled as if I were overhearing Romeo and Juliet, I would listen far into the night to all the "he saids" and "I saids" of the prodigious conversation Bess repeated with phonographic exactitude.

Bess wanted to decorate our room and proposed that we should buy a vase and fill it with grasses to last through the winter. As I had a little pocket money that fall, we selected quite a large vase at Creech's, costing, I think, a whole dollar, and gathered on our botany expeditions a choice collection of milkweed, rushes, and cattails, thereby creating a mild sensation, as it was the first thing of the sort to appear in the school.

At Christmas Bessie invited Shellie Smith, Minnie Helper, a charming girl from Due West, South Carolina, and me to spend the two-week vacation with her; and a wonderful time it was. Mr. Yates had come to escort us there, and just before we got to Greensboro he came to tell me the sad news that my trunk was not on the train and had probably gone to Goldsboro. Until it could be traced I had to wear the same black dress everywhere I went, even to parties, instead of pretty clothes like the other girls—a heavy blow for a sixteen-year-old. After several days of frantic telegraphing the trunk finally arrived, having been discovered to be at Peace all this time, keeping company with the water bucket.

But that trifling detail could not keep this from being the grandest house party ever. Not that we called it that, having never heard the term. Mr. and Mrs. Yates were the nicest kind of parents, entering into the spirit of the thing and making us feel at home from the moment we entered the house; and Bess's four brothers, who adored her, laid themselves out to give these visiting girls a good time. Moreover, there were the Smith boys, Harry, Egbert, and Alphonso, next door, who, running in and out all day long, were just like part of the family. Nobody had any idea then that these frolicking youngsters, brilliant though they were, would grow up to be president of Davidson College, a high dignitary of the church, and a college professor at the University of Virginia and later at the Naval Academy who would write the life of O. Henry.

So many good things to eat! After our meager boarding school fare how delicious these home cooked meals tasted. That first supper! Can I ever forget it? Oyster soup to begin with; then steak, thick, juicy, and tender, with gravy and hot biscuits; and for dessert, sweet potato pie. And candy! I had never seen so much in my whole life.

There were many parties, one being given by Mrs. Robert Douglas, whose husband was the son of Stephen Douglas and a Republican, but nobody seemed to mind. These parties were very different from our modern affairs, for, instead of being exclusively for the school set, they were for all ages, with no games or dancing—just conversation, which is all Southerners ever need to make it a good party. Everybody served the same refreshments —the popular new dish of sliced oranges and grated cocoanut called ambrosia, cake, and eggnog. It was at one of these parties that Shellie met Sam Dick, brother of Mrs. Douglas.

The weather was the coldest we had ever seen, the thermometer dropping to an unheard of low—14°. It was the first snow Shellie had ever seen, and when we were snowballing each other and her snowball, beginning to melt, resembled ice, she exclaimed, "Oh, my snowball is melting into ice." The house was warm and comfortable, for Mr. Yates having had several stoves put up, one could even cross the front hall without shivering.

Most exciting news was that the pond had frozen over; and the whole town tried its luck at skating, our crowd going out on a sled with sleigh bells jingling all the way. There was much tumbling down, since none of us had ever seen, much less worn, a pair of skates, but luckily no broken bones.

Will and John came to take me home for a few days, but I couldn't bear to leave the party and I wouldn't go. If it hadn't been so cold, I think they would never have let me stay behind. It was the cruelest, most selfish act of my life, and even now, I feel a pang when I think of Aunty, Mother, and Father running out when the wagon drove up and no Mary Alves got out to hug and kiss them.

The crowning joy of the whole time was going to see *East Lynne,* my first play. It was perfect. None since was ever more enjoyed. I had taken only one handkerchief, and six would have been too few. When we returned to Peace I gained quite a reputation from my impersonation of the leading lady, especially by my impassioned rendition of the line:

I am still Lord Mount Severn's daughter and your su-pe-ri-or!

This was to have consequences.

XVIII

About a year before this house party a group of the most popular girls in school had formed a secret society, all members wearing a gold pin in the center of which were the letters P.I.G. Perhaps the founders had not foreseen that they would be dubbed "Pigs," but that's what happened. They accepted the title with a laugh, continuing to invite a few new members to join this circle, weird tales being spread about the initiation ceremonies. It was a very exclusive society, and there were some very hard feelings when one of two friends was chosen and the other left out. This whole affair had created a sharp cleavage in the school, all girls not chosen seeming to lose caste.

Another group of girls, among whom were some of my best friends, decided to counteract this by organizing a second society using the initials B.B.B. and being dubbed the "Bees." The Pigs and the Bees! Somebody said Peace was getting to be a menagerie.

Being perfectly happy with Bessie Yates and my other friends, and having no money for pins and dues, I had no ambitions to be either a Pig or a Bee.

And then the blow fell. Bessie Yates, my most intimate friend and roommate, was chosen by the Bees, and I was not. My whole world fell apart. I felt hurt, bewildered, and outraged, not knowing how to act, except to pretend I didn't care, though everybody knew I did. I loathed having people feeling sorry for me—that was worst of all. It was a mean, dastardly act, and I resented it with my whole soul, feeling much as an untouchable might.

And then the miracle happened! One day I received a "missive." I use the word advisedly. It came in a large white envelope sealed with red wax, the most impressive communication I ever received except the Pope's invitation to the Vatican delivered by Messenger Extraordinary.

I had never seen anything like it. Breaking the seal with reverence, I read with utter amazement the enclosed document asking me if I would be a P.I.G. Would *I* be a P.I.G.? Would a duck swim? Scorned by the Bees, and chosen by the Pigs—the original and still the more exclusive society! The dust and ashes period ended; my cup was running over.

And what had brought about this remarkable event? Why, it was my impersonation of *East Lynne!* Both the Bees and the Pigs were going to produce plays on the same evening, and the Pigs, wishing to outshine the Bees, had chosen me for the leading part!

Sound the loud timbrel
O'er Egypt's dark sea!
Jehovah hath triumphed!
His people are free.

And then I heard that the Bees had intended to ask
me to join them and were much chagrined that the
Pigs had stolen a march on them. I would have been
much happier with them as the Pigs were much older,
and more sophisticated than I was, but I wouldn't have
let those Bees know it for the world. The great point
was that I could act natural once more with the Bees and
resume our old friendly footing without being suspected
of currying favor. Anyway it was fun going to the P.I.G.
parties Friday nights up in the gym attended by Rob and
Omega Foster, even if I did feel like a fish out of water.

And the play? Rehearsals were wonderful. I adored
them, and when the play was given, the applause and the
compliments I received firmly convinced me that I was
the star performer.

Then another group of girls, feeling left out in the
cold, decided to form a third secret society; but by this
time it had become apparent that these organizations
were a bad influence in the school; and they were sum-
marily disbanded.

Everybody not in the secret was glad to know that
those mystic letters B.B.B. were for Brains, Brass, and
Beauty, and P.I.G. for Pretty Independent Gang. It was
a happy circumstance that the gold emblem of the
P.I.G.'s with a slight change became the official Peace
Institute Pin.

XIX

I was now a senior, and the long four years of 1878-
1882 were drawing to a close. They had brought many
things wonderful and new, such as the telephone which
Mr. Johnny was one of the first to install.

There was the phonograph which we were taken to
see, and allowed to speak into. Addie Williams from

Charlotte repeated some of Miss Heffelman's famous proverbs she was always quoting; and we thought it a huge joke to hear the machine grinding out: "Never rob Peter to pay Paul" and "Procrastination is the thief of time."

We had been shocked by the news of Garfield's assassination, and like the rest of the world watched anxiously for news from the Summer White House at Elberon, New Jersey, where the President had gone to escape the summer heat.

Most memorable perhaps was going to see the impersonation by beautiful Mrs. Scott Siddons of Shakespeare's famous heroines, especially of Lady Macbeth in the sleep-walking scene. None of us will ever forget the goose flesh and the tingling of strange shivers, as with wide open distracted eyes she entered, bearing a taper; and this being laid aside, the despairing washing of hands; and the startling convolutions of her red velvet train, as roused by the knocking at the gate she rushed wildly across the stage exclaiming: "What's done, cannot be undone! To bed, to bed, to bed!"

We had been taken to the skating rink to try our luck at roller skates, some girls taking to them like ducks to water and skating expertly round and round the rink.

Most marvelous of these inventions seemed the bicycle, which had a huge wheel in front, tall as a man, and a tiny one at the back. How could anybody ever ride that! We all came out to watch Mr. Will Kerr exhibit his skill, mounting and dismounting with perfect ease, and wheeling briskly away. It didn't, and doesn't, seem possible.

Hoop skirts, the small inconspicuous kind, had come back for a short stay; and black stockings came into fashion, Nanny Anderson being the first girl at Peace to wear them. They horrified Jane at first, but not for long. Spit curls and water waves came and went, and many girls curled their bangs with tiny slate pencils, heating them in the gas jet.

Complexions were of prime importance, every girl with a bad complexion being doomed to failure. Some girls wore on their cheeks small round pieces of black sticking plaster called beauty spots. Freckles were frowned on. Everybody had a few, but Hattie Maynard, dear lovable Hattie Maynard, one of our day scholars— well, hers were countless as the sands of the seashore. Her face seemed hopeless, but Hattie tried a lotion with considerable success I was told. Nellie Hayes, a pretty girl with a nice complexion, thinking that a lotion that did so much for Hattie would do much more for her, sent for a bottle and applied it with devastating vigor to her upper lip, causing a slight defect.

Lipstick and rouge were still undreamed of as were painted fingernails.

Our complexions were still natural, except for powder and a liquid wash used by some girls.

No smoking of course, though occasionally a girl would boast of having taken a whiff from a boy's cigar.

My pigtails had given place to an intricate knot shaped like the figure *8,* and my short dresses were now long ones.

I was seventeen and a half and in my opinion grown up.

Those were my outward changes, but what about my mind and soul? Personally I felt well satisfied with my intellectual achievements, being too ignorant to know that the little I knew was nothing to brag of. I had a smattering of Latin and French, had learned how to make a few chemical experiments, had gone creditably through all the courses I had taken, never once failing. Everyone said I was smart until I almost believed it was true. And yet I was entirely unfitted to earn my own living.

As to my character, I can only say that I had very

high ideals acquired from Shakespeare, Walter Scott,
Tennyson, the Bible, Aunty, and my mother and father.
They and hundreds of others "woke me and learned me
magic." Loving sunset, dawn, clouds, moon and stars,
and beauty of words, with a vast pity for suffering, hating
all things base and ugly especially injustice, I was now
going out into the big world.

> O young mariner,
>   Launch your vessel,
> And crowd your canvas—
>   After it, follow it
> Follow the Gleam.

XX

Graduation Day was coming on apace. I had worked
hard that last term to become one of the four Full Graduates, it having been discovered that I was lacking in
Latin; and in order to graduate, I had to carry two extra
classes. My daily program was Sallust, Vergil, and Horace. Horace was the hardest, and I never could have
translated those odes and satires if the class had not
met during the noon hour and together translated the
lesson for the day. Here my memory served me well, as
I never forgot our translation.

I was also studying French, reading Racine and Cor-
neille and memorizing long passages. The good old
memory almost bogged down.

Sabra had sent me three dresses that spring, the very
prettiest in the whole school. One, a bright blue silk
brocade made with a basque, I wore to Addie Marsh's
party given for the graduates, a boy being invited for
each girl. It was also the one I wore to church on the
occasion of the Baccalaureate Sermon. My new straw
hat trimmed with wheat and a blue ribbon cost three
dollars. The sermon, by the way, was two hours long,
but though I listened very attentively, I cannot remember a word of it, nor the name of the preacher.

The graduation dress itself was a cream-colored nun's

veiling, having a V-neck in front and buttoned up the back with large round buttons looking like enormous pearls.

A third dress was a black lace bunting trimmed with grass fringe. I adored this dress, thinking that black was the last word in dress. It must be all black—no touches of white to spoil it. And so with my last pennies I bought a black ruche, basting it in the neck with great care, and, thus attired, went downstairs on Friday afternoon. Mrs. Lacy, our Lady Principal, stopped me in the hall.

"Alves," she said, "that black ruche ruins this pretty dress. Go back upstairs and put in a white one."

I went back upstairs, but that black ruche stayed where it was.

Dr. Robert Burwell called me into his sitting room and presented me with a copy of Tennyson, writing his name and mine with the date on the fly leaf. He told me he was going to miss me very much, and I almost cried. It was a solemn parting.

On the night before graduation there was a lecture by Dr. Sam Smith, son of Dr. Jacob Henry, on "Dreams." I think it was he who told us the difference between sentiment and sentimentality. "Sentiment," he said, "is thought saturated with emotion, while sentimentality is emotion minus thought."

Commencement night I pinned a cape jessamine on my striped satin blouse, giving what I felt was the last touch to the pink of perfection. Somehow it made me feel a little less shy when I stood up to declaim my French recitation, beginning with those melancholy lines:

> Percé jusqu'au fond du coeur
> D'une atteinte imprévue aussi bien que mortelle.

I'm sure nobody understood a word, but I spoke with all the pathos and ferver of my best *East Lynne* manner, and there was much applause. And one of my day-scholar friends handed up a bunch of white lilies.

And then Mr. Johnny put into my hand the precious diploma, sole recompense for four years of toil, homesickness, loneliness, and mortification almost unto death —all forgotten in this hour crowded with happy memories of fun, frolic, and friendship. All clouds had fled, leaving no wake, but instead there was an undercurrent of sadness at the thought that the life at Peace, now suddenly become dear and precious, was ending forever.

Commencement! Yes, for me it was to be the commencement of a strange new life, among strangers in a strange land.

BOOK THREE

The Promised Land

1

PIONEERING

IN THE SPRING of 1882 Father decided to move the family to Minneapolis, where my sisters Sabra and Annie were living, and resume the practice of law. It was a momentous decision; but, since his health was apparently restored, everybody agreed it was the best thing he could do, especially Sister Annie, who considered Minneapolis the next thing to Paradise.

He advertised the plantation for sale in the newspapers all over the state. No replies. Finally the one and only customer turned up, not far away from home, and the deal was completed, giving possession to the new owner the first of September. Will had already gone to Minneapolis, and as Mother was in Georgia visiting my sister Lizzie, it was decided that she would go from there to Minneapolis, visiting on the way Uncle William Webb in St. Louis. She longed to be at home with us and wrote Father a letter telling him that he never needed her more than now.

I needed her too; that last summer was a nightmare to me. Jane was teaching a model school at the University of South Carolina at Columbia, and Father and John, going away together on numberless trips, were seldom at home, which left Aunty, Loraine, and me alone in the house. I hated to see the sun go down. Aunty was too old to be afraid, and Loraine, small, slight Loraine

was never afraid of anything. I did worrying enough for
all of us.

Sam Redwine and his wife, Caroline, our two faithful
Negro servitors on whom I knew we could depend to
fight for us even unto death, were in the back yard; but
when we three were upstairs, I in Aunty's room with her,
and Loraine at the opposite end of the house, their
cabin seemed very far away. At bedtime I used to go
around locking all the outside doors—the hall doors, the
parlor door, and last the dining room door, which had
a lock the bolt of which slipped into place when turned
by the key, but the rub was that it wouldn't stay there.
When you turned the door knob again, the bolt slipped
out, the door coming unlocked. As a result I now had a
new nightmare, this cantankerous lock haunting my
dreams as had the Judgment Day for many a long year.
After I had locked up, I would get the big carving knife
out of the sideboard drawer, take it upstairs with me,
and after locking Aunty's door, lay my weapon on the
ledge near the bed where I could reach out and get it.
Everybody laughed about this.

"Even if anybody did come, what could you do with
a carving knife?" John would ask disgustedly. "Who-
ever it was, he'd take it away from you and maybe kill
you with it."

Someone has said that "being safe and feeling safe are
not the same thing." True, but being safe will not lull
you to sleep, either; you've got to have that precious
feeling of safety. And so I continued to take the carving
knife upstairs.

No use to reason with the timid; fears are not dis-
pelled by argument, for if anything can happen it may
happen. My philosophy of life was and is: " 'Cause nothin' ain't never gotcha yit, tain't no sign nothin's never
gwine to gitcha." There was the time when Sam Redwine said he was going fishing at the millpond all night,
not coming home till sun up. I made Caroline bring

her bed into the house and sleep in the front hall that night. Another night I heard a bolster that had been put on the roof to air roll off and fall on the ground. I felt no impulse to go to its rescue. As far as I was concerned, the dogs could tear it to bits. And then I heard Loraine walk downstairs, unlock the hall door, go down the front steps after the bolster, come back, lock the door, and go on upstairs.

II

Loraine and I together took charge of the housekeeping, Loraine as usual thinking up all sorts of hard jobs to be done, and I trying to argue her out of doing them —particularly picking, seeding, and drying all the Murillo cherries, it being impossible to take them to Minnesota. This was one summer, I told her, that we didn't have to dry fruit, but Loraine continued to insist that it was a sin to let it go to waste.

The Reverend Mr. William Amick, a Methodist circuit rider and a good man if ever there was one, had agreed to dry, can, or preserve the bushels and bushels of blue plums loading down our fifty-seven trees; and he was also farming on shares our cornfields, he and his nephews riding the three miles between us over and back every day to hoe and plough until the crop was laid by. And it was the prettiest crop you ever saw, the stalks, stout and tall with many ears, and broad, beautiful green leaves waving in the wind. Then came a drouth. Day after day, the sun came up like a ball of fire, setting in a cloudless sky; and as I watched those green leaves twist and shrivel I felt almost as if something human was on the funeral pyre. Night after night we sat on the piazza scanning the skies for signs of a storm, but always the lightning we saw was heat lightning, and I would say hopelessly over and over to myself, "The heavens are like brass, the heavens are like brass."

If you are born and raised on a plantation where mak-

ing things grow is the chief business of life, you feel that
a ruined crop is a sight to make angels weep. At the
World's Fair in Chicago in 1893, I was reminded of the
Amicks' corn crop as I looked at a picture called "After
the Storm," showing a group of Russian peasants regarding with hopeless misery a field of ripe wheat completely
devastated by wind and rain.

Farmers are really wonderful people who ought to
get medals pinned on their chests and statues erected in
their honor. Here they go, every year taking bread out
of their children's mouths to hold on to their precious
seed of corn and wheat, finally, after the manner of farmers, with much labor and pains putting it into the ground
where anything might happen to it, trusting the Good
Lord to send rain, sun, and dew to make a harvest. And
sometimes the crop fails. But do they stop? Well, not
often; they generally try again and again and again.
Farmers just can't give up, and a real farmer doesn't.

Sometimes, of course, farmers are idle and lazy, and
these are the ones you hear most about. John came home
that summer from a visit to a farmer at Reed Creek,
having noticed a lot of things he hadn't done.

"Why," John asked him, "haven't you put your hay
in the loft?"

"Jist hain't had time" was the ready answer.

"Why haven't you planted your corn? It's getting
pretty late."

"Jist hain't had time."

"Those oats ought to have been cut last week. Why
haven't you cut them?"

"Jist hain't had time."

"There's a hole in the garden fence where the pigs
get in. Why haven't you fixed it?"

"Jist hain't had time."

What in thunder, John asked high heaven, did he
do with his time?

One day Father called Loraine and me in for a

conference. He told us that Grandma Long's funeral sermon had never been preached, no minister he was willing to have preach it being available at the time of her death. He felt that he could not leave the state till this had been done, and he had made arrangements to have it preached the third Sunday in July. And furthermore, in honor of the occasion he had invited, besides the preacher, Mr. and Mrs. Banks Holt, Cousin Sallie King, and her sister, Cousin Annie Holt, and her husband to spend the Saturday night previous at our house, remaining until after dinner on Sunday.

There were no protests; and, much excited, we immediately began planning to do the best we could to preserve the honor of the family. I was particularly eager to preserve it in the kitchen, knowing that Cousin Sallie and the Holts would have Negro drivers who would expect to be as well fed as they were at home, no allowance being made for inexperienced housekeepers. I've always prided myself on getting along well with servants, the reason being, I think, that I always wanted to deserve their good opinion. And I think if overlings could only overhear sometimes what underlings say of them, it would do them a great deal of good. For instance, there was the driver of a Packard car who had left it in the street, partly blocking the entrance to a parking lot. The comment of the Negro proprietor was, "I reckon it took all the money he had to buy the car."

The darkies, I knew, would expect New Orleans molasses, and we had nothing but sorghum. So I decided to make some blackberry jelly, picking the berries myself in spite of chigoes, and finally had a fine kettle of juice boiling briskly away. But it didn't jell; so I boiled it some more, and still it wouldn't jell. No use asking Aunty, for poor Aunty's mind had failed very much, especially her memory. And then Mrs. Palmer appeared, having come for the mail, Loraine having taken Mother's place as postmistress.

Mrs. Palmer went out to the kitchen with me, looked at the juice boiling so beautifully, took a spoon, tasted it a couple of times and said: "Mary Alves, if I was you, I'd take it off the stove and put it in a jar. No use to keep on cooking it, for when jelly won't jell, there ain't nobody knows what to do to make it jell."

When it was time for the guests to arrive on Saturday afternoon, Loraine and I, though rather nervous, thought we had done pretty well. Together we had made all the beds, laid out towels, and filled all the water pitchers with fresh water I had drawn from the well. Mr. and Mrs. Banks Holt we had put in the middle room downstairs; Cousin Annie Holt and her husband in the middle room upstairs; and Cousin Sallie in the front bedroom with Loraine and me. The preacher, whose name I cannot remember, was to sleep in Mother's four-poster, Father taking the little bed; and John and Wes occupied the double bed in the little room off Mother's.

There were flowers in the parlor, though none I believe on the dining table, carefully set with Mother's best crocheted mats, a gift from Cousin Helen Caldwell, which Caroline had made all stiff and stark. The center of the table, I think, was honorably occupied by the highly polished castor, with all bottles freshly filled. And at each place was an individual saltcellar, also freshly filled. I had cleaned the steel knives with ivory handles and polished all the silver the day before. The room was darkened to keep out the flies, and two of Bud's little girls were coming to wield the peacock feather fans.

The stock of provisions in the pantry we hoped would last through the Sunday dinner. There had been one ham left in the smoke house, and this was the time for the sacrifice. After boiling it in some hard cider, Caroline, first scoring it, sticking in cloves, and sprinkling with a liberal hand mustard and sugar all over it, put it in the stove to bake. As we surveyed it now, all brown and crisp in a big dish ready to set on the table, we both thought Mother could have done no better. This was the *pièce de résistance* for supper, which, with hot biscuits, Mrs. Keck's comb honey, corn pudding, cucumbers and tomatoes, with cake and green apple floating island, we hoped would satisfy our guests.

For breakfast there would be cold ham, Dixie biscuits with honey, and stewed corn. With an orchard full of peaches, plums, pears, apples, and cherries it never occurred to us to serve fruit, a custom to be acquired later.

For Sunday dinner we had secured from Mrs. Burgess, the miller's wife, four large pullets, still in the coop since we had no ice. These, fried, with rice and chicken gravy, corn on the cob, string beans boiled with some of that good ham fat, tomatoes and cucumbers, and cake, peaches, and cream for dessert, we felt was a dinner good enough for anybody.

Everything went off very well. As Grandma had been dead eight years, the occasion was not exactly a sad one, and there was much fun and laughing, Father as usual keeping everybody holding his sides. He carved the ham in thin, succulent slices, urging everyone to take more, and told us when he was a boy tomatoes, then called love apples, were considered poison since they belonged to the deadly nightshade family. They were his favorite vegetable now, and eaten even at breakfast.

Wesley made a fine impression on the Holts with his handsome face and agreeable manners, as indeed he did everywhere, even in Hillsborough, where manners were considered next to godliness.

Loraine and I met on the back platform very early the next morning; everything was all right we thought, except there was simply not enough cake left for dinner. Making a cake on Sunday was something never before done in our family, and Loraine thought it should not be attempted now. I persisted, however, beating the eggs very carefully lest I waken the Holts; and it was all mixed and baked before Caroline appeared to get breakfast.

I never knew what Caroline served in the kitchen. "I give 'em plenty," she told me, "and dey licked it up. Dey knows we all is quality."

Cousin Annie helped Loraine and me wash the breakfast dishes, and Cousin Sallie made the beds and straightened up in Mother's room.

When we went upstairs to dress, Cousin Sallie, in her beautiful dress and hat, was a great contrast to poor Cousin Annie, whose dress she tried to brighten up with a lace collar.

We all got off to church in good time, leaving the dinner to Caroline. As for the sermon, I can't remember a word of it.

III

In August, Jane came home full of the good times she and Dr. Vance had enjoyed in Columbia, especially at the home of Mrs. McMaster, where they had been frequent guests. However, Jane's spirits, oppressed by the impending changes, were not up to their usual mark. I heard her telling Father one day that she didn't think John and I would ever earn a living. Father himself, riding the crest of the wave, took her to task, telling her to dismiss all fears. "Why, Jane," he said, "here am I, sixty-eight years old, starting out in a new country without a single misgiving."

Things were now easier for everybody; and soon after that Cousin Jim Webb came from Hillsborough to help us pack the few things we meant to take. Of course every stick of furniture was to be sold, even Mother's four-poster given her by Grandpa Webb, and the brass andirons, a wedding present from Grandma Webb. The house we were going to was heated by stoves and too small for furniture as big as ours, even if we had had money enough to pay the freight. I watched Cousin Jim pack the barrel of crockery, handling expertly the black and white English china Mother had inherited from her father. I showed him an old teapot I had long claimed, cracked and a little yellow from age, but beautiful to me, wondering if it was worth taking along. "Yes," he said, "it is a rare old piece." A museum piece, he called it and tucked it away with special care. We took the silver, of course, Mother's big Bible with the Apocrypha, her guitar, and the very thick volume containing her choicest music.

The only pictures slated to go were Sabra's crayon drawing, "The Wedding Ring" and Uncle Edwin's portrait. That, of course, should have been packed flat, it being an oil portrait; but Father decided to roll it—a fatal error, for when unrolled the paint had cracked so badly that it practically all came off, and there was nothing left to do but burn the remains.

IV

Father was very busy making plans for the members of the family to be left behind. Our house, so long a haven of refuge for so many people, was going to be one no longer. There was Aunty. It was impossible to take Aunty to that new country, and it was finally decided to leave her with Uncle Tom and Aunt Rob in Hillsborough. Her small capital was used to build a special room where she could have her own furniture; and there with people she loved and her own things about her, she would feel happy and at home. Three of the cousins agreed to give ten dollars a month each for her care; so we all felt that Aunty was well provided for. When Cousin Jim returned after packing for us, he took Aunty back with him, and her things followed in a wagon. It was a sad last parting. I never saw her again. Her flowers had to be left behind, as Aunt Rob had no greenhouse and could not be burdened with their care. I don't think Aunty ever missed them. Dr. Bill Staley bought the orange and lemon trees which had been such a boon to the sick, and I was glad in a way that they remained in our neighborhood.

Mary Shepherd had a position to teach school, but there was Loraine. Where could she go? What would become of Loraine? That problem was finally settled by sending her to live with my sister Lizzie in Rome, Georgia.

John, who was determined to be a lawyer, was to take the money he had earned and enter Judge Dick's law school in Greensboro, afterwards taking the state examination for admission to the bar.

Jane, who was returning to Peace, was not going with us; and when she saw Father so busy looking after everybody else and apparently feeling no concern at her being left behind, she said to him one day: "You are thinking about everybody but me; why don't you think about me sometimes?"

"Why, Jane," he said, looking at her in the utmost astonishment, "you can look after yourself!"

That was Father all over—thinking about the helpless and what must be done to help them—and doing it.

What Matthew Arnold said of his father in the poem "Rugby Chapel" is just as true of mine.

After a day of blinding storm when the host of the inn asks the "stormbeat figures" whom they brought in their party, whom they had left behind in the snow, they answer sadly:

> 'We bring
> Only ourselves! We lost
> Sight of the rest in the storm.'
> But thou would'st not *alone*
> Be saved, my father! *Alone*
> Conquer and come to thy goal,
> Leaving the rest in the wild.

ANNIE WEBB LONG
Always the life of the party

JOHN HUSKE LONG, Lawyer

Witty and humorous, he set the table in a roar

Still thou turnedst, and still
Gavest the weary thy hand:
. . . .
Therefore to thee it was given
Many to save.

V

Father, being impatient to get to Minneapolis, left
early and was spared the horrors of the sale. He had
cleaned out his desk, crammed with letters from all the
important people who had been his friends, and, nobody thinking they should be preserved, had burned
them, together with a barrel full of Confederate money.

I was to follow with Miss Abby J. Wiggin, a Minneapolis girl who had come to North Carolina on a visit,
and under her competent guidance, I had my first
glimpse of the great world. I had never seen a streetcar,
there being none in North Carolina, nor any town larger
than Raleigh with only nine thousand, nor any building
bigger than the State Capitol.

In Washington we stayed at the National Hotel,
which far outshone the McAdoo House in Greensboro,
and when I saw the Capitol my eyes almost popped out
of my head. But what impressed me most was the green
grass I saw growing everywhere, especially in those circles
around the trees. Green grass in summer! That was
a miracle!

Down the Potomac we sailed to Mt. Vernon, more
beautiful than fancy could paint. Up the path to the
tomb where grew a weeping willow transplanted from
the grave of Napoleon at St. Helena, and then into the
house, gaping at the picture of Washington, Nellie Cus-
tis's harpsichord, and the huge iron key of the Bastille,
presented by Lafayette.

We left for Chicago on a very early train. As we
walked to the station, I wondered at Miss Abby's uncanny
ability to find the way and was thrilled to my inmost
core by the early morning roar of a great city waking up.

It thrills me even yet. We traveled on the Baltimore and Ohio, looking out at Harper's Ferry from the back platform, Miss Abby and I with very different feelings about John Brown. It was a day of wonders and strange beauty —clouds, mountain peaks in sunlight and shadows, swift flowing rivers, green valleys, and nestling villages. That night in Ohio a party of boys and girls boarded the train; among them one named Pearl; and my ears were assailed by those Western voices rolling the "r" as they called her name. It sounded like Purrl, and I didn't like it.

We stopped a day in Chicago, not so impressive or beautiful as Washington. We rode the Cottage Grove Cable Car, sitting in the "Grip," to Oakland Avenue, where at a little stone house we boarded the horse-drawn bus for a trip through Washington Park, seeing a marvelous flower display of the flag, the huge face of a clock, and a flight of steps, at the top of which were the gates ajar. The bus drove right in the huge circular stable for all the park horses, each of which had its name in big letters over its stall.

We had dinner that night at the home of the Fowell Hills, who lived near Stephen Douglas's monument. They were Quakers, and Mr. Hill was a native of North Carolina, his sister having married Father's first cousin, Dr. Alfred Lindley, of Minneapolis. After a practically sleepless night followed by a day of sightseeing, I was almost in a state of collapse, so sleepy that my eyes would shut even at the dinner table. I made desperate efforts to keep awake, not succeeding any too well—nodding and coming to with a start. The Hills, whom I was to know well later, were the kindest people in the world, and I think they understood.

Besides all this fatigue, there was an overpowering wave of homesickness as I suddenly realized I had left my old home far behind and was now going to a new country where everything would be strange—and there was no going back. I had crossed the Rubicon, but unlike Caesar I had no sustaining dream of conquest. I was down in the depths with all the waves going over me. I could just manage to keep back the tears.

Up bright and early the next morning, I was much excited over crossing the Mississippi River, the Father of Waters. This I felt to be a great event. Deeply interesting, too, were the Pillsbury and Washburn flour mills looming black and ugly—scene of a great explosion of which Sabra had talked so much; and my first cataract —The Falls of St. Anthony. The motto "Pillsbury's Best" appeared on every flour sack and barrel, and when the twin boys were born to Mr. Charles Pillsbury, headlines proclaimed them—Pillsbury's Best.

As Miss Abby was the niece of Mrs. Richard J. Mendenhall, she was met by a coachman with carriage, into which with her Western energy and expertness she hustled me and my belongings, depositing me at my new home. As it was Sunday the whole family were there to welcome me to this strange new world.

VI

Our house in Minneapolis was the last one in a tenement row on First Avenue South between Fifth and Fourth streets where Powers Department Store now stands. "Tenement" suggests a slum, but that was the name given then to all rows of houses and implied no opprobrium. In the houses opposite dwelt some of the "best people."

There was Mr. Samuel Gale's gray stone mansion in the wall of which was a tablet in memory of a cat buried underneath. Few people ever got by without stopping to look. And next to it on the corner was a handsome wooden house painted brown, belonging to the trustee of a local bank. Every so often a plainly dressed woman knocked at the door, but never entered. But she kept on coming, for she needed the signature of the owner to free her husband from the penitentiary at Stillwater.

And finally she obtained it, her husband nobly redeeming the errors of his past.

There was a car track in front for what was called the "Dummy," a train of ordinary street cars drawn by a regular engine that rang a bell and blew a whistle. The terminal was in front of our house, and there was some arrangement for switching the engine. Besides making regular stops in town the Dummy ran to Minnehaha Falls and Lake Minnetonka.

All other houses in our row were occupied by a boardinghouse run by Mrs. Baker, a gentlewoman who had seen better days. Each house had a little porch in front, and nothing could have been uglier—a life saver though on hot summer evenings. On the Fourth of July the next summer the thermometer registered 104—unusual! I was to discover that all disagreeably hot weather was "unusual"—and that all those perfect days of bracing air, like wine—warm but not hot, cool but not cold, when it is a joy to be alive, were "regular Minnesota days."

However, the house suited our purpose well enough, and we were glad to have a roof over our heads. Since it was just two rooms deep, there was plenty of light and air. Downstairs there was an entrance hall big enough for a hatrack with a mirror into which I always took a last look going and a first one coming; double parlors with folding doors, a dining room, and beyond that, a one-story kitchen opening on an alley. Across the alley was a little house—combination woodshed and Chick Sale. Yes, the sad truth was that this house was as devoid of plumbing as the one back home in North Carolina. The dining room was marred by a sink, at one end of which was a pump connected with a cistern which supplied us with drinking water having a strong limestone taste. Horrible stuff! I was haunted at night by dreams of our old well. And then somebody told us of a spring on the East Side free from that limestone taste. Thirst-

ing like desert pilgrims, Will and I set out one night to
find it, drinking deep draughts of water pure as crystal.
It was a warm night and by the time we had walked the
two miles back home we were just as thirsty as when we
had left two hours before. "A ridiculous mouse had been
born."

Then there were three bedrooms on the second floor,
two more and an attic on the third. Newly furnished
throughout. My sisters had done all that on credit, and
I thought the furniture perfectly beautiful. Mother had
bought the parlor set—a sofa, one easy chair, the kind
called a patent rocker, and two straight chairs of black
walnut upholstered in a brocade of dazzling loveliness
in my eyes. It cost ninety dollars, and Mother was going
to pay for it by working button holes at three cents
apiece. The button holes came to her all stitched, and
for cutting them, she had a pair of buttonhole scissors.
The silk twist to work each button hole was carefully
measured off so that none was ever wasted. Dear patient
Mother! But she was glad of the work. Just as at home
her hands were never idle; she hadn't held them then,
and she certainly never held them now, being busy from
morning to night. Sister Annie kept the house, and we
had a fine Swedish maid at three dollars and a half a
week; so there were no household cares to interrupt.

Most important were those three rooms on the second floor, for we depended on them to pay the rent.
Luckily, it was easy to rent rooms, in spite of their having no modern conveniences. Minneapolis was a boom
town; it had doubled its population in two years, and
people were still pouring in, especially young men.
Then, too, we got the overflow from Mrs. Baker's boardinghouse, many of them theatrical people from Shake-
spearean companies like John McCullough's.

Never shall I forget Frankie, one of the little princes
in the tower—the sweetest, most darling little boy I have
ever seen. Frankie's mother was an actress, too, and it

turned out that she was the very one who had played in
East Lynne back in Greensboro and whom I had imitated
so successfully in boarding school that I was invited to
join the P.I.G.'s. Frankie had a birthday and I took him
uptown and bought him some candy.

"Are you going to be an actor when you grow up,
Frankie?" I asked him.

"No," he said scornfully, "I'm going to be a *gentleman*."

The roomers were nice people and opened a new
world to me. There was the beautiful Mrs. Downey with
hair so golden everybody thought it was blondined. She
told me it was natural, and I believed her. She wore
hoopskirts—not then in fashion, and when she went on
Nicollet Avenue every head was turned. No rouge
though. Only the demimonde wore rouge. She had
eloped when only fourteen with Mr. Downey and was
now about twenty-five. A creature of beauty and romance. I saw no fault in her and dogged her footsteps.

The G.A.R. came to town that fall, singing "Hang
Jeff Davis on a Sour Apple Tree" and "Marching
Through Georgia"—songs unpleasing to the ear of a
Southerner. We girls had sung that first song many
a time at Peace; only instead of Jeff Davis, we had said
Abe Lincoln. They knocked at our door for rooms;
and Sis Annie and I moved into the attic and rented them
ours at a fancy price. We did the same thing during the
state fair; not having a penny of my own, I would have
slept on brickbats to help pay the family bills.

The fact is that things hadn't turned out as Father
thought they would. He had received a small down
payment from the sale of the plantation and taken notes
for the rest, due at long intervals. He had not yet begun
to practice law, and was now sick in bed. Jobs were
scarce, and Will was still looking. We were all of us
really dependent now on my two sisters, and feeling it
keenly, not because of anything those two generous darl-

ings had said or done, but because we didn't want to be dependent. Sister Annie's salary as a teacher in the public schools was seventy dollars a month—the maximum, and she paid forty of this for her board. Our roomers paid the rent, but all other expenses were still to be met; and Sister Annie's forty dollars didn't go very far.

The rest of the heavy responsibility Sabra assumed, gladly, I may say because she loved us and meant to make this venture a success. She was now the leading dressmaker of the city, and her earnings were considerable, but so were her expenses. Sabra grudged us nothing and spent her money freely, in the true pioneer spirit, believing firmly in final victory.

VII

Nobody in Minneapolis seemed to have any doubts of success. Who could help believing in a town where so much building was going on? Just a block from us on Nicollet Avenue between Fifth and Sixth streets the Syndicate Block, to be the largest building in the town devoted to stores and offices, was in process of construction. *Syndicate* was a new word to me, but I discovered that it was so named because a number of men calling themselves a syndicate were the owners. It was to be occupied by many firms and individuals whose names would become household words. Among these was Bradstreet, an interior decorator whose word was henceforth to be law and gospel, though his preachments went far beyond most people's ideas. To have your house decorated by Bradstreet was to be at the top of the heap.

Quinlan, that was another name to become famous; and a new dry goods firm known later as the Minneapolis Dry Goods Company occupied the corner at Fifth and Nicollet opposite Hale's—Hale's, to Minneapolis then, was what A. T. Stewart's was to New York. Farther down on Nicollet between Third and Washington was

Goodfellow's, another important dry goods store. Another big building contracted for was the Skiles-Lindley block on Nicollet between Sixth and Seventh streets. Nicollet was now undesirable for residence, and so Dr. Alfred Lindley and Mr. Tom Skiles had had their houses moved to residential districts, and together had erected this building on the land made vacant, each owning half. And still farther uptown, owned by the Donaldsons, was the spectacular Glass Block, not so important then, though much talked of and destined as a firm to rank with the best.

Out in the Eighth Ward jerry-built houses were going up rapidly, financed, it was said, by Menage, a speculator in real estate. Not long afterwards he built a large office building on Washington of red sandstone, with glass floors in the corridors so as to lighten the building. Menage's career was soon to end, but Minneapolis was on its way to greatness bidding fair at even that early day to outstrip its hated rival St. Paul.

VIII

On Seventh and Nicollet the New Westminster Presbyterian Church was rapidly nearing completion. Already the congregation were worshiping in the Sunday school room underneath the auditorium, on the ground floor. There were no pews, the audience being seated in chairs. As I entered one Sunday morning, everyone was standing up and I inadvertently moved one of these empty chairs. When the occupant, not knowing this, attempted to sit down, he fell on the floor, greatly amusing his wife. They were two very prominent people, Mr. Charley Thompson, an elder in the church, and his wife, formerly Kitty Harris. I didn't know them then, but though I became well acquainted afterwards, it never seemed worth while to mention this incident.

Dr. Sample was the pastor then, a saintly man idolized by his congregation, though he preached a doctrine too strict for most to follow. He set his face against Sabbath-breaking, condemning newspapers and picnicking—a sport few could resist, there being so many lakes in easy reach. He described these picnickers returning after a Sunday spent in the country as "physically jaded and spiritually demoralized."

This church was to become one of my addictions; at one time I was attending six services on Sundays. The family had a word for it—Religious Dissipation.

Even the rich really went to church in those days, and the Heffelfinger pew was always full on Sunday morning, Mrs. Heffelfinger marshaling before her Nellie, Fannie, Frank, Charlie, and Pudge, the future football star at Yale.

Plenty of things went on during the week to absorb your time and energy. Waiting on a church dinner with other young people can be as much fun as going to a dance. We washed the dishes too, but not the way Aunty and I used to do. And those New England dinners with oyster soup, baked beans, brown bread, and pumpkin pie tasted powerful good.

More fun than anything else were the enterprises for raising money. There was Ezibizione, a project to put the Missionary Society in the red practically guaranteed by Mr. Harper, a young man of artistic proclivities after the manner of Oscar Wilde. Those in the know pronounced this name Etzy-Bitzy-Ony, but John insisted on calling it—Ezi-Bizi-One. It was to be a great art exhibition featuring the art of all countries—Greek, Italian, French, and Dutch. I was asked to be in the Greek Section in charge of Dr. Hunter, who held rehearsals at his house, it being finally decided that we were to reproduce a Greek frieze. All we would have to do would be to wear Greek costumes and to pose as directed. These rehearsals were great fun, Dr. Hunter living up to his reputation as a wit and Mrs. Hunter serving coffee and

scalloped oysters before sending us off out in the cold.
And it was cold. Way below zero as I remember it.

A hall was hired for the occasion and booths erected
for all the different countries, plus a booth in which to
serve coffee and doughnuts. A lifesaver it proved to be.
There were five performances. Practically everybody in
the church took part, and it was so well advertised that
the townspeople turned out in droves in spite of the below zero weather, the receipts totaling twenty-five hundred dollars. I had contracted a severe cold, and since it
was a sheer impossibility to wear at the same time the
Greek costume and a red woolen undershirt, my cold
did not improve. The family was determined to put me
to bed, but only paralysis could have kept me at home.

It was a great show, acclaimed as a great artistic success, and it looked as if it were going to be a financial
one. But there had been expenses—those things cost
money you know, and the profits turned out to be twenty-
five dollars!

I had begun to find out that here, in Minneapolis,
Republicans were in the place that Democrats had in the
South. When I asked a young man at a church sociable
if he was going to vote for Mayor Ames, who was running on the Democratic ticket, he replied, "Is thy servant
a dog that he should do this thing?"

Much waving of the bloody shirt even in church,
where I heard Robert E. Lee compared to Judas Iscariot
and the marching of Sherman's army to the marching
of the Lord of Hosts. My brother-in-law, who had been
in Columbia, South Carolina the night Sherman burned
it, was indignant. "There was no crime," he said, "that
Sherman's army did not commit."

IX

Father had been steadily growing worse, and the
doctor gave us little hope of his recovery. Sabra was
obliged, however, to take her usual fall trip to New York
to get the new styles and buy the latest trimmings. Un-

less she did that she could hardly run her business. It was a heart-breaking farewell. They both broke down and wept when she told him good-by, not knowing whether they would ever see each other again. Father kept saying, "Sabra, Sabra."

Poor Father! He had come with such high hopes. I remembered his saying to my sister before leaving North Carolina, "Jane, I am sixty-eight years old, but I'm starting out to begin the practice of law in a strange city without a fear or even a misgiving." And now he was sick unto death and full of anguish about leaving Mother and me dependent. He had saved others; himself he could not save. Soon after Sabra's return he died, on October 29, the anniversary of my sister Lizzie's wedding. The first snows fell on his grave.

We all put on black; it was customary, and it suited our feelings. Mother had a long, heavy crepe veil that fell almost to the bottom of her skirt and nearly blinded her. Wearing that veil was a sort of martyrdom.

Letters began pouring in: grief-stricken ones from John, studying law in Greensboro, and from Jane, teaching at Peace Institute in Raleigh; from Sister Lizzie in Georgia; and from Loraine and Mary Shepherd. Their names were among the last on Father's lips. When "Uncle William" died, they lost a second father.

From Cousin John Norwood in Hillsborough, himself a lawyer of renown who had known Father long and well, came the finest tribute, I believe, ever paid any man —an unpremeditated out-pouring of his heart in a letter to my sister Jane, now in the archives of the University of North Carolina.

I knew your father as you are aware, intimately and well, from his boyhood to the close of his life. He was just and up-right in all his dealings: doing unto others as he would they should do unto him: amiable, pleasant, and a universal favourite among all his acquaintances. He had no enemies. All who *knew* him admired him. All who were *intimate* with him, loved him. In his profession he had deservedly a high standing. He gave satisfaction to his clients in his profession, because he served them faithfully and well.

In the Court House he was a beautiful model of what an advocate should be. True, faithful and jealous for his client, and at the same time demeaning himself courteously and respectfully to the other party. No abuse of parties or witnesses. He studied well his cases, and his arguments were always listened to with peculiar interest by judges, jurors and bystanders. While William Long was speaking, the court house was full. All wanted to hear him. And this arose much from the fact that in addition to a direct, clear, and forcible exposition of the law and facts of his case, there was an inimitable vein of his own peculiar humour running through the whole.

Every hearer was delighted with this pleasantry; and his cause was greatly helped by it.

He was a noble man. As gentle, amiable, and kind as a woman; but carrying within himself at the same time all the spirit, strength, and firmness of the true man. I have known but one William Long.

Nor were such private tributes the only ones. The Raleigh *News and Observer,* on December 9, 1882, carried a sketch by Samuel F. Phillips, which said in part:

I have said that Mr. Long had many of the characteristics of the Friends. In the first place he was above all things himself a *friend*—true, sympathetic, sturdy, self-forgetful. Then he was a man of marked simplicity in habit and manner—in food, dress, speech and behavior. He appeared to be, and was, perfectly sincere, and at the same time was gentle and unobtrusive. He was fond of social intercourse, and himself a very bond of the bar society in his circuit. The infectious and innocent humor which enlivened his addresses to the jury, and his talk around the fireside at times when he had surrendered an evening to the briefless barristers and other friends who thronged his room—crowding chairs, tables and couch—was perhaps the characteristic by which he was most commonly known, but charming as we felt him to be in this mood, his friends and those who had occasion to seek advice from him, marked him for traits of as great excellence upon the serious side of life. He lent a ready and interested ear to any matter, professional or other, about which his opinion might be desired, and he brought to [this] duty the exercise of a well poised judgment. His sympathy and tact rendered him a persuasive advocate, and his candor and cour-

tesy gained the ear of the bench to an exceptional extent in the
time of those excellent and lamented magistrates who made the
Circuit Court of North Carolina venerable in the decades which
preceded the war. . . .

It is indeed when we recall the names of those who were
Long's friends, in a special sense, that one feels how strong he
was. Let *noscitur a sociis* be applied to him. Ruffin, the great
Chief Justice, who has done more for the lasting fame of the
State than any other of her citizens—the Moreheads, Gilmer,
Badger, Graham, Jonathan Worth, Charles Manly—I mention
only a few; of such were the men who sought his company, and
enjoyed it, and whose partiality, in turn, was appreciated by him
as an immediate jewel of his soul.

Father died with a deep sense of failure, but in reality
this last act of a life spent in serving others was the very
best thing he could have done for his family. I shudder
to think what a life of frustration would have been our
fate had we been left to struggle along on the plantation.
In bringing us to the Promised Land he had succeeded
beyond his dreams, for he had given us opportunity—
the greatest gift one can bestow—the opportunity to get
an education and employment.

X

Winter set in early this year with heavy snow; the
paper caps on bottles left by the milkman rested on
mounds of ice, and sleigh bells were tinkling all over
town. Every afternoon the sports and beaux joined the
parade on Portland Avenue, generally in their one-horse
single sleighs, though occasionally a two-horse one went
dashing by. Crowds of spectators stood on the sidewalks
to watch not only the fancy driving but the pretty girls
sitting beside the drivers, although of these young ladies,
wrapped in furs to their chins and wearing fur caps
down over their ears, nothing was visible except rosy
cheeks.

One of these spectacular drivers was "Oyster" Mack,
who ran a fish market and lived in a showy red-brick
house with marble trimmings. He had a fatal facility for

getting himself before the public in a disagreeable light. There was a magician showing at the Academy of Music who claimed he could make an omelet in a man's hat without leaving a trace. "Oyster" Mack made himself exceedingly disagreeable in expressing his doubts, but was finally persuaded to hand up his hat. The magician broke in several eggs, violently stirring them up, then, to the huge delight of the audience, returned the hat, saying, "You were right, sir; I can't do it."

It was a long, cold winter with one hundred and ten consecutive days of sleighing. Men wore buffalo overcoats down to their ankles and tied handkerchiefs over their noses—their mustaches being covered with icicles. Practically everybody wore earmuffs and heavy fleece-lined overshoes called arctics. Policemen who walked a beat twelve hours kept their feet from freezing by wearing instead of shoes inside their arctics a felt sock which did not impede circulation. And all the little boys and girls and even some ladies sported leggings. People were always saying, "It's so dry you don't feel the cold." But whether you felt it or not, if you were exposed to those low temperatures very long, you would find on coming in that ears, cheeks, or nose had been nipped.

I had never before worn anything extra in winter except a flannel petticoat or a balmoral; now even woolen stockings, high-necked, long-sleeved, long-legged red flannels seemed flimsy in these icy blasts. My new winter coat had a high fur collar to turn up over my ears, and Sabra made me a cloth muff trimmed in fur to match and bought me a pair of fleece-lined gloves. They still have those low temperatures in Minneapolis, but the people there now look just as they do on the streets of Chicago, New York, or even cities in the South.

It was a strange new world. Mother and I were both homesick, and we clung to each other like drowning persons. The people seemed to me as cold as the icicles, with queer customs such as having a stable actually attached to a dwelling house. I was astonished to find men helping with the housework, one man actually coming home every Monday afternoon to help his wife hang out the clothes. When I commented on this, I was told that Northern women did not wait on men as their sisters did in the South. I began to wonder.

XI

As there was nothing I could do to earn more than a mere pittance, Sabra decided to send me to the University of Minnesota, hoping to prepare me to teach in the public schools. In those days the expense would be very little—fifty cents a week for carfare—Saturdays were still the Saturdays of yore, and the tuition only five dollars a year. Of course there would be a few textbooks— a source of intense worry, and, hating to ask for money, I was tempted to select courses that required no textbook.

When I went to consult the authorities, I found that I lacked the proper entrance requirements and was given examinations. The one on American history floored me completely, and I got zeros on those questions about the Missouri Compromise and the Dred Scott Decision, neither of which I had ever heard of.

I was finally permitted to enter as a "special student," but the freshman class kindly allowed me to attend their meetings, pay dues, and buy a pin. Class organization was a brand new idea to me.

Nobody helped me plan my course, the result being that I did it very badly.

Not many buildings on the Campus in the year of 1882. I am certain of only two, Main and Chemistry, but think there may have been a physics building also. The Main Building, of gray stone with a tiny tower, was not as imposing as Peace. Here were the library, recitation rooms, and the parlors.

Professor Downey was by far the finest of my teachers in discipline and instruction. Everyone was always so eager to do his best for Professor Downey that there was never any disorder. He dealt in sarcasm, but it was always so witty that the victim laughed with the rest of us. As a teacher he must have been a wizard, or anyone as poor in math as I was could never have passed in higher algebra and conic sections.

My other teachers that first year were all dreadful bores except Professor Maria Sanford, whose originality and enthusiasm put her in a class by herself. Not much to look at, judged by beauty parlor standards. Her thin, straight hair, drawn back from her face, was twisted into a tight little knot. She was a Quaker, but her plain black dress was even more devoid of feminine charm than a Quaker lady's. You got used to this and didn't mind. Anyway, that wonderful, infectious laugh made up for everything. In my day everybody liked her and enjoyed her. She kept a boardinghouse of great renown and always arrived at her class breathless.

Her hobby was enunciation. As I never sounded my *r's,* she disapproved strongly of my careless Southern style, illustrating with an anecdote the value of precise speech.

A soldier on his way home after the war, becoming tired and hungry, went up to a man sitting on his front porch and asked, "Won'tcher please gimme sumpin' to eat?"

"Certainly," he answered, "just go round to the kitchen door and ask the cook; she'll fix you up."

Shortly after this another soldier came along and asked the man the same question: "Won't you please give me something to eat?"

"Certainly," he said, "I'll be glad to. Come right into the dining room with me. Dinner is just about ready."

Many honors have been heaped upon her, in life and after death. Her personality was unforgettable; and tucked away in her niche of fame, she rests more securely perhaps than many others wiser and greater.

I had begun to feel that people in Minnesota didn't appreciate the South; it was, I felt, a much misunderstood region, and when President Folwell announced that Mr. Sam Hill would speak on North Carolina at Chapel the next morning, I was ecstatic, thinking, "Now they'll know what's what." For this gilded youth, rich, tall, handsome, and popular, a graduate of Harvard and a rising young lawyer, had been born in my own county of Randolph, his father Dr. Richard Hill being one of those Quakers who had greatly prospered in Minnesota.

Mr. Hill, however, had no words of praise for his native state. He dwelt only upon its backwardness, poverty, and its high percentage of illiteracy. According to him, North Carolina was at the bottom of the heap. I could have torn him limb from limb. But you can't down a Tarheel. As I marched out thumbs down, chin and head were both up.

At another Chapel talk the introductory remarks by President Folwell in presenting his brother still linger in my memory. He began by telling us that the teaching profession was grossly underpaid. Here was he getting only four thousand dollars a year while his brother often received that much as a single fee. If teachers were to continue receiving low salaries, people of brains and ability would naturally enter other professions. Prophetic words!

The most noteworthy student of this period was Oscar Firkins, who had graduated at the age of sixteen and was always being pointed out as a prodigy. Slight, undersized, peering from behind enormous glasses, his looks belied tales of his genius. Still a student at the University, he could generally be seen poring over a huge pile of books in the library. However, he had plenty of sense, became an excellent professor in the English department, and his poetry was published in the leading magazines. Others remember him as a scholar, but I by the poem beginning "Little Greek that shines my shoe."

That winter in February the Emma Abbot Opera Company came to town for a week's stay at the Academy of Music on Hennepin and Washington. It was the only decent theater in town, the only other being the Opera Comique, frequented only by men. Emma Abbot's father, Mr. Seth Abbot, a short, stout man with white hair and whiskers, was a familiar figure about town, being a prominent real-estate operator.

Sister Annie invited me to go to the Saturday matinee; and the opera—the very same which Owen Meredith had praised in our Concert Recitation "Aux Italiens,"

> Of all the operas that Verdi wrote,
> The best to my taste is the Trovatore.

It was my first opera, and I loved it. "Things seen are mightier than things heard." But this was both seen and heard as Leonora sobbing down below

> That voice rang out from the donjon tower
> 'Non ti scordar di me, non ti scordar di me.'

It thrilled me that afternoon, and it thrills me now, as it still does the audiences at the Metropolitan Opera House in New York.

Minneapolis was soon to have another theater on Sixth Street next to the Syndicate Block called the Grand Opera House. Here I was to see all the old favorites given by the Chicago Church Choir Company and the Boston Ideal Opera Company, as well as the new masterpieces *Robin Hood, The Mikado, Patience* and *Iolanthe.* Oscar Wilde himself came to Minneapolis, and people began to speak of the sunflower with respect.

Minneapolis, being only a night's ride from Chicago, was a great show town, and singers and players all came to make their exits and their entrances in our new opera house. And a great procession they were: Patti, Mantell, Modjeska, Clara Morris, Fanny Davenport, Frederick

Ward, Sol Smith Russell, Robson and Crane, Lawrence Barrett, Salvini, and Edwin Booth.

It's worth being old to have heard Edwin Booth in *Julius Caesar* and *Hamlet*. All those long speeches that had seemed rather dull, like "What's Hecuba to me" suddenly came alive, and you found yourself hanging on every word; and the scene between Hamlet and his mother, "Come sit you down and let me wring your heart," you felt was forever unsurpassed and unsurpassable.

We were often hard up, but thank goodness we always thought money for theater tickets well spent.

The second winter the sophomore class decided to celebrate with a sleigh ride to St. Paul, where we would be entertained by two of our members. We picked probably the coldest night that winter. And it was the longest for the West Side girls: Miss Amy, Ada Kiehle, and myself, for whom the sleigh called first about six o'clock. This two-horse vehicle, though having a canvas cover and a floor deep in straw, offered little protection from the cold as we sat huddled together on the two long benches on opposite sides. There was no chaperon, but we needed none. We couldn't have been more circumspect under a searchlight than we were in this dimly lit cavern. There is a story of a girl on a sleigh ride who, telling her escort nobody loved her and her hands were cold, was informed, "God loves you, and you can sit on your hands." We girls were illustrating the spirit of this advice by using muffs for our hands and sitting on our feet.

Once arrived in St. Paul we were soon thawed out, dancing with such vigor in the grand right and left that one of the boys told me that his hands were "sweaty." Disgusting word, I thought, remembering the Hillsborough adage, "Horses sweat, men perspire, and ladies glow."

On the way over we had sung a song about taking ninety-nine blue bottles down from the wall, and on the way back we hung them all up again. I reached home at five in the morning and was back at the University in time for my class at half past eight. Tired, but happy. All of us had no better sense than to think we had had a grand time.

I longed passionately now to go on and graduate, but lacking guidance I was still a special student with no regular standing; and a talk with the registrar convinced me my case was hopeless. And so, in spite of Sabra's protests, I said what I thought was a final farewell to Minnesota.

2

ON BECOMING A BREADWINNER

I WAS JUST twenty when I applied for my first job as
teacher in the Minneapolis public schools. I felt I ought
to take my turn earning my own living; and though
Sabra urged me to go on and graduate, I decided to take
the plunge. After two years in the University I hoped
I was now fitted to be a grade teacher.

The man I had to see was Mr. Orson V. Tousley,
who, after several years' absence as minister to some
Scandinavian country, had now returned to resume his
duties as superintendent of the Minneapolis public
schools. Before his return, I had talked the matter over
with Mr. Moore, the affable assistant superintendent,
who had assured me that the University was just the
place to prepare for becoming a teacher in the grade
schools.

Mr. Tousley, a man with a reputation for being
merciless and harsh, was dreaded and feared by teachers
in general. There were few who did not tremble when
he entered the schoolroom on a visit of inspection, and
some teachers had been known to faint. However, I
had no particular fear as I set out one cold January afternoon to call on this tyrant and ask him for a job. Every
word of the conversation that followed was indelibly
engraved upon my memory.

His first question after I had made my wishes known
was: "Have you gone to the Normal School?"

"No. I have been two years at the University."

"That's bad. To teach in a grade school you ought to have gone to the Normal."

"Well, I came to see Mr. Moore, and he told me to go to the University; and now you tell me I ought to have gone to the Normal. What can I do about it now?"

"I'll ask you a few questions. Do you feel any fear of a few questions?"

"No, none at all."

"You don't? People usually feel some trepidation when they come in here."

"Well *I* don't. *I* don't feel the slightest." My spirits were rising. It was true! I wasn't afraid of him. Somehow I liked him.

"In the sentence 'How do you do?' how do you parse the first 'do'?"

I thought of Mother. This was why she had made me do all that parsing.

"Auxiliary of the second 'do,' " I told him.

"Who wrote 'Thanatopsis'?"

I almost giggled. That was one of Mr. Tousley's favorite questions. One teacher, on being asked that, inquired, "Mr. Tousley, did you say 'Thannytopsis,' or 'Fannytopsis'?"

"William Cullen Bryant," I said remembering my *National Fifth Reader* and "Where Rolls the Oregon."

"Who wrote *The Lady of the Lake?*"

What luck. My favorite poem that I knew almost by heart. "The stag at eve had drunk his fill." "Hail to the chief who in triumph advances." Roderick throwing down his shield, come one come all, and "Snowdown's Knight was Scotland's King." It was really funny.

"Walter Scott," I replied.

"What is the formula for squaring the sum of two quantities?"

That, too, was easy. "$A^2 + 2ab + B^2$." I rattled it off.

"What is X exponent zero equal to?" thinking, no

doubt, that this would be a poser. And it's a wonder it wasn't. It's about the only thing I remembered of higher algebra, which I had taken the year before. That somehow had stuck.

"One," I answered triumphantly.

"Who wrote *The Federalist?*"

That was a poser. I had never heard of the book.

"I don't know."

"Well," he said, "not many people know the answer to that. I guess you'll do. You go home, and when I want you, I'll send for you."

I thanked him and departed. I had met the enemy and he was mine. I didn't tread on air going home; I swam. The family was surprised and delighted. They hadn't thought it would be so easy.

II

The notification arrived two weeks later informing me that I was to report February 1 at the Garfield School, Eighth Avenue South and Twenty-fourth Street. I was to be an assistant at fifteen dollars per *month*. Not quite independent yet; partly, though, for Sister Annie told me I could now pay the milk bill, one dollar a week, leaving me eleven dollars for carfare, etc. Not many et ceteras! Milk was cheap—twenty quarts for a dollar. We used top milk for cream. My March pay check, without any previous notification, read $25.00; and Sister Annie told me I could now also pay the ice bill; and of course save money enough to carry me through the summer. I didn't mind. Twenty-five dollars a month! I felt rich —richer than I ever have since. I went uptown and bought Mother a box of out-of-season strawberries and some lemon drops, her favorite confection. And I opened a savings account at the Farmers and Mechanics Bank, depositing five dollars.

When I received my reappointment in June, my salary was raised to forty-five dollars. Too good to be true, but it was. And at Thanksgiving that year, my salary check read fifty dollars. I have never understood these raises—they came unsolicited and unexpected, like manna from heaven. I have always believed that they were due to the direct interposition of Mr. Tousley, my special providence, but why I cannot tell. That first interview was my last. He had visited my classroom only once, when I was having a reading lesson. Gone, never to return, was that gay brash feeling of "no trepidation" of a few weeks before. Now I was trembling. There was no seat for him—I offered him mine, but he refused with a wave of his hand, and leaning against the opposite wall stood, dark and saturnine, chin on hand, like Browning's giants at a hunting, finally stalking out in the middle of the lesson without having spoken a word. We all breathed again. The children had been good; they did their best, and I was grateful. I had tried to do mine also, but was not at all sure I had succeeded. After that I saw him only from a distance, at teachers' meetings. Occasionally I heard echoes from his question-and-answer method. One teacher, on being asked to explain the proverb "Silks and Satins put out the kitchen fire," told him that those materials were not very combustible and smothered the fire.

But he had been my good angel, setting my untried feet on the road to independence. And for this he received my undying admiration and deepest gratitude; for life is not worth living unless you can make a living —something I did from that time forward.

As a matter of fact I hadn't deserved those raises. Mr. Tousley had been right—I should have had normal training; for having attended only private schools, I knew nothing of public-school children and their addictions to spitballs, notepassing, and making hard-to-locate noises. Incidentally, no noise that I am not responsible for stopping ever disturbs me now. I knew nothing of their idea of considering teacher Public Enemy No. 1,

and doing everything possible to embarrass or catch her
out. I encountered that at my very first class, a seventh-
grade history lesson. It must have been a Roman history
class, because it concerned Hannibal; and I found myself repeating the story of how Hannibal, when crossing
the Alps, dissolved the barriers of stone by pouring over
them heated vinegar. "Where," one of the girls asked
in a now-I've-got-you-in-a-corner voice, "did he get the
vinegar?" It was a good question, one *I* had never
thought of asking, and the explanation I gave was not
entirely satisfying. The best I could do was to say that
as Hannibal knew that he would have to get rid of
rocks, he had taken the vinegar along for that purpose.

I became great friends with the teachers, who found
me an amusing personality. One of them, Miss Stevens,
sister of Mrs. Philip Winston, the first white child born
in Minneapolis, was always asking me to say "door";
I didn't say "do" but my two-syllable "doah" always
sent them into gales of laughter.

Another teacher I remember well was Miss Cox, who
had a strange objection to holidays, claiming the children
needed that extra time for lessons. When I told her I
had never finished *Uncle Tom's Cabin,* she brought me
the book the next morning. One of the teachers, Mallie
Sprague, was new like myself, but she was fresh from
Normal School at Potsdam, New York.

III

The Garfield School stood on the edge of a prairie
across which many of our children came to school. The
winter of 1885 was one of the coldest. As I remember
it was thirty below zero most of the time. One of my
duties was to stand at the front door with a bucket of
snow, scrutinize the nose, ears, and cheeks of each child
as he entered, and if I saw any yellow spots, clap thereon
a handful of snow to thaw them out. I had a two-and-a-
half mile ride on a street car theoretically heated by a

stove at the front, but I was always half frozen by the
time I got to Twenty-second Street, the end of the car-
line. The remaining two blocks were torture.

It was an eight-room building, and my classroom—
long and narrow, was between the sixth-grade room and
the seventh-and-eighth-grade room. There was one window, in front of which was my desk, and there were
benches on three sides for my pupils. A third door
opened into the hall—to admit classes from the fourth
and fifth grades. I taught reading, arithmetic, geography,
history, and something called "general lesson"—a sort of
melange of physics, botany, and zoology. One of the hardest things to explain was how the system of valves operated to lift the water up to the spout when pumping. I
couldn't do it now, but I was very glib then, though I
didn't understand it very well. Luckily, one of my pupils, a wonderful boy named Lyle Greenfield, made a
pump using a lamp chimney so that one could see exactly
what went on inside a pump, with the result that every
pupil became letter perfect, and Lyle, the hero of the
hour, was asked to exhibit his pump in other rooms, I
getting much of the credit for his brain.

I had a hard time keeping ahead of my seventh grade
arithmetic pupils, many of them like Harry Kennedy
having mathematical minds, which I had not. Decidedly
not. The fact that I had successfully studied algebra,
geometry, trigonometry, higher algebra, and conic sections was due to my really remarkable memory. Once I
had learned how to solve a certain problem, I could do
any other like it; and my custom was to memorize all
problems in the current book. No rule, however lengthy,
daunted me—not even the one in higher algebra a whole
page long divided into sections. Matthew Arnold says,
"We forget not because we will, but because we *must*"
and my "forgettory" has been quite as good as my
memory.

Notwithstanding all the years I had spent on mathematics I now encountered one little problem that seemed brand new—namely, "Twelve is three-fourths of what number?" It floored me completely and believe it or not, it still floors most people. Try it on anyone you know and see what happens. Will, who was a wizard in math, set me straight, and I worked out a way to make the meaning clear to my pupils. First I asked them: If three apples cost twelve cents what do four apples cost? A simple sum all could work—answer sixteen cents. Next I told them fourths was the name, just like apples, and that if three-fourths equaled twelve, one fourth would be one-third of twelve or four, and four-fourths or the whole number would be four times four, equaling sixteen. With a little patient drilling even the dullest child finally understood. I maintain that twelve is three-fourths of what number is a stupid way of putting the question. Why not ask: If three-fourths of a number equals twelve, what number does four-fourths equal? To be a good mathematician one must understand the language.

The hardest hour of the day was the one spent in the primary room to allow the primary teacher to visit the other lower grade rooms. It requires special training and special gifts to be a good primary teacher, and I had neither. Try as I would, the pupils often got out of hand. Sammy was a horrid little nuisance, always having his hand in the air. "Well, Sammy," I said crossly, "what do you want now?"

"You ain't strict enough with us," he informed me.

It is a sound pedagogical principle, and I began with Sammy, putting his hand down hard.

Discipline was my weak point, and without the advice and guidance of Miss Mary Stahl, the one principal I ever knew who did her best to help a new teacher find herself, I wouldn't have lasted out the year. One of the brightest stars in her crown is there because of what she did for me. After four years in the Garfield, Miss Stahl was appointed principal of the new Clinton, and there I was given the sixth-grade room.

One of the hardest jobs in the world is being a room teacher. Very like being a poor man's wife who besides being able to cook, wash, iron, scrub, sew, and do everything else that needs to be done in a home, including the care and bringing up of children, must also be the sort of financial expert who can make one dollar do the work of two or more, never getting into the hole—and never, never losing her temper.

My room had two classes of course—6B and 6A, one of which must quietly study while the other recited. Besides the regular branches of reading, writing, arithmetic, geography, grammar, spelling, general lesson, and gymnastics, one had to teach drawing and singing. Each of these last two branches had supervisors who laid down the course in special teachers' meetings, and also at intervals visited each room, putting both teacher and pupil through their paces. They were really super; and if we had known the word, we would have added "duper." The teacher visited first would circulate notes reading "So-and-So's here."

Being practically tone deaf, not even able to carry a tune, I found singing the hardest to teach. Goodness knows I had tried hard enough to sing, and Mother had done her best to teach me, but it was not any use. Mary Shepherd sarcastically greeted all my efforts with the lines:

> Swans sing before they die;
> 'Twere no bad thing,
> Should certain persons die
> Before they sing.

Fortunately all sixth-graders already knew how to sing by note, such prowess seeming to me miraculous. That anyone can look at a note and then sing it is something I have never been able to understand. I would blow my pitchpipe, beat time with the ruler, and they

MARY ALVES LONG, Aged Twenty-four

THE WEDDING OF MARY LONG PORCHER TO HER COUSIN,
DR. WALTER PEYRE PORCHER
Minneapolis, September 29, 1897

were off singing a song never before seen! They loved to sing "rounds," always coming out even. However, under my instruction, they did not improve; and the supervisor did not approve of my teaching.

Minneapolis schools prided themselves on being progressive and introduced two new branches into the curriculum—each having supervisors: sloyd for the boys, and sewing for the girls. Sloyd was a kind of scientific whittling which I had to learn from A to izzard. I had never owned a pocket knife, and the only whittling I had ever done was sharpening a pencil, which by the way I did very badly.

Mother had taught me how to sew, and though fine sewing was beyond me, I could and did make my own shirtwaists and cotton dresses and lingerie. But there were new wrinkles to the sewing taught by the supervisor, Miss Susie Sirwell. Threading a needle became a new and special operation. On the principle that there should be no waste motion, the thread must be held firmly in the left hand and the needle in the right to avoid unnecessary transfers. Just try for yourself threading a needle in this way and see how you like it.

First break off the thread—a major operation. The scientific way of performing that is to grasp the spool in your right hand; take the end of the thread between the thumb and forefinger of the left hand, and, holding on to it for dear life, unroll with your right hand until the thread is the desired length and stretched as tight as possible—then, presto, with a quick, determined thrust of the right thumb, break the thread. Now lay down the spool, pick up the needle, hold it tight, and with thumb and forefinger of the left hand insert into its eye the thread. A sigh of relief follows.

Ten years of this kind of thing began to pall upon me, and finally became intolerable. Must I spend the rest of my life in uncongenial toil? There was always some additional burden. Free textbooks for instance.

Teacher must see that they were not abused. They had to be given out, condition carefully noted in a book, and compared on the return. That year night school was held in our building, and each night every pupil had to gather up his books and deposit them on the floor of a closet across the hall from whence they were retrieved in the morning amid more or less confusion. I hadn't been very well that winter, and one Friday afternoon following a session with sloyd I suddenly arrived at a momentous decision. I would resign, go back to the University, graduate, and become a high-school instructor, teaching at the most only two subjects. Words can never tell the delight that filled my whole being as I left for home knowing I was never to return. My mind was fully made up.

At dinner that night I broke the news to the family. What a family! They agreed with me one hundred per cent and proposed a delightful plan. I was tired and worn out, they said, and needed a rest. I must go to visit the cousins in Alabama for the rest of the winter and spring, and enter the University in the fall. They would see me through. Mother, who had recently spent a winter in Alabama and knew the cousins well, would write and tell them I was coming. John said the thing to do was to go by way of New Orleans. Mardi Gras was the following Tuesday. I must leave the next night for Chicago, arriving in New Orleans Monday night, see the Mardi Gras, stay as long as I liked, and then go to Alabama. Before we left the dinner table, it was all settled.

My clouds had all dissolved into thin air. I dressed and went off to my Friday card club with a light heart, feeling much as if I had gone to heaven, and played whist with a fine abandon. When I said my prayers that night, I thanked God for my family. And for the Promised Land! It had dealt wonderfully with us. Our whole family was now in Minneapolis and more prosperous than we had ever dared to hope. John was doing well as a lawyer, and Will had gone into the real-estate business with John as partner. They now had five apartment buildings, one having forty apartments. Will's letterheads bore under his name the words "Landlord and Builder," than which he said nothing could be bigger or better. We had all helped, putting all our resources into this venture. Mother had contributed two thousand dollars which Father had left her, Sabra lent the money to buy the first lot, and the rest had given whatever we had. Of course they didn't own the buildings outright. Each had a mortgage, which worried no one as under the system of financing it would be eventually paid off.

It was a happy day when we had moved into the first building, the apartment having two parlors, four bedrooms, and a bath on the first floor; and a maid's room, dining room, and kitchen in the basement. Our first bathroom! Oh, happy day! It made our hearts rejoice. And those sweet morning sounds of sizzling and pounding steam pipes! Our first central heating! We tasted to the full the joys of waking in a warm house with a warm bathroom awaiting our ablutions. What is the heart of a home?—bathroom or furnace room? Is the possession of such things prose or poetry? Prose or Poetry? Those who have lived in Minnesota without both would answer Poetry. It takes both for a well-ordered existence, and there is no poetry in discomfort and inconvenience.

But better than comfort is the happiness that comes from belonging to a united family. And that ours was. Each was ready to sacrifice for the other, and we were all pulling together for our common welfare. Love made our world go round.

3

FRESH FIELDS

IT WAS BITTER cold that Sunday morning in February, 1894, when I boarded the Illinois Central train in Chicago for New Orleans, but my heart was light; for there would be no school on Monday, nor for many following Mondays. I think I felt somewhat as Christian did when the burden on his back rolled away. Anyhow, I had left my City of Destruction far behind.

When we waked up in Mississippi, it looked like summer, there being no snow and ice—but a pleasing warmth on the back platform when we stepped out to watch the pickaninnies standing on their heads or scrambling for pennies. Mississippi is not a scenic state, but the day was passed pleasantly enough in playing whist with Mr. and Mrs. Williams, a delightful couple from Grand Rapids, Michigan, and an agreeable young man Mr. Williams had found for a fourth.

The Williamses, like myself, had no reservations, and a telegram from the Gruenwald said "No vacancies." So on arrival we all went to the Hotel Royal, where we found the same situation. Mr. Williams and the other men decided the only thing to do was to go in search of rooms, leaving Mrs. Williams and me to guard the pile of luggage. At one o'clock they had not returned, and Mrs. Williams was frantic, convinced that they had surely been robbed and murdered.

A young man returning from the Comus Ball, seeing

our plight, introduced himself to us as Mr. Gaylord from
Memphis and offered us his room, saying he could sleep
with a friend. Eventually this offer was accepted, the
men returning from a fruitless search. They planned to
spend the night at a Turkish bath or on a cot in the
parlor. The room was the worst I had ever seen, the
soot-blackened walls reminding me of our old kitchen
in Randolph. The bed was a single one, but we needed
no rocking that night to put us to sleep.

Fun looking for rooms the next morning in warm
sunshine, with roses in full bloom. Soon becoming located in a rooming house on Clio, we returned to watch
the mummers and the floats from a balcony offered us by
a jeweler through the good offices of our partner at whist.
I thought to myself that things like this never happened
in the cold frozen North.

Left to my own devices on the departure of the Williamses for Pass Christian, I became an indefatigable
sight-seer, haunting antique shops, the French Quarter,
and cemeteries, reading hundreds of inscriptions and
remembering only the beginning of one, "Four Commonwealths claim him." This was inscribed on the tomb
of Albert Sidney Johnston, killed at Shiloh, who next to
Lee and Stonewall Jackson was my favorite hero.

I treated myself to dinner at Antoine's, marveling at
the contrast between the sanded floor and the huge white
damask napkins, and, being shocked at the prices, departed unimpressed by the food I had chosen because it
was cheap. Not so good, I thought, as that served by Miss
Pitt at her boarding house on Clio and St. Charles. Miss
Pitt was one of the aristocracy, and her oyster pie of alter-
nate layers of pie crust and oysters was made by a recipe
handed down in her family. Good to the last bite!

The warm weather hadn't lasted long, and the grate
in my immense room being about as big as a man's handkerchief, I was always half frozen by the time I was
dressed. How good it was to enter Miss Pitt's dining

room and, sitting with my back to a blazing grate fire, eat sausages and biscuits kept hot over the coals for late-comers!

II

At the end of two weeks I departed for Alabama. As I crossed Lake Ponchartrain there was a blazing sunset, and I kept repeating to myself a poem I had recently learned:

> Sunset and evening star,
> And one clear call for me. . . .

Southern railroads seemed to run in the interest of hotels, it being impossible to go any place without stopping somewhere while waiting to change trains. It was about eleven o'clock that night when my train reached Meridian, where the Negro porter escorted me to the hotel and back again after a few hours of uneasy slumber to catch the four o'clock train to Demopolis.

All my life I had been hearing tales of Alabama. Tales about snakes! There was the cottonmouth snake; and, thinking it was a cotton boll and trying to pick it, people would get bitten. Equally frightening was the story about Aunt Betsy, who had walked up to find a snake in her bed. There was the story of a man returning to North Carolina who, fearing robbers, exchanged his money at the bank for a draft on the bank in Raleigh. He was given his draft, also a letter to the bank, and was asked if he would be so kind as to carry a small iron box. When he presented the letter and draft, the cashier asked if he had not also brought an iron box.

"Oh yes, here it is," he said, taking it out of his pocket.

"Well it's a good thing it is here, for without this box your draft could not have been honored," was the astonishing reply. The man was naturally amazed at finding that had he been robbed of this box, his draft would have been no good.

Here in Demopolis I was to visit three first cousins, none of whom I had ever seen, and being a self-invited guest, I naturally felt a little uneasy at my reception. Fears all unfounded! In the Deep South hospitality was unbounded.

Demopolis, I found, had a strong French flavor. The story went that Marshal Ney had escaped and settled here with his followers, which explained why so many places bore the names of Napoleon's victories: Marengo, Arcola, and Linden. And there were many French dishes such as daube—a roast of beef marinated in vinegar and richly spiced. Burr artichokes, which puzzled strangers like myself, were considered a great delicacy.

The show place of the town, "Blandwood," though falling to pieces, was deeply interesting. There were holes in the roof and weeds were springing up through the rotting floors, but the proportions of the rooms were still magnificent—lofty ceilings, fluted columns, and even marble statues. It has since been restored.

III

My first host, originally from Hillsborough, was Cousin John Cox Webb, who had married Miss Sallie Creagh, one of Alabama's belles. People like them just don't live any more; the environment which produced them has gone forever. Cousin John told me of a dreadful summer when he first came to Demopolis; Miss Sallie Creagh wouldn't say Yes, and the heavens wouldn't send rain; the cotton crop seemed doomed. So he went back to Hillsborough on a visit, forgetting all his troubles; and when he returned the cotton crop was a lollapaloosa and Miss Sallie said Yes.

He had prospered greatly since then, owning besides the cotton gin and warehouse the Cheshire-Webb block, the local skyscraper three stories in height. When one of the young cousins in Demopolis came to St. Louis during the Exposition in 1904 and we took her to see the tall buildings of the town, she said, "You ought to see

the Cheshire-Webb block." He also had several cotton
plantations on the outskirts of the town, one of the sights
being the Negroes marching from one plantation to the
other, carrying their hoes, and singing as they went.
This was the Black Belt of Alabama, so-called, I thought,
because there were so many Negroes there, but the real
reason was that the rich soil was so black. Cousin John
used to rise every morning at seven, riding on horseback to visit all these plantations, and returning for
breakfast at nine o'clock with his family. It was a very
devoted family, everybody admiring everyone else, and
nobody criticizing.

Those were pleasant evenings spent by fires of can-
nel coal, talking or playing whist. Whenever many high
cards fell on the same trick, somebody was sure to exclaim, "Big stars fell in Alabama." There was a wonderful music box bought in Mobile, with a large repertory
of tinkling tunes; and Willey Creagh, the eldest daughter, would sing the new songs, accompanying herself on
the piano.

IV

The great event of my visit was Willey Creagh's
wedding in April. The dress Sabra sent me for the
occasion was the prettiest there. It was white silk with
broad green stripes, and around the low neck falling
over the big puffed sleeves was a wide flounce of embroidered chiffon.

As I had come from a big city, Willey consulted me
about the refreshment for the marriage supper. Suppos-
ing everyone would stand up as they did in Minneapolis,
I advised against serving anything that could not be
eaten with a fork or a spoon, such as chicken salad and
ice cream. When Cousin John heard of this he went off
the deep end. Invite people to his house and have them
stand up! Over his dead body! So the side porch was en-
larged to form a room big enough to seat the two hundred and fifty guests. As it was to be a white and green

wedding, the rough pine boards were covered with white cheesecloth and green Venetian blinds filled the window spaces. We brought in cartloads of Southern smilax from the swamp, draping it over the banisters, windows, and the improvised altar in the bay window.

The day of the wedding an old darkey out in the back yard was barbecuing sheep and pigs. The menu as finally served was oyster soup, roast turkey, the barbecued sheep and pig, chicken salad, and ice cream and cake. Fifty pounds of sugar had been used in icing the cakes adorned with flowers and pillared temples. I had never seen such elaborate creations. The highlight to my mind was the barbecued meat of sheep and pig roasted whole over a trench full of coals. Champagne flowed like water, and next morning everybody was explaining how he knew he had not drunk too much, one man saying he had been able to unlock his door, and another that he had put his hat straight down. Everybody explained, except Mrs. Glover, renowned for her wit. Her story was that when she and Mr. Glover reached the hotel, it was going round and round. After standing there watching it a while, she said, "Look out now, Sam; next time it comes around, let's jump aboard."

I loved all the cousins. Aunt Betsy, now an invalid, lived on the plantation with Cousin Helen and Cousin Will, who had run the plantation and brought up the whole family. He was an old man now, with a line of language in addressing the Negroes I believe unequaled. He liked his biscuits hot, and when Diana handed the plate round would take only one, waiting impatiently for her to bring a second turn fresh from the oven. He was a keen observer of birds and told me about a jay which, devouring a grasshopper, ate all the best portions, handing the legs to his son and heir.

Cousin Helen was raising turkeys, the problem being to keep the hens from stealing their nests. To prevent this a little darkey was detailed to follow each hen and watch where she made her nest. Cousin Helen was a devoted aunt, adoring all her nieces and nephews, inventing formulas for sick babies and keeping a watchful eye on their actions.

"Look out, Sam," she said to her sister Pattie's son as he stood resting his chin on the open muzzle of a loaded gun; "do you want to blow your head off?"

Cousin Pattie Houze had been a great beauty; now one no longer, she was the sweetest woman I have ever known, and I adored her. She had a wonderful cook—everything being done to please Mr. Houze, who liked things just right. Every meal here was a repast.

These Alabama cousins were all adorable, and I bade them good-by with an aching heart, never again seeing any of my generation.

v

On my way back to Minneapolis I stopped at Bellbuckle, Tennessee, to visit my cousins John and William Webb, formerly of Oaks, where they had attended Mr. William Bingham's school. They were not my first cousins, but, as near as we could figure out, only seventh; however, as far as congeniality and affection went, they were double-first.

Here in this tiny hamlet these two brothers conducted the Webb School, one of the most successful schools in the South, with a reputation for turning bad boys into good ones. The school was limited to two hundred boys, a number never exceeded even if the applicant was the son of the richest and most influential man in the state. Its graduates were recognized even at Yale and Princeton as men of exceptional character and scholarship, particularly in Latin and Greek. Both brothers were men of unique personality, John noted for his scholarship and William, known as "Old Sawney," for his original methods of discipline which only he could use.

When a boy came to Bellbuckle, he was told that

WILLIAM R. WEBB—"Old Sawney," of the Webb School,
Bellbuckle, Tennessee

The only Don't in his Gospel of Do.

Boys, don't do things on the sly. A brave man never does things on the sly. Whenever you get the consent of your mind to do in the darkness a thing that you wouldn't do in the broad daylight, you're a coward, and you'll stay a coward until you cultivate a spirit of openness. I despise a coward. Everybody does.

I despise the Boston Tea Party with its disguise. I refused to join the Ku Klux unless they would go in the daylight.

I wouldn't. I wouldn't. I wouldn't for all the world — I wouldn't do anything on the sly. Let your actions always be such that if the keen sunlight of publicity were turned in, it wouldn't make you ashamed.

Boys, don't do anything on the sly.

THE ONLY DON'T IN "OLD SAWNEY'S" CREDO

while there he must not lie. If he broke his word, he would be expelled. As there was no dormitory, the boys roomed in private homes, each being required to give his word of honor that he would not leave his room during the night. If any emergency arose, he was to go to Sawney's house, tell his story, and get permission. Another regulation was that no boy was to be at the station when trains arrived. It was a funny sight, people said, to see the boys loafing there turn their backs and walk away when they heard the whistle of the approaching train. They were also told they had to learn their lessons or be whipped. Given ten words to learn, if you spelled nine correctly, you were whipped, on the theory that if you could learn nine, you could learn ten.

When Mrs. Childress of St. Louis heard that her sons had been whipped, she took the next train to Bellbuckle, determined to take them home. But the boys wouldn't go. They said Old Sawney was great fun, and they would rather take some whippings than leave Bellbuckle.

The school lacked almost everything in equipment considered essential elsewhere. The various schoolrooms were not equipped with desks, nor even provided with chairs, each boy taking his chair from one classroom to another.

The "unusual" characterized Old Sawney's handling of the various problems. For instance, one boy had been attacked and beaten by several others. Easy enough to punish the offenders; the question was how to do it in some spectacular way that would strike home.

"Could you," Sawney asked the victim, "have licked these boys if they had come at you one at a time?"

"Oh, yes, Mr. Webb, I could," he answered.

So all the classes were suspended, the boys seizing their chairs and hastening to the trial scene. Old Sawney explained just what was going to happen as a result of boys banding together to attack one boy. Each culprit, given a hickory switch, took his turn with the boy who had been attacked, all of them being ignominiously defeated. This, he told me, disposed of that problem for the rest of the year.

Another time it was a case of a big boy beating up a little one, the whole school being again witness to the proceedings. Old Sawney addressed the culprit, pointing out how shameful for a big boy to attack a little one.

"You wouldn't dare," he said, "to hit a big boy like Jim Clark here."

To his amazement the bully accepted the challenge, striking Jim Clark lightly on the cheek; Old Sawney thought his case was lost. But Jim Clark, to everybody's astonishment, knocked the boy down, telling Cousin Sawney afterwards, "I wasn't going to let him get away with it, Mr. Webb."

But his was not a negative philosophy; uprightness and square dealing were his theme; "the only don't in his gospel of do" was "Boys, don't be sly." And he wouldn't join the Ku Klux Klan because they wore masks and rode at night.

He was notoriously untidy himself, but his pretty wife was always beautifully dressed. He told me that when courting Cousin Emma he invited her to go buggy riding, intending to pop the question. Just as he was about to speak, he looked down and, seeing his shoes not blacked and the shoe strings untied, he was speechless.

At the Paris Exposition in 1889 my sister Annie caught sight of him, neither knowing the other was there. Without saying a word she went up and began straightening his tie.

He had the courage of his convictions, advocating prohibition in spite of threats on his life. Cousin Emma told me of a night of terror. Returning on a late train from Nashville, she was surprised that he was not at the station to meet her. Neither was he at home. Suspecting foul play, she called the police and a search was organized lasting way into the night. As she sat there alone, suddenly the door opened, and Cousin Sawney appeared, looking very sheepish. His story was soon told. He had sat down in the station to wait for her, heard the whistle and seen the headlights; then inexplicably he had fallen asleep and had just waked up.

His passion for prohibition never left him. Appointed Senator to fill out an unexpired term, he made just one speech on the floor of the United States Senate, eloquently pleading the cause of prohibition.

His creed was cheerfulness no matter what the circumstances. He told me the story which had given him this guiding principle. During the last days of the Civil War when his company was encamped one rainy night in an open field, the only ration issued was parched corn. As, cold and hungry, he munched his share discontentedly, feeling completely discouraged, he heard a pounding going on and, looking to see what was happening, noticed an elderly man cracking his corn with a flint rock. "I only got one tooth," he explained cheerfully, "so I hafter crack my corn up."

VI

When I returned to the University of Minnesota, determined to get my degree, I found a friend in Professor Clark, who taught Latin, never forgetting to ask every class the perennial question, "Who chased whom around the walls of what?" As I still lacked many entrance requirements, he advised my sending to Peace for records in the subjects taken there; and on receiving them, I found myself a junior with regular standing.

Having decided to teach English and Latin, I specialized in those subjects. Rather mortifying to find myself a classmate of Paul Jocelyn, my star pupil in sixth grade at the Clinton School. I had to work hard to keep up with Paul, fresh and up-to-date in Latin while I had grown rusty. Young Professor Pike, one of the up-and-coming members of the faculty had a new wrinkle.

Translating was not enough—we must speak Latin as students did in French and German classes.

In English I was having seminars with Professor McClumpha in Browning and the novel. We did Browning up brown—nothing too obscure for our nimble minds —*The Ring and the Book,* "Bishop Blougram's Apology," and "Sordello"; we understood and explained everything. In the seminar on the novel the students were asked to review books by authors ranging from Fielding down to modern times. The story of *Adam Bede,* assigned to a young Scandinavian, sounded very much like the *Police Gazette.*

Oscar Firkins was doing excellent work in teaching composition and declamation, requiring us to deliver the speeches we wrote. He praised my oration on Robert E. Lee, but lit into a story I called "The Telltale Heart" which he said was too full of physiological details to have any literary value. Recognizing his sincerity and ability, I agreed with this criticism.

VII

And then a new star appeared in the firmament— Robert Herrick at the University of Chicago, famous not only for writing best sellers, but for teaching composition. So I made another momentous decision. After finishing my junior year I would go to the University of Chicago, study under Robert Herrick, and graduate from this much-talked-of institution. There was, however, a great obstacle—one of the entrance requirements at Chicago was physics. So I registered for that subject under Professor Frederick Jones, a born teacher. He saw how hard I was trying; without his sympathetic efforts, I never could have comprehended the mysteries of mirrors and polarization.

Professor Clark, who had done so much to help me, considered my going to Chicago sheer disloyalty; but I had put my hand to the plough, and I wouldn't turn back. Jane lent me three hundred dollars, and John gave me a new bicycle; and, taking what clothes I had and my precious twenty-six and a half credits, I matriculated at Chicago in October, 1897.

The tuition seemed excessive after Minnesota, and I discovered that if I took more than three majors a semester, I would have to pay extra—a heavy blow, as I lacked one-half credit to make up the thirty-six required for a degree. In this emergency I found that a course in Bible under President Harper, which met every Sunday morning from nine to ten o'clock through two semesters, cost nothing and would give me the half credit I lacked. It seemed a bonanza; and so it was, for I had to count pennies in those days when I was living on borrowed money. But it spoiled a lot of precious hours. Every Saturday night when I wanted to be gay there was a Bible lesson to study; and it certainly took the edge off Sunday, which to me was a day of rest.

I was thankful for Mother's precept to keep the Sabbath holy, which, except for Dr. Harper's Bible lesson, made Sunday an absolutely free day. While other girls darned stockings, washed their hair and lingerie, or studied lessons, I remained a lady of elegant leisure.

VIII

I liked all three of my professors that first semester. Our psychology textbook by William James as taught by Dr. Warner Fite was more interesting than the novels of his brother Henry James. Truth, Dr. Fite said, was the foundation virtue. Without that, there was nothing on which to build.

Dr. Fite liked teaching in a coeducational school, complaining that in the woman's college where he had taught the young ladies swallowed everything he said whole, but picked him to pieces.

Like me he was new to Chicago, never before having been farther west than the Hudson River, and as we often met while exploring Jackson Park on our bicycles, I listened eagerly to his stories of campus life in the East and here in Chicago. There was the story of Professor Royce's new carpet, the subject at Harvard of much unfavorable comment. When Mrs. Royce answered the doorbell one day, a little boy asked if he might see the carpet. After gazing intently for some time, he rose and remarking, "It don't make *me sick*," departed.

John Dewey, whose "progressive" methods were exciting attention everywhere, was the most-talked-of man on the campus. His children called their parents by their first names and were encouraged to show initiative. When the Deweys returned one night, they found the faucets removed from the kitchen sink and water on the floor rising rapidly. "John," said the boys, "don't say a word; get a mop."

A recent story represents him in a new light. He accepted the dinner invitation of a young couple on the condition that he might go home at nine o'clock. When the hour arrived he looked at his watch, but made no move to go. After repeating this performance at intervals until midnight, he was still there, his hosts worn out, and wondering. Suddenly exclaiming, "This is your house; I thought it was mine," he snatched up his hat and dashed off home.

Other people much in the limelight were Professor Trigg, who proclaimed that evil was just as good as good; and Thorstein Veblen, whose book *The Theory of the Leisure Class* threatened to turn the world upside down. His idea that *emulation* was the guiding principle of life leading people to "conspicuously consume" explained why a rich man, unable by himself conspicuously to consume as much as he liked, married a wife to deck out in jewels, furs, and fine feathers.

Topping everyone else head and shoulders was Professor Von Holst, accorded by graduate students the reverential awe a heathen has for his god. I crept into his class one day, thrilled to hear this oracle speak of some dry-as-dust historic event with flashing eyes and deep feeling of an Edwin Booth playing Hamlet. The great man, however, lacked a sense of humor. He was told the story of a Jewish boy who, seeing a five-dollar gold piece lying on the counter of a drug store, swallowed it. The druggist sought to recover it by the aid of a stomach pump, but all he got back was two dollars and a half. Dr. Von Holst did not smile, saying severely that the story was absurd, as everyone knew that a stomach pump could not raise metals. Mrs. Von Holst backed up her husband, remarking fatuously that Dr. Von Holst was an authority on stomach pumps.

Professor Fite was a liberalizing and salutary influence in my life, making me less dogmatic. When I told him I could not understand how anybody could be a Catholic, he said, "Miss Long, I can't understand how anybody can be a Presbyterian!" His book *The Theory of the Individual* won him a place on the faculty of Princeton. Dr. Fite's theory, as I remember it, was that the individual is the Supreme Court from whose decision there can be no appeal. If a thing seems right or wrong to you—then for you it is right or wrong.

My Latin teacher, Dr. William Gardiner Hale, was one of the Grand Moguls of the University, receiving seven thousand dollars a year. He taught us Latin by the lecture method, seldom calling on anyone to recite.

When I went to register for English Four, a class in composition and a prerequisite for English Five with Robert Herrick, for whose sake I had come to Chicago, the Registrar frightened me almost to death by his doubts of my qualifications. Feeling my whole future at stake, I went into battle resolved to do or die, soon winning an easy victory.

The teacher of English Four, William Vaughn Moody, said to be the youngest member of the faculty at the age of twenty-eight, was about five years younger than I, but I was well content to sit at his feet accepting his dicta as law and gospel. He could be caustic on occasion, a criticism on one of my themes being "trite, trivial, and commonplace." This might have slain me had he not liked much of my work, often reading my daily themes aloud in the class. I wrote a fortnightly theme about "Aunty," his comment being that here was rich material. I had complained in one daily theme apropos of a devastating criticism that it was difficult to soar with a ball and chain attachment; his written comment in reply was "but you can dig very nicely."

I finished English Four with flying colors, and as Mr. Moody was living with the Herricks he had told Professor Herrick about my work. Professor Herrick had the reputation of being a savage critic, often making his students weep. Having never seen him until I entered his class, I was amazed to find a youthful, cherubic-looking individual rather than somebody resembling an ogre. Could harsh words issue from those smiling lips? They could and did. "A daily theme is a daily theme written between six P.M. and six P.M." This was an ultimatum delivered harshly at the beginning of class every day; and if that daily theme was not deposited in the iron box marked "Daily Theme, Herrick," standing at the entrance of Cobb Hall by six P.M., the hour for collection, it was a lost opportunity. No redress.

At first I disliked him, but not for long, for I became an ardent worshiper. He had sensed my antagonism, but not the worship, and at the first interview he said to me, "Miss Long, you have no confidence in me, and therefore I can do nothing for you."

"Why, Professor," I exclaimed with the deepest sincerity, "I believe every word you say."

After that all went smoothly. I took not only English Five but English Six, receiving A's in both.

And the next year the heroine in his novel, *The Web of Life* was named "Alves"; whether after me or not I never knew. I had three namesakes now, a cousin and a colt, both in Alabama, and a character in a Chicago novel. And a very disreputable character she was too, according to Walter Scott's standards—and mine.

Cousin Sawney's daughter, Alla Webb, wearing no distinguishing mark that anyone could observe, appeared at a party where every one represented a book, but no one ever guessed that she was *The Web of Life.*

IX

I lived at Kelly Hall, the smallest of the women's dormitories, but considered the most exclusive. Dean Marion Talbot was the Head. A strict disciplinarian, together with a committee of the girls themselves she formulated rules for our conduct, the principal one being that anyone expecting to be out after ten o'clock must obtain a key. A rule frequently broken by absent-minded people like me who forgot to ask for a key. Poor Miss Hall! Her room was nearest the front door; and if looks could kill, those who rang after hours would all have dropped dead.

Would you believe it? There was no rule against smoking, which was not strange, for in 1897 girls had not begun to smoke. However, there was a rumor that the odor of tobacco smoke was profaning the sacred pre-cincts of Kelly Hall, not an unfounded rumor, the of-fender proving to be the granddaughter of the donor of a prominent university building bearing his name. This did not save her from being sent to Dr. Harper, who laid down the law of "No Smoking." Pretty and popular, she was a forerunner of the modern girl, frankly announc-ing that she planned to taste every joy of life, barring none.

Many graduate students lived at Kelly, some younger, some older than I, all at first regarding me—an under-graduate in the thirties—as one born out of due season. In the beginning I regarded the graduate-student species with awe, but soon discovering that though I could not match learning with them, I could match wits, we be-came "good fellows well met."

These women, some of them already Ph.D.'s *summa cum laude,* were very human, always ready to joke and laugh even about Walt Whitman, taken on the campus, for the most part, very seriously. Dr. Dora Wells's verdict was that there was every leaf in the *Leaves of Grass* except the fig leaf. And Dr. Grace Darling's comment on a young instructor was that if he were a bear, the noun *cub* would describe him, together with the adjective *unlicked.*

To test our sense of humor Miss Isabel Bronk related the following anecdote, at which one was supposed to laugh, though very few ever did.

At a dinner party a young man on being asked, "Do you know that you are rubbing your head with a piece of lettuce?" replied, "Oh, am I? I thought it was spinach."

Miss Sophonisba Breckinridge, regarded by all as a "topnotcher," was able to discuss the gold standard and even weightier matters with the professors themselves. She was the head of the table where I sat very humbly listening to her theories of life. She talked much of her father, an orator described as silver-tongued. He believed one should use the telegraph freely, a commonplace idea now, but in those days when the telegram was a harbinger of woe or death, a revolutionary suggestion. "Why," he asked, "sit in suspense waiting for letters when you can telegraph?" Sound advice which I was to remember later.

Dr. Eleanor Hammond, fresh from Oxford with all the brilliance of a falling star, came that spring to be a "docent"—lowest place in the faculty hierachy, beginning with full professor, associate professor, assistant professor, instructor, and so on down to docent, who received no fixed salary, but was paid so much for every student.

The great Professor Trigg had begun as a docent, but, attracted by his revolutionary ideas, so many students flocked to his classes that the University found it cheaper to make him a professor.

Dr. Hammond regarded me askance until she discovered that I too was a Jane Austen fan, knowing all of her novels practically by heart and adoring Elizabeth Bennett and laughing at Mr. Collins and Lady Catherine deBourgh. That proved the tie that binds, though she had many other attractions for me, such as reading Kipling with "rhythm." "Gunga Din, Din! Din! Din!" became a classic.

In Oxford Dr. Hammond was invited to tea by a professor's wife.

"Miss Hammond," she said, "I have been trying to locate Chicago, but cannot find it on my map."

"That's strange! Let me see your map."

When unrolled, it was the map of Canada.

We had many tastes in common, and spent many a "frabjous day" together in the enchanted realms of Jackson Park.

My room in Kelly Hall overlooked the Midway, crowded every afternoon and evening with a continuous stream of carriages and bicycles. I wrote a daily theme about it for Professor Moody comparing the recurring phenomenon to an endless belt going round and round. At night I would lie in my bed listening to the lessening roar of the great city, suddenly increased by the Illinois Central train thundering by. I loved it, noise and all. Chicago and most of all the University had got into my blood. What seemed routine—meals, classes, daily themes, bicycling by Lake Michigan, a ride on the grip of the Cable, the sing on the steps of Haskell Museum were the pearls in my Rosary.

x

Egyptian relics were displayed in Haskell, exhibit number one being The Lady Meribah—three thousand years old! And she looked her age. Kipling must have had her in mind when he penned "a rag, a bone, and a hank of hair."

But those old-fashioned "sings" on the wide stone steps, spring evenings, when everybody sang were something to remember, always ending with our beautiful Alma Mater song, "The City Gray."

Nowadays, gathered round a sunken fountain, you listen to the quartettes of the various fraternities, instead of roaring at the top of your lungs the ditties of those early days:

> John D.
> Rockefeller he
> Gives all his spare change
> To the U. of C.
>
> Oh we came here in the autumn of 1893;
> We spent our days in research work
> Our evenings at the Fair
> Cobb Hall was then the the only place
> Where we could daily flunk
> And in the dear old Drexel Dorm
> Was the only place to bunk.

Could it be possible this beautiful university was only four years old?

How fast this City Gray had grown! Now men undergraduates could also bunk in Snell; graduate students and professors in the building next to Cobb; and women in Beecher, Kelly, and Foster. Besides these, there were five other buildings on the Campus, all named for donors except the gym. Cement walks, so straight and proper, and also many untidy, disfiguring "short cuts," connected all these buildings. Professor Fite's theory was "Do no paving until after the short cuts are made, then pave the short cuts."

XI

Spring in 1898! There was a war going on. The first American victim was Worth Bagley of North Carolina, whose family I had known so well in my Peace Institute days. His place in North Carolina's hall of fame is secure and honored. I was the most patriotic person on the

Campus—that is if patriotism means an *overweening* confidence in your country's ability to win. Except me, everybody, especially the Ph.D.'s, seemed to have doubts. My faith never wavered. "Haven't we always won?" I asked. "Remember Paul Jones? Of course we'll win," I insisted, never doubting that Fighting Bob Evans and the *Oregon* would round Cape Horn in time to strike a blow for freedom. It was a delightful frame of mind.

Dean Talbot's mother, fearing Boston would be bombarded, had fled in a panic to Chicago, and when called on to cheer her up by playing whist, I never refused, though my schedule that last semester was terrifically heavy.

It wasn't classes that kept my nose to the grindstone, Professor Herrick's English Six being the only stiff and exacting course—daily themes and a weekly chapter on an imaginary biography of John Donne written in the archaic English he would have used. The other two majors—Bible with Dr. Richard Moulton and a lecture course I had deliberately chosen because they were notoriously easy and required no textbooks. My object—not learning but credits. And the reason—I had decided to take the spring examinations offered by Chicago to applicants for a position in the high schools. This meant hours and hours of study. I had been warned that these examinations were fearfully difficult, even Ph.D.'s like Dr. Amy Tanner having failed to pass the last one; and neither she nor anyone else thought a mere undergraduate such as I had the slightest chance.

But having decided to pitch my tent henceforth by the waters of Lake Michigan I rushed boldly in. The four subjects I chose: history, English literature, physical geography, and French, requiring not logic but memory, were admirably adapted for cramming, which I now set myself to do every spare moment, besides the two early morning hours from five to seven, reserved for this special task.

The Class of June, 1898, met according to custom one afternoon a week during the last semester with President Harper in his library—a delightful room lined with books. These informal sessions of talk and tea were considered the high spot of our sojourn in the University. President Harper was a fine caterer; every mundane soul looked forward to the "eats," consuming with gusto salted nuts, cucumber sandwiches, cheese crackers, and crisp cookies; and the tea, hot and fragrant, with plenty of lemon and sugar, loosened our tongues. Nothing seemed too sacred to be discussed, everyone speaking freely of what was on his mind.

"Is there any immediate prospect of the University's endowment being increased?" is the one question I remember, perhaps because the answer struck my funnybone.

"Yes," said Dr. Harper, "there is. A rich man has recently made his will leaving Chicago a very large sum; and he is now in California for his health."

The tempo increased as the day for graduation drew near—a melange of daily grind and frolic.

Dean Talbot invited us all to a tallyho ride to Lincoln Park and back—a munificent excursion for there were three tallyhos so that all might sit on the top deck. I looked in wonder at the few who chose to sit inside. Tastes differ.

There was also a farewell party given by Dean Talbot for Rena Cobb, Dr. Harper's secretary, who was returning to live in Boston. Everyone was asked to write a jingle about Miss Cobb, the best to receive a prize. It was won by a young instructor in the physics department, Professor Robert Millikan, now become famous, who turned in this gem:

> Had I a Muse to-night 't would sob,
> Had I a heart to-night 't would throb!
> But Muse and Heart have fled, begob!
> They wait in Boston for Miss Cobb.

Two tense days were spent in taking the public school examinations at the West Side Division High School. I wrote feverishly, coming home limp but jubilant, feeling certain I had passed both history and English literature, in the end sure of having passed everything but French, but hoping my average would bring me to the passing mark. Not until the middle of July would I know the result; in the meantime I possessed my soul in patience.

Every Saturday afternoon our foursome went on a picnic, bicycling to one of the parks. When we started to Lincoln Park, there was a stiff north wind blowing.

"Let's go to Garfield Park instead," I suggested, it being due west.

"No," objected Dr. Fite, "we planned to go to Lincoln Park; so let's go there."

And we did, bucking the north wind all the way. Going home the wind had changed, and we bucked the south wind all the way back.

Moral. Figure it out for yourself. The moral I would write is: "Make sure of the present; and go with the wind when you can."

Convocation Day came at last. Our class marched in the grand procession, trailing those of high degree, gorgeous in the hoods of scarlet, blue, or gold. Wearing a borrowed cap and gown over my white shirtwaist suit, I received my diploma with a thankful heart.

As my dear friend Miss Pauline Moxley chose not to attend the graduation exercises, I volunteered to take her diploma also; but when I arrived at Kelly Hall, I did not have it, nor, though I sought it carefully with tears, could I find it. A diploma cost ten dollars, and ten dollars just then seemed a vast sum. When I told Miss Moxley, she asked me why on earth I had taken her diploma. Why indeed? It had seemed the natural thing to do at the time; but I resolved never again to be meddlesome.

As I lay down that last night on a pallet in Rena Cobb's room, my own having been assigned to a newcomer in the summer quarter, my last waking thought was of my own precious diploma. Only a piece of paper, but someday it would anchor my ship in a safe and pleasant harbor.

Next morning the sun was casting long shadows on the campus as I turned my back on the University, going home to wait for news from the Chicago Public School Examinations.

XII

The family welcomed me home with open arms, regarding my diploma with deep respect. It was the first university diploma in our family since Father had received his from Chapel Hill about sixty years before; and I laid the two together side by side in the top drawer.

Darling Mother! She had made me a graduation present—a rug she had knitted of silk carpet rags with two enormous wooden needles. Too precious to lay on the floor, it would serve as a scarf on a table. I thought it was perfectly beautiful and told her so.

All this time I had been worrying over Miss Moxley's diploma, and great was the relief when I heard it had been found.

Shortly after this a letter came telling me of my grades in the examinations: History 97, English Literature 94, Physical Geography 90, French 40, English Composition 88. This last mark was obtained by judging the English I had used in answering the questions.

That dratted French! It had brought my average down, but any way it was over eighty, and made me eligible for appointment to the Chicago High Schools. The election would be held the last Wednesday in September. And so I settled down to this second wait of six more weeks.

And then the unexpected happened—I received an offer from the High School in Helena, Montana, to teach the next year at a salary of one hundred dollars a month. This had come through Professor Herrick, who, being asked to recommend an English teacher, had selected me.

I had to make a decision then and there. Here was a bird in the hand. If I let it go, I might not get another. Prudent counsels prevailed, and I wrote to Chicago withdrawing my application till the following year. But I wasn't happy about it, though putting on a brave front. "No use taking Mother's rug as I'll be back so soon," I said when packing my trunk. But when I saw her disappointed look, I stowed it in, declaring I couldn't bear to leave it behind.

The day I left for Helena, I felt as if I were turning my back on paradise. As I went down the front steps, I turned for a last look at Mother sitting at the window looking as sad as I felt. At the station a handsome boy greeted me cordially. It was Ed Quist, one of my bad boys at the Horace Mann School, who wanted to draw all the time, and as he never made any trouble when drawing, I finally gave up and let him draw. Bygones were bygones with him, and he greeted me like a long-lost friend. I felt almost cheerful as he wrung my hand at parting. The amazing thing is how often these bad boys turn out to be such fine men.

The day was scorching hot, everybody on the train trying to get comfortable. It was my first experience on a tourist sleeper, chosen because it cost thirteen dollars less than a Pullman; and I looked in amazement at men in shirtsleeves and women wearing Mother Hubbards. My opposite neighbors were a Home Missionary and his wife with their six children bound for their new home in Oregon. The eldest child celebrated her ninth birthday on the train, and the youngest was a baby in arms. The father took excellent care of the baby, boasting about what a good nurse he was. They were to have a parsonage and his salary was six hundred dollars a year. Something wrong somewhere!

Everybody including myself had brought provisions to last through the journey, some cooking regular meals on the stove in the tiny kitchen at the entrance, even frying onions. We had hardly started before a large woman spread a white cloth on the table set up by our porter, and began unpacking a huge basket, setting out fried chicken, hard-boiled eggs, sliced ham, cucumber pickles, pumpkin and apple pie, doughnuts, and an enormous cake covered with grated coconut frosting. After a hearty meal, she carefully repacked the basket, repeating this performance three times a day without any noticeable diminution of the contents, like the widow's cruse of oil. It was all very clubby, every one chatting away exchanging life histories, as people do when thrown together by chance.

The mountains were white with snow the day I arrived in Helena. A beautiful sight. I lived with two other teachers in a little house on the side of Mount Helena. The New England mother of one of the teachers kept house for us, and we had a Chinese cook who served the best clam chowder and blueberry pie I ever ate!

The view was magnificent. Mountains do something to you; after a while you feel you can never live without them. From our perch we saw the town cupped in by the mountains, and beyond it the grassy plains stretching thirty miles away to the Missouri River flowing at the foot of a long range of jagged mountain peaks. It was a cold winter, and the bed of embers kindled on the snow-covered peaks by the rising sun those bitter mornings warmed only my heart.

When it snowed in Helena the flakes didn't come down vertically, but blew in horizontally from the surrounding mountains.

XIII

The next summer I went back to Chicago, resolved to risk all on getting appointed to one of the high schools. Professor Robert Lovett, in charge of the office placing graduates, had heard of me through Professor Herrick, and offered me a position in the Normal School at

Bloomington at twelve hundred dollars a year. But I refused, and after interviewing Mr. Nightingale, the high-school superintendent and leaving him my address, I went back home to wait for the election that last Wednesday in September.

It was a long wait, but the day finally came, and when I went to bed that night I confidently expected a telegram in the morning. It didn't come, either that day or the next. By noon Friday I was pretty desperate, when suddenly I remembered what Miss Breckinridge's father had said: "Why wait for letters when you can telegraph?"

I composed my telegram, as I thought, very diplomatically—"When and where shall I report for duty?" —and calling a friend in the telegraph office, I asked him to rush it.

The answer came back in an hour. I was afraid to open it. We had company in the parlor; so I went off alone to the back of the house and, opening it, read:

"Report at the John Marshall High School, Kedzie and Adams, at nine o'clock Monday morning."

That moment was the height of something or other in my life. As Mr. Dooley said, "All was happiness and a cottage organ."

That fall one day in November I received a letter that had been returned to the Board of Education, and finally to me. It bore the address 11 East 17th Street— my Minneapolis address—but instead of Minneapolis, Minnesota, it read Chicago, Illinois. When I opened the letter, it proved to be the notification of my appointment. Blessings on Miss Sophonisba Breckinridge!

When I talked the matter of my salary over with Dr. Nightingale, the Superintendent of High Schools, he told me frankly that he was going to put me in the lowest group at the next to the highest salary, and that when I reached the maximum of twelve hundred dollars, the only way to get into the next group was to be lifted there

by a member of the School Board. Fortunately, however, by the time I had reached the maximum by the
slow process of a yearly raise of seven and a half dollars
a month a new superintendent had arisen who changed
all this by offering an examination to all those eligible
for a transfer. As I had no board member up my sleeve,
I hailed this innovation with delight, and shortly after
Christmas began studying for this fateful test.

As this was the first examination of the kind, nobody
had the faintest idea of what the questions would be
like. As I was an English teacher, I decided to become
familiar with all reading required of the students, and
among other things read for the first time all twelve
books of Homer, discovering what I proclaimed was the
origin of consolation prizes as the loser in a chariot race
was given a mule.

No matter how tempted those spring afternoons to
collect companions for a drive in my Model T Ford to
the shores of Lake Michigan or to one of the many forest preserves, I went religiously home, studying faithfully from four to six. And every Saturday I settled down
for a three-hour session from nine to twelve, before
going to lunch at the Chicago College Club and a matinee afterwards.

One Friday it was announced at school that there
would be a lecture by a noted educator for all high-school
teachers. As the examination was drawing near, I settled
down to study as usual that Saturday morning when suddenly a startling thought assailed me: suppose one of the
examination questions should be taken from this lecture
just to see whether the teachers had attended?

Snatching my hat, I started off at high speed, arriving
just in time to hear the lecturer describe what he called
the long and short circuits. If a teacher asked a question and the student responded orally, that was the short
circuit—entering the ear and coming out at the mouth.

If the answer was written, that was the long circuit—
entering the ear and coming out at the hand.

When I finally took the examination, for which an
hour and a half was allowed, there were ten questions,
the first one being a request to prepare an outline for
teaching *Silas Marner.* I got so interested in doing this
that when I finished there was only a half hour left.
I almost threw down my pen and walked out. How
could I possibly answer nine questions in half an hour?
However I began to write furiously, and possibly illeg-
ibly, and believe it or not the tenth question was—"What
is meant by the long and short circuit?"—the very thing
that would have stumped anyone who had failed to attend the lecture. The passing mark for the examination
was eighty, and my average, had I not been able to answer that question about the circuits would have been
seventy-two instead of eighty-two—just two over the
mark.

The ways of Providence are said to be past finding
out, but I could not help feeling that here had been a
direct intervention in my behalf.

XIV

Fresh fields and pastures new. Life was just beginning! Back in my beloved Chicago, all sorts of experi-
ences were to come—instead of sloyd, teaching *Macbeth*
and *Hamlet;* graduate work at the University; life in a
Chicago boarding house; an apartment of my own with
what I called my Near Family.

And finally there was leisure, something I had never
known. After thirty-five years in the schoolroom I decided to retire at the age of fifty-eight, and go to Europe
for a year and a half. So many fresh fields! Paris, London, Switzerland, the Rhine, Oberammergau, Italy,
Egypt—and back to Italy, Paris, and London. Spring in
the Forum wreathed in wisteria and roses. Redbud trees
lighting up the Palatine Hill like enormous pink candles

—Holy Week in Rome, Westminster Abbey, Oxford, and Stratford on Avon.

Then back to fresh fields in America. On the Adriatic returning home I was asked by a sweet Englishwoman where my home was.

"In St. Louis," I replied, "but I have never lived there."

Strange but true, for I was now going to live with Will, Jane, and Sabra, who had moved there from Minneapolis. Here too were many cousins, especially Julia Brokaw and that beloved and unique personality, Annie Huske Webb.

The Show-Me State! You have to live in this state to know how much it has to show. It was on the map long before Lindbergh made his lone-eagle flight to Paris. French explorers, De Soto and Marquette, sailed by on the river, and other Frenchmen following gave to its civilization a strong French flavor, characterized by humor, gaiety and, let me add, food of a goodness one can never forget. From a hill in Forest Park the statue of St. Louis, Louis IX of France, overlooks the city that bears his name.

Not far from St. Louis, Daniel Boone's old home, restored with all its beautiful paneling, stands near the Judgment Tree, where Boone dispensed justice under three flags. The Lewis and Clark Expedition started from St. Louis, and there in Bellefontaine Cemetery, overlooking the Mississippi he knew so well, is the tomb of Meriwether Clark. Nor is Mark Twain its only famous author; a host of others have won distinction in every field of literature. Neither is it an anticlimax to mention the Cardinals and the Davis Cup, an international prize given by a St. Louisan.

The Show-Me State! It showed me a cause. A great woman leader said if you have a cause your life will never lack interest or savor. Boredom will pass you by. My fourteen years in St. Louis gave me a new zest for living.

COLONEL ROBERT BINGHAM AND W. R. WEBB ("Old Sawney")

ROBERT WORTH BINGHAM
Ambassador to Great Britain

I loved St. Louis, and I loved the people. Chicago took second place, but in Chicago I had had no cause. Four commonwealths claimed Albert Sidney Johnston. I claimed four commonwealths: North Carolina, Minnesota, Illinois, and Missouri. I talked glibly of my four native states. When I rose to address an audience in Wilmington, North Carolina, I said I used to be a native of North Carolina, and, horrified, hastened to add "and still am."

With my new-found leisure life became an intoxicating venture, passing through in bewildering succession one open door after another. Membership in the St. Louis Wednesday Club meant many new friends, including Mrs. Frederick B. Hall. But the greatest honor and opportunity of my life came when I was appointed National Chairman of the International Relations Department of the National Federation of Women's Clubs.

Though I was new in the cause I found others like Mrs. Philip North Moore, Bishops Ivan Lee Holt and Scarlett, Mrs. George Gellhorn, Forrest Donnell, now a United States Senator, and many others, old in their allegiance. Nor can I forget Mrs. John Green, whose Foundation in memory of Mr. Green brought Winston Churchill to Westminster College, where he shook the world by his pronunciamento about the Iron Curtain.

It is said sarcastically that English women love committee meetings. Well, I found committee meetings with people like these as interesting as a matinee. And the cause! It is the greatest of all causes. World peace with liberty, justice, and BREAD. For peace to be durable, must be endurable. Man cannot live by bread alone, but he cannot live at all without it. There is and there should be no peace in a world of hunger. "Give us this day our daily bread" is a prayer for peace. One cannot work directly for peace any more than for happiness. Each depends upon conditions—and those we can work for. The question is to discover what those conditions are.

In St. Louis the evening paper called the *Star* had for

its slogan: "Don't say paper; say *Star*." And don't say peace, but say the Marshall Plan, or something else without which you cannot expect peace.

My cause led me in 1926 back to Europe, where I planned to spend August in Geneva studying the League of Nations. There I was to have the amazing good fortune to be present when Germany entered the League and to hear Briand's thrilling speech as he proclaimed in French which even I could understand, "Our two countries have had enough of war."

As I intended to visit several countries, I wrote to my cousin Robert Bingham asking for a letter of introduction to our various embassies, which I thought might prove useful. Not only was this letter forthcoming, but there also arrived an invitation to visit him in a castle he had taken for the summer in Scotland. He hadn't seen me since my Peace Institute days, but he knew well and dearly loved my sister Jane; and so I felt this to be a tribute to her memory, for when she died he had written me a beautiful letter, now in the archives at Chapel Hill, saying she gratified his pride in North Carolina and in kinship. One of life's little ironies was that I had to decline this invitation as my plans for travel did not include the British Isles.

Paris that summer was a wonderful place to be. For one thing the King of Morocco had come and was to march with all his cohorts down the Champs Élysées. I had tried before to see a parade in Paris from the sidewalk and was determined this time to find somebody who would give or sell me a ticket to a window overlooking this spectacle. After many fruitless efforts, someone told me to try *Vogue*, which gave me, not one, but four tickets without charge, though of course I insisted on giving a generous tip, which was not refused.

The first fruit of the letter of introduction was an invitation to the Fourth of July celebration at the American Embassy in Paris, a most delightful affair with music from a French band loaned for the occasion, and an unforgettable highly decorated table in the dining room, loaded with every variety of French confection and all sorts of colored drinks. How nice it was, I thought, to be getting some recompense for all those loathsome income taxes. Best of all was meeting our Ambassador, Mr. Herrick, who in his hail-fellow-well-met Western way mingled freely with his guests, telling us amusing stories.

A few weeks later, the night before I was to leave on an early train for Amsterdam to attend a meeting of the International Federation of University Women, at about half past seven o'clock when I came to dinner, worn out with sight-seeing and dreading the packing still to be done, the waiter handed me a letter with many apologies for its being a day late, as it had been delivered by mistake to the hotel next door. It proved to be a letter from Cousin Rob inviting me to dinner at the Hotel Crillon that very night at eight o'clock. What a blow! And me with a most beautiful Paris gown of lace and chiffon! That disappointment still rankles.

But compensation was to come, though years afterwards. The summer of 1936 my cause led me again to Europe, this time to Brussels, where I went to attend the Rassemblement Universel pour la Paix, represented by the letters R.U.P. plastered all over the city. This was called by Lord Robert Cecil and Pierre Cot in a desperate attempt to save the League of Nations.

From there I went to London to visit a dear friend. When I gave my passport to the customs agent at Dover, I suddenly realized that I had forgotten to get my English visa. Would I be sent back to Belgium? My look of horror must have impressed the agent, for he told me to go on to London, where I could get my visa the next day. My fervent love for England and the English became undying worship.

Rob Bingham was now our Ambassador to England, and great was my delight to receive an invitation to luncheon.

I had acquired at the court dressmaker's just the hat and dress for the occasion; but my coat! It was unspeakable, a sport coat mussed from being slept in on trains and being splashed on the voyage from Belgium by waves big enough to disconcert even the English.

When I went to get my things from the court dressmaker and told her of my invitation, she was as much thrilled as if it had been from the King himself to Buckingham Palace. When I said, "But look at my coat!" she solved my problem by lending me one of elegant black cloth with a Persian lamb collar. Arrayed in this I felt as elegant as Miss Sue May Kirkland of Hillsborough would have looked.

And what an interesting time we all had at the luncheon. Rob's conversation would have graced any gathering, and I too had something to contribute, since all were interested to hear about the R.U.P.

As for the food, it was the best America could produce. When I said, "I bet this is the only place in London to-day where they are feasting on sweet-pickled peaches," Mrs. Bingham exclaimed, "and on Kentucky ham."

The Bingham family was well and favorably known in England long before Cousin Rob became Ambassador there, as I was unexpectedly to discover by the long arm of coincidence, strangely enough, in Italy, where I went by the roundabout way of Turkey and Greece—countries of such inexhaustible interest that even in a lifetime one could hardly do more than scratch the surface.

Anyway, I walked through the same Lion Gate Agamemnon passed when he went to Troy; visited Epidaurus, where a wild ass capered over the rows of seats in the great stadium of such marvelous acoustic properties that the faintest whisper on the stage could be heard in the last row at the top. My companion, Professor Bates of Culver, Indiana, and I tested that statement. Climbing to the summit, I listened to Lincoln's speech at Gettysburg, and then descending I declaimed Marco

Bozzaris' famous appeal to his soldiers battling with the Turk:

> Strike, for your altars and your fires;
> Strike! for the green graves of your sires,
> God, and your native land.

How could anybody miss going to Delphi? And I didn't, even though it meant taking a little dinky cargo boat to Italy, instead of a big fast steamer. We were a small party, including an English officer and a British playwright, besides Professor Bates and me. The hotel in Athens had given us the greatest quantity of delicious food, so much that I offered some sandwiches to a Greek boy traveling on a donkey. The Greeks being a very self-respecting people, I had trouble getting him to accept, and he insisted on giving me a pomegranate in return, which I thankfully ate, marveling at the wisdom of nature in growing a fruit so full of juice in this dry and dusty land where no rain had fallen for a year. When I agreed to take my first trip with the American Express, I said, "Now if it rains I won't go."

"Oh, it won't rain," the young man declared.

"How do you know it won't rain?" I asked skeptically.

"Well," he replied, "I've been here a year and it hasn't rained yet."

After lunch we crossed the road to inspect the kitchen of the little hotel over there. It was a large room more like a big shed with no doors, with a dirt floor of course, and on one side the stove, pots and pans, etc., and in the rear a stable for mules, horses, and even a goat. A big pot was boiling away, and the odor as I leaned over to look was most appetizing. I was inclined to be shocked, of course; but after all the stories I've heard of restaurant kitchens in the United States, I think the Greek one was probably more sanitary, this being, at least, open to inspection.

The English officer entertained us with an account of the attack on Corfu, ridiculing Mussolini for making

such a display of force. The English, he said, would have
found a corporal's guard sufficient to obtain surrender.

That afternoon at Delphi, as we were sitting outdoors, a Greek couple arrived, the man riding the donkey. Dismounting, he threw the reins to his wife, who
took charge of the little ass, while he sat down for a chat
with us.

After a very good dinner at the Delphi Hotel we
made our pilgrimage to the Oracle, an uncertain moon
dimly lighting our path to the top, where down in the
underground recesses of the Temple we listened to tales
of the Python so weird that we felt that fabled serpent
might still be alive. I think we were all glad to reach
the hotel without an encounter.

A last look from my balcony at the moonlit sea, and
down to the ravine where Daphne, to escape the amorous
god, became a laurel bush, then to bed and deep, dream-
less sleep.

Suddenly I was waked by a voice in the next room
exclaiming in thrilling tones, "Keep back! Keep back!"

Could it be the Python? Going to the door between
the rooms, I called, "What is the matter?"

A rebuking voice answered angrily, "It was only a
bad dream. Don't make a fuss."

As if I had! I thought crossly.

But the next morning at breakfast a little English girl
atoned charmingly with many apologies.

On the way back to Athens we stopped for a way-
side luncheon by that old marble lion still guarding the
Boeotian plains after centuries of watching.

A strange sight on the way was hundreds of turkeys
being driven to market at Athens. Truly a death march,
but one which roused pity in nobody.

The journey from Brindisi to Rome seemed never
ending. After the junction for Naples, I found myself
all alone in my first-class compartment, something I had
been warned against, as so many solitary travelers had

been found murdered on reaching their destination.
However, as every station displayed a sign bearing huge
fasces, I thought trustfully of Mussolini and, snuggling
down in my red velvet chair, was soon asleep. It was almost midnight when, waking, I looked out the window,
and there in the distance blazing with lights was the
"city of my soul." Ecco Roma! What a thrill!

Of course at the hotel nobody had stayed up to greet
me, but in my room welcoming me was a vase full of
beautiful pink roses, with a lovely note from my British
friend, Mrs. John Gray, a very recent bride.

Mrs. Gray, whose husband, long a resident of Rome,
had received the title of Commendatore for distinguished
services during the war, had of course a large circle of
interesting friends and, wishing them to hear my story
of Germany's entering the League of Nations, invited
them to tea. Among the guests was one everybody called
the Vestal Virgin as she was always in the Forum gathering information about the vestal virgins. Another,
Donna Felicia, who had married a member of the noted
Cenci family, was the daughter of Governor Yates of
Illinois. When I told her of my amazement at seeing
cornfields in Roumania as large as those in Illinois, she
said that Roumania had sent men to learn about corn-
growing in Illinois, where her father had supervised
their instruction, sending them back well versed in the
best methods known and practiced by Illinois farmers.

Shortly afterwards Mrs. Gray took me to spend the
day at Tivoli with her friends the Hallams, who lived
just opposite the falls in an old house once a monastery,
now with everything changed for comfort and convenience, a very charming home. Peeking with awe into
the Catacombs, I discovered nothing more alarming than
the winter's supply of coal. This house had the added
distinction of having originally belonged to Horace, and
one room on the ground floor, empty and damp and with

a few lines of network still on one wall, was preserved
sacred to his memory.

At dinner almost everything served had been raised
on the estate: chickens, olives and olive oil, vegetables,
grapes, wine, and honey. Mr. Hallam, who had once
been headmaster of a boy's school in England, told us
that Colonel Bingham, Head of the Bingham Military
School at Asheville, North Carolina, wishing to draw
the United States and England closer together, had offered a prize to the school contributing the best essay on
how this could be done. His school had won the prize,
and at the celebration of this event Colonel Bingham's
son, Judge Robert Bingham, had presented the prize
with an appropriate and eloquent speech. Mr. Hallam
then said he wondered if Colonel Bingham was still living; and I, who had been listening with open mouth,
was delighted to tell him that he was and also of my
cousinship.

After dinner we went to see the Villa d'Este, where,
because of the recent rains, all the innumerable fountains were in their glory. Nowhere else are there such
fountains, nor such cypresses. We returned to the Hallams' for what was a truly high tea, with sandwiches and
an enormous cake covered with white icing. We tore
ourselves reluctantly away, sure that there was never such
another "spend the day."

That night I sat up late writing Colonel Bingham a
long account of this red letter day.

One little incident on the through express to Paris
cries out to be told.

Carefully locking the door of my single stateroom,
I climbed into my berth, sure nobody could come in.
I waked suddenly to find two men bending over me.

"Customs," they said.

"What, customs in the middle of the night!" I
exclaimed.

"Yes, Madame, we cross the frontier here."

"LONGACRE"
Columbia, South Carolina
The Author's home, in her "fifth commonwealth"

BRECKINRIDGE LONG
Ambassador to Rome, Assistant Secretary of State

So I sent them out, promising to open my bags and call them.

Painfully I dragged them all out, placing them on top of my berth, and opening them up. Then, putting on my kimono, I opened the door. Only the conductor stood outside. On my invitation to enter, he shook his head, saying, "Customs is finish."

When I returned to St. Louis, the American Association of University Women appropriated nearly a hundred dollars for me to visit all the Branches and tell them what I had learned there. I found audiences rather indifferent and even hostile, but they were not impervious to wit and humor, which, plus a good story, won a hearing for my logic.

A popular one was about a woman who had fallen into a river. A man trying to rescue her grasped her by the hair, but her wig came off. Next he seized her foot, and off came her shoe. Then he reached for her arm, which was wooden, and that too eluded his grasp. He felt discouraged. "Madam," he said, "I'm willing to save you, but I must have a little co-operation."

Moral: It takes international co-operation to save the world.

And now only two of us were left, the oldest and the youngest—Sabra and I. Together we came to live in South Carolina. I had boxed the compass! Almost.

Here in Columbia, we joined our niece and her husband, Cadwallader Jones V, in their home, "Longacre."

I had first heard of Columbia from my brother-in-law, Charles Porcher, who had been there the night it was burned by Sherman. Charles, who had run away from school when only sixteen to join the Confederate Army, had been sent that night to deliver a note to his commanding officer in Columbia. He hitched his horse to a post, but when he came back, the horse was gone and Columbia was in flames. Somehow in that night of horror he managed to escape and rejoin his regiment.

A few landmarks miraculously remained for many years, including the house where Lafayette, proudly escorted here by a troop all mounted on white horses, spoke to the cheering multitudes below.

Everyone knows of the charm and historic interest of Charleston. Charles talked much of the time when he lived there with his parents, who entertained so many guests that the cab drivers, thinking their home rivaled the Charleston Hotel, nicknamed it the "Little Charleston."

Charleston he considered impregnable from the sea. Though bombarded for seven hundred days by a gun called "The Swamp Angel," it never surrendered until Sherman arrived in his march from Atlanta to the sea.

A source of many anecdotes was his eccentric uncle, Mazyck Porcher, who, waxing very indignant at a New England summer resort before the war at comments on *Uncle Tom's Cabin,* said, "You people who condemn slavery should remember that the finest character in the book is Uncle Tom, himself a slave, and a product of slavery." On being introduced to Harriet Beecher Stowe, he instinctively put out his hand, and then withdrew it, saying, "Madam, I respect you, but I cannot shake the hand that produced such a false picture of the South."

During the War Sherman's soldiers tied him to a tree and made him watch his house being burned to the ground. He was a great churchman, and one of his friends, perhaps wishing to test his faith, asked him, "Do you ever pray for those Yankee enemies of yours?"

"Yes," he said, "I do, night and morning. I pray God that He will abate their pride, assuage their malice, and confound their devices."

That, I often thought during the last war, was a good way to pray for Hitler. And now Joe Stalin.

Cadwallader Jones's boyhood home in Columbia is

still remembered as a center of hospitality, fun, and frolic.
When he went to bed alone he often woke in the morning to find some chum beside him. He was glad to return
and hang on the wall at "Longacre" the sword given by
Lafayette to the first Cadwallader Jones and handed
down to other Cadwalladers.

One of his heroes was Wade Hampton, whose statue
stands in the State House Grounds not far from Houdon's
of Washington. The pillars of Hampton's home, all that
remain of the house burned by Sherman, form a local
shrine frequented by many pilgrims. One of the great
moments, perhaps the greatest, of Hampton's life was
the dispersing by his fiery eloquence a mob bent on at-
tacking the Negroes. There is a very unusual monument
in the little town of Fort Mill, South Carolina, erected
in a little triangular park near the depot, by Simms Elliott
White. It bears two inscriptions: one, "To the Women
of the Confederacy"; the other, "To the Slaves of the
Confederacy in Commemoration of Their Fidelity to
Their Mistresses." When the men of the family had all
gone to war there were many forebodings of what might
happen to the women they left behind. And this monument is a fitting tribute to the devotion of the slaves who
everywhere in the South proved faithful to their trust.

During World War I when a train full of soldiers
stopped at the depot in Fort Mill, one of them, a Carolina mountaineer, seeing a group of loafers sitting on
the foundation stone of the monument, yelled, "Say fellows, stead of settin' on history, why don't you jine up
and make some?"

Prosperity came to Mr. White and to his descendants,
for his grandson, Elliott Springs, is spoken of as the greatest manufacturer in America.

And now let me sign off with the story of one last
fling. What better way to end could there be than with
a visit to Churchill's and Shakespeare's England? In the

spring of 1949 my English friend, Mrs. John Gray, urged me to return to England, my most beloved country next to my own; and so I decided to squander my dollars there instead of in the North Carolina mountains. And I'm glad that I did, for it's a wonderful thing to be in a country where age is an asset rather than a liability. In crowded buses people would stand so that I might sit; and when I asked my way, people—even college professors hurrying to classes—would stop and go with me to show me where to go. It's amazing what total strangers will do for one.

And it was good to have brought home to one what the English had really suffered. Not since 1939 had they had enough to eat. Even in 1949 eggs and many other things were still rationed. But I never heard any complaints about such scarcities from the English themselves. It was left for us tourists to declaim on such matters.

The natives, in fact, were unbelievably cheerful. I said to a charming woman from Winchester, a favorite target for bombs in wartime, "You are the gayest person I ever knew."

"It's because there's no bombing," she said. "What a nuisance that was! Some nights we would have to go to the shelter again and again. And during the day, whether washing our hair, mixing a cake, or watching the oven, we would have to skedaddle to that shelter. And when I told my husband good-bye in the morning, I never knew whether or not I'd ever see him again. It's because there's no bombing! A crust is plenty."

It made one's heart ache to see the awful results of the bombings. More than once I found myself thinking, with tears in my eyes, "What a night of horror this must have been!" But it was amazing how much was left. Nelson was still aloft unharmed in Trafalgar Square; those lions had guarded him well. And from the bridge where Wordsworth stood when he wrote the famous sonnet, one could still say, "Earth has not anything to show more fair."

Yes, I drank deep of beauty—and also of fun. It was worth the trip to see Olivier as Sir Peter Teazle in *The School for Scandal* at the Old Vic. Gracie Fields and her brother Tommy in the music hall were an added fillip. Tommy's singing reminded one of Harry Lauder. And his jokes! He could even joke about that impossible bread I ate for the four months of my visit.

Fun, too, to go to the Fourth of July celebration at the Embassy, where we sat under a huge marquee drinking punch and eating cake and watching celebrities, including Danny Kaye, the center of an admiring throng.

Something better than fun to attend the unveiling of a stained glass window to Milton right next to Sir Walter Raleigh's in St. Margaret's and to see T. S. Eliot, reading one of Milton's sonnets in tones so low that only those up close could hear him.

Very impressive, too, to watch our ambassador on Decoration Day lay a wreath of roses on the tomb of the Unknown Soldier in Westminster Abbey.

Never to be forgotten was the sight of the whole royal family on Trooping the Colors Day. After soldiers and the band came King George in his chariot, and behind him riding horseback the Princess Elizabeth, not accompanied—to the surprise of the uninformed—by her husband, he not being royalty, but by her uncle the Duke of Gloucester. Much craning of necks to see Queen Elizabeth and Princess Margaret Rose, gay in pink and blue hats and dresses. Finally, on their return, the whole family (except Bonnie Prince Charlie) came out on the balcony of Buckingham Palace and responded with many bows to the waves of applause. Nor was it exactly an anticlimax to see Queen Mary, stately as always, in furs and silks leaving Westminster Abbey accompanied by Governor Dewey.

And the greatest thrill of all, after we had stood for

ages at St. Paul's, was to catch a glimpse of Winston Churchill, the man of the century, taking part in the celebration of the Boer War, in which he was a newspaper correspondent.

As I looked down from the plane for the last time on that country where there had been so much "blood, sweat, and tears," I could only think that it was indeed "this blessed plot, . . . this England."

Now I am the last of my family, but my cause came with me to South Carolina. Here in this field, working with others who love this cause as I do, the morning hour still has gold in its mouth. And the cause! It is still the greatest of all causes—World Peace with Liberty, Justice, and BREAD. A cause, now that we have atomic bombs, that should rally all mankind to its banner.